Guerrilla Metaphysics

Guerrilla Metaphysics

Phenomenology and the
Carpentry of Things

GRAHAM HARMAN

OPEN COURT
Chicago and La Salle, Illinois

To order books from Open Court, call 1-800-815-2280 or visit www.opencourtbooks.com.

Open Court Publishing Company is a division of Carus Publishing Company.

Printed and bound in the United States of America.

Library of Congress Cataloging-in-Publication Data

Harman, Graham, 1968-
    Guerrilla metaphysics : phenomenology and the carpentry of things / Graham Harman.
      p. cm.
    Includes bibliographical references and index.
    ISBN-13: 978-0-8126-9456-7 (pbk. : alk. paper)
    ISBN-10: 0-8126-9456-2 (pbk. : alk. paper)
    1. Phenomenology. 2. Philosophy, Modern. 3. Metaphysics. I. Title.
B829.5.H37 2005
110—dc22

2005013757

Contents

Introduction

This book calls for what might be termed an *object-oriented philosophy*, and in this way rejects both the analytic and continental traditions. The ongoing dispute between these traditions, including the sort of "bridge building" that starts by conceding the existence of the dispute, misses a prejudice shared by both: their primary interest lies not in objects, but in human *access* to them. The so-called linguistic turn is still the dominant model for the philosophy of access, but there are plenty of others—phenomenology, hermeneutics, deconstruction, philosophy of mind, pragmatism. None of these philosophical schools tells us much of anything about objects themselves; indeed, they pride themselves on avoiding all naive contact with nonhuman entities. By contrast, object-oriented philosophy holds that the relation of humans to pollen, oxygen, eagles, or windmills is no different in kind from the interaction of these objects with each other. For this reason, the philosophy of objects is sometimes lazily viewed as a form of scientific naturalism, since it plunges directly into the world and considers every object imaginable, avoiding any prior technical critique of the workings of human knowledge. But quite unlike naturalism, object-oriented philosophy adopts a bluntly *metaphysical* approach to the relations between objects rather than a familiar physical one. In fact, another term that might be employed for object-oriented philosophy is *guerrilla metaphysics*—a name meant to signify that the numerous present-day objections to metaphysics are not unknown to me, but also that I do not find them especially compelling.

Guerrilla Metaphysics is the sequel to my previous book, *Tool-Being*. The central thesis of the earlier work is that objects exist in utter isolation from all others, packed into secluded private vacuums. Obviously, this can be no better than a half-truth about the world: if it were the full story, nothing would ever happen, and every object would repose in its own intimate universe, never affecting or affected by anything else at all. *Guerrilla*

1

Metaphysics is an attempt to tell the other side of the story. It needs to be shown how relations and events are possible *despite* the existence of vacuum-sealed objects or tool-beings. The subject matter of a carpentry of things in object-oriented philosophy is the shifting communication and collision between distinct entities. What this carpentry speaks of is not the physical but the *metaphysical* way in which objects are joined or pieced together, as well as the internal composition of their individual parts. But since the vacuum-sealed nature of objects makes direct communication impossible, all conjunction or coupling must occur through some outside mediator. For this reason, the classical notion of occasional cause needs to be partially rehabilitated, despite its recent centuries as an object of philosophical ridicule by scholars and novices alike. The revival is only partial insofar as I will not recommend a traditional occasionalist theory based on a God who directly intervenes in the motion of raindrops and dust—a theory in which the deity is openly invoked but the divine mechanisms are left in darkness. The new term to be used is *vicarious* cause, and it requires no theology to support it. *Any* philosophy that makes an absolute distinction between substances and relations will inevitably become a theory of vicarious causation, since there will be no way for the substances to interact directly with one another.

The first root of this book, then, is the need to complete the picture of the world sketched in *Tool-Being* by shifting attention from objects to their interactions. The other root lies in the intriguing possibility of a revival of phenomenology—a resurgence not of its lingering idealist biases and barren technical catechism, but of its fascination with the carnival of the world. For more than a decade I have been disappointed by the direction of recent continental philosophy, which is preoccupied almost entirely with written texts and minor modifications to historical narratives already posited by others. While the banner of phenomenology still flies here and there, it too often has the smell of mothballs about it, and is utilized more as a means of summoning forgotten terminology from the dead than as a way of returning to the things themselves.

Yet there are clear exceptions to this rule. Above all, there is the small group of figures who might be unified under the label of *carnal phenomenology*. Amidst all the repetitious manifestoes and dry meta-descriptions of human consciousness, we also find the works of Merleau-Ponty and Levinas. In the writings of these authors, we encounter the lascivious warmth of the sun and air and the mystery of strange flashes at midnight; we adjust our postures to the resonance of bird calls and acoustic guitars; we enjoy bread or raspberries, and respond to the demands of orphans. One living author who speaks in the same style as these figures is Alphonso Lingis, who began his professional life as their translator. Almost alone among contemporary philosophers, Lingis takes us outside all academic disputes and places us amidst coral reefs, sorghum fields, paragliders, ant colonies, binary stars, sea voyages, Asian swindlers, and desolate temples. As far as I am aware, he is also the one who coined the phrase "the carpentry of things," and so contributed to this book's subtitle.

In all three of these authors, we find ourselves mesmerized by the objects in the world, rooted in a carnal setting where our bodies meet with the voluptuous textures of entities. Their similarity of intellectual style is easily sensed by any reader. All of them work within a phenomenological idiom, and all follow an insight of Husserl with which he is too rarely credited: namely, objects always lie beyond any possibility of total presence. And for this reason, the carnal medium in which we dwell can only be some sort of elusive ether or medium of nonobjective qualities, though not just of raw sense data. Merleau-Ponty calls this medium the flesh; Levinas calls it the elemental; Lingis calls it the levels. Each of these conceptions has its own virtues and its own possible drawbacks. By discovering an apparent nonobjective realm in which objects nonetheless sparkle and recede, all of them shed some light on the glue that binds the material of perception.

But over the past few years, it gradually became clear to me that this sensual medium of the carnal phenomenologists is really just the *human* face of a wider medium that must exist between all the objects of the world. If the intentional objects of perception are linked with their qualities by means of this ether of loose carnal properties, the same turns out to be true of the relation of an inanimate substance with its own qualities, and of all such substances with each other.

The fleshly enjoyment described by the carnal phenomenologists is not just the poignant arena of sensitive human experience, but evidence of a global ether that makes the entire network of entities possible. And the same problems posed by the interaction of two vacuum-sealed objects or tool-beings can already be found in the relation between an object of perception and its various profiles and shadows. The twin themes of vicarious causation and carnal phenomenology had previously been confined to two distinct manuscripts, but I no longer find it possible to separate them. The carpentry of perception is only a special case of the carpentry of things.

*   *   *

Part One of this book follows the carnal phenomenologists at work, charting their most general breakthroughs and shortcomings.

Chapter 1 disputes the claim of Dominique Janicaud that phenomenology becomes concrete only by remaining on the surface of experience and not postulating depths beneath the phenomenal world. Although phenomenology likes to regard the dispute between realism and antirealism as both fruitless and *passé*, it is fully implicated in one side of this conflict—the wrong side, in fact.

Chapter 2 follows Husserl's paradoxical insight that what we encounter *directly* in perception is neither objects nor raw qualities. Intentional objects never become fully manifest, and therefore never enter perception in the flesh. Yet sheer perceptual quality never exists without some sort of object-oriented form. For this reason it remains unclear what the stuff of perception really is, since it is neither form nor matter, neither object nor quality. Whatever this carnal ether may be, Husserl places us squarely in its midst, though without ever letting it extend above or beneath the phenomenal world experienced by humans.

Chapter 3 shifts to Levinas, who establishes an elemental medium of *enjoyment*—one that never disappears into some remote equipmental purpose, and which for him is made up of pure qualities without objects. Yet enjoyment is always enjoyment of something specific: we do not bask in a shapeless medium of qualities, but rather amidst sunlight or the company of an old friend. In this way, even enjoyment is unable to escape the link to objects. On a related note, Levinas strikes me as too willing to grant human beings the *exclusive* right to break the anonymous rumble of being into specific parts, as though the world in itself without humans were a single massive chunk—much as with Anaxagoras, for whom only *nous* could break the *apeiron* into pieces.

Chapter 4 considers Merleau-Ponty, whose concept of the flesh is meant to disintegrate the distinction between subject and object: as he famously puts it, the world looks at me just as I look at it. Unfortunately, there is always a human being involved in Merleau-Ponty's description of flesh, which makes no allowance for any interaction of pine trees with snowflakes when there happen to be no humans in the vicinity. Indeed, he often shows flashes of explicit contempt for any possibility of a world without humans. To this extent, his model of the flesh remains trapped in a philosophy of access that it otherwise helps us to escape.

Chapter 5 considers the recent work of Lingis, perhaps the sole living representative of the carnal school, and probably the most colorful personality and most talented stylist of his generation of philosophers. In his marvellous book *The Imperative*, Lingis begins by fusing Merleau-Ponty's theory of perception with the ethics of Levinas, showing that both are essentially structured by imperatives. But of even greater interest for the present book, Lingis also pushes carnal phenomenology in a tentatively *realist* direction with his conception of the levels of the world. For Lingis, the carnal medium is not something permanently fixed along a thin wedge between human self and inanimate world, as remains the case even in Merleau-Ponty's later work. For Lingis, carnality exists less between myself and the things than *in the things themselves*—and always at a very specific level to which I must adjust myself. Humans are not the preciously unique site of carnal reality, but only supple vehicles built to explore the various levels on which carnality is found. With our tools and bodily organs we explore the levels of a conversation, a dangerous forest, a seedy waterfront, the Karakoram Range, the works of a poet, the keys of a saxophone, or the patterns on a fish. These levels fill up the world with or without my permission, and merely summon me to enter them—just as any given restaurant or opium den enacts its style in the world even when I refuse to enter. The flesh does not first appear when humans arrive on the scene, but is already there linking the parts of the forest to one another as they invite me into their midst.

Part Two of the book links carnal phenomenology with the general standpoint developed in *Tool-Being*.

Chapter 6 reviews the basic features of objects or tool-beings as identified in the previous book. Objects withdraw absolutely from all interaction with both humans and nonhumans, creating a split between the tool-being itself and the tool-being as manifested in any relation. And along with this rift between objects and relations, objects are also split in themselves between their sheer unity as one object and their multiplicity of traits. The intersection of these two axes in the world leads to a quadruple structure whose mechanics have never even been suspected, let alone carefully mapped.

Chapter 7 reviews four basic problems that *Tool-Being* noted in object-oriented philosophy. Three of these can easily be unified under the broader theme of occasional cause, renamed *vicarious cause*, so as to avoid the inevitable connotation that occasionalism means God intervening everywhere at every second. The fourth problem concerns what separates genuine entities from any bizarre and arbitrary conglomerate of things that someone might dream up; in classical terms, it is the problem of substance and aggregate. More generally, since it is possible to identify four separate and noncommunicating poles of being, it is necessary to describe how crossovers between these poles *do* occur.

Chapter 8 takes *metaphor* as a starting point to study the interrelation between unified perceptual objects and their numerous tangible properties. By examining the theories of Ortega y Gasset and Black, we find that metaphor creates a strange tension between the two chief moments of the sensual thing.

Chapter 9 does much the same thing with *humor*, through an examination of Bergson's essay on laughter. Metaphor, humor, and several other types of experiences are all seen to belong under the more general heading of *allure*. Allure differs from normal perception by somehow putting the relation of the two moments of the thing at issue for us, by openly severing a thing from its qualities.

Part Three marks the conclusion of the book, and unites the carnal ether from Part One with the vicarious causation of allure from Part Two.

Chapter 10 reviews the most crucial features of the preceding discussions. First, what we are looking for is the mechanism by which a thing becomes severed from its qualities, whether in the allure of beauty, the elusiveness of objects for perception, or the simple strife between an object and its own properties. Second, the world is not naturally carved up into one fixed layer of objects and another permanent space of qualities; the space of perception, like the space of the world itself, is filled with numerous different levels, each of them filled entirely with objects. Finally, the key question must be asked: if the world is made up solely of objects, how do interactions occur at all, given that an object has been defined as that which resists and exceeds interaction?

Chapter 11 considers the three different sorts of metaphysical bond that result from the four poles of objects. The *sensual* bond marks the tension between the unified object of our experience and the numerous sensuous qualities that seem enslaved to it at any given moment. The *physical* bond is the same tension insofar as it plays out in the heart of things themselves rather than in the things as relative to perception. The *causal* bond concerns the interaction that occurs between separate objects despite their ultimate withdrawal from one another. But all three of these bonds are nothing other than forms of vicarious causation, since all are concerned with links between isolated poles of reality.

Chapter 12 examines the question of whether the sensual world belongs only to humans and the higher animals, or whether it is present for plants and inanimate objects as well. It also makes an initial effort to apply the results of this book to the problem of space and time. This brief effort works in the shadow of a more comprehensive book on object-oriented philosophy, which will consider many of the traditional problems of metaphysics.

The vast majority of this book was written between the summer of 2001 and the fall of 2003. For reasons still unknown, it was written most easily at dusk, which may help to explain the general tone of its most prominent passages. Electronic mail sent to the author at toolbeing@yahoo.com is guaranteed a response.

PART ONE

The Carnal Phenomenologists

"A thing exists in the midst of its wastes."

—EMMANUEL LEVINAS,
Totality and Infinity

[1]

Concreteness in the Depths

The carnival tent rustles in the evening breeze, disturbing the moods of those who approach. Inside the tent are swarms of humans and trained animals; there are jarring sounds, strange ethnic foods, and shadows. For a few moments the music of a concealed organ is countered by the rumble of thunder, as emaciated dogs begin to whine. A small fight breaks out, soon to be halted by a sneering, scar-faced man. Suddenly, hailstones strike the roof of the tent like bullets, frightening everyone: the visitors, the fortunetellers, the unkempt and corrupted security guards, the monkeys sparkling with costume jewelry. At long last, the organ player's morbid inner anger takes command, and he begins an atonal dirge that will last throughout the storm.

All of this can be explained by atoms. Each of the human and inhuman objects in this scene is made of physical material integrated into ever larger units that generate new emergent properties. Weave enough of the right molecules together and you have a durable canvas tent, strong enough to resist the force of iceballs from the sky. The taste and smell of the food are easily explained as the action of physical particles upon the human or animal nervous systems, which send chemical signals through the spine, transmitting useful information about the external world. Ultimately, perhaps all of the living creatures in the tent are nothing more than complicated tools, products of the hidden genes that build up entire organisms so as to compete for survival and reproduction with the rival organisms that house competitor genes. The fear felt by everyone during the hailstorm would simply be an inherited reflex mechanism that enhances the probability of our taking shelter, preserving our genes and allowing them to survive into the next generation. Everything that happens in the tent can be explained quite naturally. Even the storm had been predicted by meteorologists several hours ahead of time, and should have been no surprise to any but the least-informed. Moreover, the apparently ominous situation I have described did not unfold in some nameless fantasy space of German Expressionism, but a few miles east of Geneva, Ohio, late in the presidency of Ronald Reagan, across the street from a bakery and an insurance agent, in a dull vacant lot of three-dimensional geometric space no different from any other. It is a completely natural event.

But phenomenology forbids us to describe the carnival in this way. For this philosophical school, the dark circus of Geneva is not primarily a natural set of atoms and chemicals and genetic codes and geometric locations that could be used to cut more complicated aspects of the experience down to size. Before explaining the elements of our world by means of any favorite theory, we are supposed to focus diligently on the only thing that is truly given: the experience as such. What I feel at the carnival is a numbing fear, not the movement of chemicals through my nerves. What I hear is the lumbering melody of the organ, not sound waves traveling through space and causing my eardrum to vibrate. We are asked to suspend belief in any hidden causes or secret powers, to focus only on what immediately shows itself when we are trapped in the carnival tent in the storm. We are asked, in other words, to let the phenomena speak for themselves. Whereas science seeks to explain the world by way of natural objects that bump into other natural objects, phenomenology recommends a step backwards into the world as it appears, prior to the employment of any such theories. This raises a key philosophical problem, one that puts at stake the relation of philosophy not just to the sciences, but to realism in general. Namely, when phenomenology replaces natural objects with phenomena, we should ask whether it thereby reduces the world to appearance alone, bracketing any deeper reality out of existence. We need to know if it is possible to speak of a layer of the world that eludes appearance, or whether this is merely a relapse into the sort of theory that phenomenology must always oppose.

Dominique Janicaud considers this issue in his dispute with those French phenomenologists who attempt a kind of "theological turn."[1] For these theologians, some element of the Beyond must penetrate the closed circle of visible phenomena. But for Janicaud this is anathema—as he sees it, the theologians have abandoned intellectual rigor and kidnapped Husserl's philosophy to serve their own dogmatic plans. When Janicaud insists that phenomenology must remain concrete, what he means is that it must stay confined to what verifiably appears, or at most to those general conditions that make all appearance possible. In his own words: "phenomenology and theology make two."[2] And: "between the unconditional affirmation of Transcendence and the patient interrogation of the visible, the incompatibility cries out; we must choose."[3]

In what follows, it will become necessary to refuse *both* of these options, inasmuch as they share a fundamental mistake. When Janicaud replaces the object with the phenomenon, when the theologians replace it with a barely effable Beyond, *both wrongly agree that the individual object is something that needs to be replaced*. What disappears in both of these standpoints is any reality of entities as genuine forces to reckon with in the world, as real players exerting influence outside themselves even while hiding behind their exposed surfaces. That is to say, both Janicaud and the theologians see no way to preserve objects at the center of philosophy without delivering the world to reductive scientific explanations. For this reason, both begin by checkmating the reality of objects in favor of dogmatic assumptions of their own. If phenomenology and theology make two, I propose that we add a third: an object-oriented philosophy. I only regret that Dominique Janicaud, who listened generously to the first version of my argument at a conference in Rotterdam, is no longer able to make counterarguments to this final version.

Those who knew the disarming gentleness of Janicaud the man might be surprised at the biting edge of his polemic against the theologians. Polemical writing in philosophy no longer enjoys its previous level of acceptance, and is now often dismissed as the product of incivility, aggression, even jealousy. Against this attitude, we should appreciate the clarifying tendencies of polemic—always the favored genre of authors frustrated by the continued clouding of an important decision, whether through fashionable cliché or dubious conceptual maneuvers. In Janicaud's monograph "The Theological Turn in French Phenomenology," a gracious personality speaks in tongues of fire. And not against minor opponents: Emmanuel Levinas, Jean-Luc Marion, and Michel Henry are the primary targets of his annoyance. While phenomenology can exist only as "a patient interrogation of the visible," the impatient theologians are accused of firing off wild rounds of pistol shots, importing metaphysical baggage and even religious prejudice into what ought to be a remorseless intellectual pursuit. Each of Janicaud's critiques sheds different light on the choice he demands from us: phenomenology or theology. For the purposes of this book, it will be enough to consider his criticism of Levinas.

A. The Most High

In claiming that phenomenology has been hijacked by the theological turn, Janicaud points to Levinas as the mastermind of this operation: "*Totality and Infinity* is the first major work of French philosophy in which [the] theological turn is not only discernible, but explicitly taken up within a phenomenological inspiration."[4] He will eventually deny Levinas's claim to be a phenomenologist at all, arguing that this philosopher's obvious apprenticeship to Husserl is outweighed by his apparent relapse into the very positions that phenomenology overcomes. What he most objects to in Levinas is an "impatience to attain the beyond," expressing his "astonishment before [the] metaphysical flight"[5] of an author quick to abandon the promise of the phenomena themselves. Whereas phenomenology tried to subordinate hidden natural causes to the lush particularity of the visible world, Levinas seems nostalgic for the world-in-itself of metaphysics. As Janicaud cites him: "All knowledge, as intentionality, already presupposes the idea of the infinite, the *nonadequation* par excellence."[6] For Levinas, any human encounter with reality fails to exhaust the fullness of that reality, and cannot avoid reducing it to its own terms, the terms of the Same. The space of nonadequation is that of a reality forever eluding the kingdom of presence: it is the Infinite, the Other. But for Janicaud, phenomenon and infinity make two; there is no "real" world to which the phenomenon ought to be adequate in the first place. On this basis he views Levinasian infinity as a reactionary concept, one that summons up all the ghastly phantoms of naive realism: "What strikes us as [Levinas's] essential violence . . . is the act or surplus of the idea of the infinite."[7]

Clearly annoyed, Janicaud can barely tolerate Levinas's claim that intentionality in Husserl is a kind of adequation. This claim, he says, "leads us to question the very coherence of [Levinas's] thought,"[8] since it seems that Levinas is accusing Husserl of the kind of realism that phenomenology has already left in the dust. "For Husserl, the suspension of the natural attitude implies leaving behind all ontological realism . . . intentionality in Husserl is not at all reducible to the adequation of thought and object."[9] In passing, it should be said that this is a clear misreading. When Levinas sings the praises of "nonadequation," he is not accusing Husserl of holding that the phenomenon is adequate to some sort of external object, but rather that it is adequate *to itself.* In other words, Levinasian "Infinity" is designed not to outsmart a realism falsely imputed to Husserl, but to undercut a phenomenalism ascribed to him quite understandably.

But Janicaud wants to have it both ways. Even while lamenting the "violence" of any surplus beyond appearance, he also decries the claim that Husserl is trapped within appearance at all: "This is an artificial operation, one that Descartes and Husserl were able to do without: for these thinkers, in discovering in me the idea of the infinite, I discover also that *my subjectivity* exceeds the representation I have of it."[10] I place the phrase "my subjectivity" in italics because it gives away the game so early. Levinas simply asks us to note the insufficiency of phenomena and recognize the surplus that lies beyond them. Janicaud sidesteps this request by claiming that the sought-after surplus can be found only in the transcendental *conditions* of intentionality, which hide from view in overflowing all that is immediately visible. But this only proves Levinas right: what Janicaud wants to do is to strip all surplus from the outer world and pack it into the living room of the human subject, even if part of it always remains hidden behind the furniture. The world's pulsating landscape of palm trees, lizards, obsidian, salt, motorboats, and viruses is granted no hidden layer whatsoever. For Janicaud, it is true that the *human perception* of these things may contain layers and horizons hidden from view, but any claim that the salt has an inner life apart from its series of appearances can only be a relapse into realism—also known as "metaphysics." The present book waves the flag of metaphysics proudly and openly, rejecting the misgivings of Janicaud and others.

But this is not to say that Levinas gets it entirely right, either. Janicaud is certainly correct in sensing a duplicity in his rival's position: "Levinas specifies [that] 'The infinite does not first exist and *then* reveal itself. Its infinition produces itself as revelation, as positing its idea in *me*.' But if this revelation is subjectivity . . . what sense does it make to claim that it does not involve, precisely, intentionality?"[11] It is strange indeed that Levinas both points to an infinity outside all appearance while *also* implying that this infinity has no independent life and exists only *within* appearance. If the infinite exceeds the specific visible contours of the world, then it also ought to inhabit some part of the world *outside* the restricted circle of human being; otherwise, the Infinite remains within the loop of intentionality, and Janicaud is right to question its value. Although I would not join with Janicaud in questioning the "coherence" of Levinas's thought, a certain ambiguity is present here concerning the status of any extrahuman world, as will be described in chapter 3 below. For Levinas, the drama of finite and infinite takes place solely at the intersection between human intentionality and whatever lies beyond it. There are passages in his writings which state that individual things have a substance that our perceptions or uses of them fail to exhaust, but no passages where he speaks of an Infinity in the relations of these things to one another. For Levinas, Infinity is never an issue between the forest and the flames that burn it, or even the rotten pineapple and the birds that devour it. Infinity is a uniquely human burden, one that does not belong to relationality in general.

At this point, a related problem catches Janicaud's eye. Insofar as Levinas tends to bring Infinity back into the human fold, downplaying the notion of manifold individual surpluses lying in various individual things, he tends to regard Infinity as a single Holy Other. It is not just that appearances are inadequate to a reality lying behind them: for Levinas, they are inadequate in comparison with a "*Most* High," which Janicaud is obviously right to identify with "the God of the Biblical tradition."[12] As might be expected, this only adds fuel to his polemic: "[Levinas] supposes a metaphysico-theological montage, prior to philosophical writing. The dice are loaded and choices are made; faith rises majestically in the background."[13] When the Other and the Most High are joined by "Desire," Levinas is accused of trying to intimidate philosophy with capital letters. Rejecting the all-or-nothing choice that seems to be in the air, Janicaud denounces the "defection from phenomenality"[14] that sent Levinas, lickety-split, all the way to God: "His phenomenology is then above all negative, but ultimately precious—precious for its sense of passivity irreducible to all apophantic discourse and representation."[15] In many ways this is an oversimplification. Among other things, Janicaud's critique shows no trace of the Levinas of the 1940s and his masterful descriptions of concrete phenomena, descriptions often found in the later work as well. But by the same token, Janicaud is not just drawing caricatures: it is clearly the case that Levinas tends to make Infinity a One, and that all routes toward the One quickly seem to be headed for a *Highest* One. Although I have always been an admirer of Levinas, there are long stretches of Janicaud's polemic where it is hard to disagree.

We should join with Janicaud in remaining wary of the single *De Profundis* of Levinasian theology. When Levinas undercuts the presence of all phenomena with a single mighty stroke of divine Infinity, once and for all, this maneuver certainly ought to disappoint us. But there is little to be said for Janicaud's alternative, which merely flattens the world into what we *see* of the world: epistemology by another name, at the expense of all metaphysics. It is no more convincing when he tries to increase the sophistication of this move by avowing (with Jan Patočka[16]) that there is indeed something beyond appearance, but that it lies entirely within the hidden conditions of possibility of the human observer. While the stark disparity between Levinas and Janicaud becomes obvious from all the fusillades of the latter, there is one point on which they could hardly agree more: their conviction, adopted from Husserl, that an object can mean nothing other than a natural empirical object as described by the sciences. For both of them, with the occasional exception of Levinas, individual objects are only phenomenal silhouettes, not real entities with autonomous power and quality. Janicaud is so good as to admit this openly. But even for Levinas, it turns out most of the time that no *specific* entity may lay claim to infinity: the single Most High sits upon a single throne. Notice that whichever of these two camps one enters, phenomenology or theology, objects are reduced to the lackeys and menials of a unified lofty power. Even if this power allows for a bit of concealment beneath the phenomenal realm, it is never a hidden layer of the things themselves—it is either God, or the transcendental conditions of the human subject. There may be times when phenomenology and theology make two, but in this respect they are blood brothers. And on this score at least, both are equally worthy of rejection.

B. A Hidden Agreement

The discord between Janicaud and the theologians should not obscure their shared basic suppositions. At the outset, the theologians want to point us toward a transcendence beyond the phenomenal sphere, while Janicaud resists this attempted "hijacking" (*his* word) and tries to prevent his adversaries from "wringing phenomenology's neck" (*his* phrase). But scratch the surface of both positions, and we find a striking coincidence of views: for there is a sense in which the theologians do not want transcendence at all. Michel Henry openly admits this, with his claim to a theology of radical immanence. In similar fashion, Levinas often suggests that the infinite exists only through its intrusion into consciousness, while Marion tends to seek pure giving in an internal saturation of phenomena rather than in a transcendent space beyond them.

Now, Janicaud is clearly wrong to imply that these authors are not real phenomenologists. In their shared wariness toward any independent extraphenomenal things, they are actually *too* loyal to Husserl, and nothing like the realist Neanderthals Janicaud imagines. Even when they do approach something like transcendence, it is not a transcendence of the things, but more like an inarticulate lump of infinity, a brooding concealed monolith that dwarfs the nullities known as specific entities. Infinity has little actual role in these philosophies besides haunting our awareness, and seems largely inoperative outside the sphere of human consciousness. Indeed, as soon as we arrive at the point of reflecting on particular cigars or mangoes, the theologians think that philosophy has already been lost. In a word, the theologians are loyal adherents of the Copernican Revolution in philosophy, reducing all of reality to the terms of human *access* to it. From time to time they reach vaguely for a God-beyond-access, but even their fleeting successes give us a single triumphant Infinite rather than a plural reality of individual things. Hurricanes, whips, zebras, chemicals, and weddings are still permitted to be individuals only within the *phenomenal* sphere. Any attempt to step outside this sphere is assumed to give us only the single pistol shot of the Infinite Other.

Janicaud offers equally rough treatment to the things. Even while crying out against the neglect of the phenomenal sphere, even while praising *en passant* the lascivious delights of Merleau-Ponty's prose, his real interests lie elsewhere. What Janicaud presents as the true path of phenomenology is really just a program for further technical description of the conditions of possibility of human access, possibly spiced up with historical accounts of the metaphysical biases of the Western tradition—which all starts to sound an awful lot like mainstream Heidegger scholarship. In a sense this actually makes Janicaud more conservative than the theologians, who at least try to inject their amorphous Infinite directly into the things, thereby gaining at least a fighting chance of invigorating them. But on the whole, both camps leave the phenomena as dust in the wind. Phenomena do nothing but sit around in a floodlit human space, passively encountered by pure observers or, at best, handled by engaged historical agents. For fear of regressing into scientific naturalism, fire loses its power to burn houses and melt ore, and the moon is reduced to the literary descriptions of poseurs. For fear of scientific reductionism, gravity loses all power over bodies, and brains lose all power over minds. The natural object disappears from philosophy, just as Husserl demanded. Janicaud and the theologians are united in compliance with this demand before their quarrel even begins. They should at least stop accusing one another of not being real phenomenologists; everyone's loyalty to the cause is perfectly clear from the start.

C. Unnatural Objects

Phenomenology asks us to retreat to a point of neutral description, setting aside all explanatory theories of atoms, chemicals, and waves of sound. Given that no direct access is possible to the scientific objects just mentioned, we confine ourselves instead to the manifest properties of the world as it appears. The object is stripped of all independent power and considered only insofar as it flares into human view. Both Janicaud and the theologians embrace this procedure, and in this respect they are one. But they also resemble each other in a less fortunate respect: namely, both groups offer a primarily *negative* concept of phenomena. For we might ask what is actually accomplished by the return to phenomena in both groups. Regrettably, the central purpose of the turn toward the phenomena is apparently nothing more than to suppress all extraphenomenal aspects of the things. Almonds and rain are no longer secret powers lurking behind appearance, as they still are for science and metaphysics, but only luminous personae crowding a narrowly human space. At the very moment that concrete phenomena attain their apparent philosophic triumph, they are abandoned by both of the camps that claimed to defend them.

This having been done, the scene of philosophy is shifted elsewhere. Maybe it shifts toward a single infinite Other that outstrips all specific phenomena, as with Levinas in his less interesting moments. Maybe it moves toward a single "pure call" prior to all determination, or a radically immanent life that weaves through the phenomena even while trumping them, as with Marion and Henry, respectively. Maybe it rejects the infinite altogether, and turns back toward the very conditions of human access to the world, or toward the encrustations of history that shape our view of the world, as Janicaud recommends. But in all such cases, the status of concrete things is eroded. And although Janicaud is weary of those who claim to be truer to the spirit of phenomenology than Husserl himself, it is not hard to be truer to its spirit than these self-proclaimed phenomenologists, who place themselves *anywhere but* in the things themselves. It is high time that the phenomena be treated as something more than polemical devices for undercutting the purported naiveté of realist dupes, since the things themselves are supposed be the key players in phenomenology, not just hired guns or temps.

The time has come to pursue a model of the things as autonomous objects, not just as humanly accessible phenomena. Recall the carnival tent flapping in the cold Ohio wind. We can imagine that Maurice Merleau-Ponty is now inside the tent, milling about with the various entertainers and criminals, performing sensitive work of description on this troubling scene (as he certainly would have). But stranded in the storm a hundred yards away, Moritz Geiger sees the tent quite differently: as an ominous cone-shaped bulk that promises warmth even while triggering fear. Various dogs, rats, and moths encounter the tent in ways that we humans can only begin to imagine. The tent is always able to *surprise* any of the entities that observe it, or to be described in new and unorthodox ways. This indicates that the currently accessible features of a thing do not tell the whole story about it. The tent is more than an appearance, because it is many different appearances at once to many different creatures. Beyond that, it is even more than all of these appearances put together, because it might harbor qualities that no current observers are equipped to detect, as if they were all nothing but snakes slithering across an undiscovered tomb.

But neither is the tent equal to all of the *possible* appearances it might generate, because these are still nothing more than appearances for *other* entities—and it is not my *perception* of the tent that shelters the carnival from injury in the storm. The tent-object is something, and that something simply does not have a phenomenal character. Nor does the tent merely partake in some hidden unified "Infinity"—after all, the tent-object is not the same as the snake-object or monkey-object or hailstone-object. What is concealed in each of these cases is something completely different.

To repeat, the tent is neither a phenomenon nor any set of phenomena, but a real force throwing its weight around in the world and demanding to be taken seriously. Any *appearance* of the tent is only an appearance *for* some other entity, and such an appearance cannot possibly step in for the thing and replace it in its labors amidst the world. That is to say, the tent-for-Merleau-Ponty or the tent-for-Geiger cannot step into the world and do all the work that is done by the tent itself, since such appearances are never more than thin slices of the reality of any given thing. *The tent itself is an object, not a phenomenon.*

The naive perspectivists who dominate our era of philosophy will claim that this is a reactionary step, sheer regression into a metaphysics of naive realism.Whereas Husserl's heroic achievement was to deflate natural objects and replace them with accessible appearances, some will say that my argument is trying to revive some transcendent phantom X lying outside of appearance even while generating it. Others might ask, and *have* asked, whether moving from phenomena to objects is a way of renouncing philosophy and returning to empirical science, as if to say, "Welcome back, brain cells, atoms, acid, billiard balls—and feel free to reduce philosophy out of existence." But suspicions of this kind are only a symptom of the quarantine mentality of contemporary philosophy, which obsessively fears taking any steps outside of the human sphere. By restricting oneself to transcendental conditions lying outside all nonhuman reality, by walling off concrete things and their powers from the ontologist's playroom, philosophy has withered from a theory of reality into a theory of human *access* to reality. And phenomenology is no less guilty of this step than Anglo-American philosophy of language. Both schools approach the things themselves with a series of dithering preliminary steps that never seems to end.

The point is that there is still another kind of object besides the natural kind: we might call them *unnatural* objects, most of their features already foreshadowed in this chapter. In the first place, these objects are not phenomena, since by definition they are always more than any appearance or set of appearances by which the things signal to us. This is my answer to Janicaud. In the second place, there is a *multitude* of such objects, an underground layer of innumerable rock-objects and flag-objects and tree-objects, all of them exceeding and withdrawing from rocks, flags, and trees as we know them. The infinity beneath phenomena is many, not one. And this is my answer to the theologians. Having abandoned the phenomena for a world of countless real objects, it might seem that we are now back to square one of pre-Husserlian scientific naturalism. To counter this assumption, I will show how an unnatural object differs from a natural one.

This is actually not so difficult, given the strange status of causality that results from what I have said. From the naturalistic standpoint, ignoring for now whatever complications one might wish to infer from the quantum theory, causation is essentially a physical problem of two material masses slamming into each other or mutually affected through fields. One object becomes directly present to the other, whether through physical contact or some other form of causal intimacy. But there is also a *metaphysical* problem of causation to go along with the physical one.

Consider the plight of Merleau-Ponty and Geiger as well as the many insects and mammals in their respective interactions with the carnival tent. In each of these cases, the tent-object remains something different from whatever these entities encounter of it, since none of them ever fully plumbs the depths of the tent. But somewhat astonishingly, the same holds true not just for these *living* entities, but also for the inanimate hailstones and breezes and rays of lamplight that strike against the tent. Here too, the tent remains independent of any encounter between it and any entity at all. But this implies that *no two objects can encounter each other directly*. Given that an object always remains aloof from its dealings with the world, causality can only be *indirect*, can only occur through some medium other than the things themselves, since these forever elude any sort of relation. It will need to be shown concretely how two objects can be absolutely hidden from each other *and* capable of affecting one another. Considered in this paradoxical light, objects are strictly "unnatural," not natural, since they withdraw even from the brute relational system of nature.

There is another typical feature of naturalism that phenomenology understandably wants to avoid. I refer to the tendency of physical explanations to assert that one privileged layer of the world is more real than the others: as if brain cells were real and daydreams merely derivative, as if neutrons or quarks were more real than birthday parties and sports leagues. The tent-object that lies behind all of our perceptions of the carnival tent is reminiscent of what used to be called a *substance*. The problem is that traditional realism used substance as a kind of celebratory title granted only to a certain privileged class of objects by means of some standard, different for each philosopher: whether it was those things that existed by nature, those regarded as metaphysically simple, or those considered to be physically indestructible. The theory defended in this book sees objects as existing not just at some ultimate pampered layer, but all the way up and down the ladder of the cosmos, so that all realities gain the dignity of objects. This is my way of preserving phenomenology's horror at reductionism, and its demand that everything in the world be taken on its own terms. What I disagree with is simply the notion that to reduce an object to its encounter with humans is to take it on its own terms.

In the case under discussion, the substance or object is the carnival tent itself, apart from any of the relations or effects that link it to the rest of the world. Other objects have surprises in store as well: lemon meringue, popsicles, Ajax Amsterdam, reggae bands, grains of sand. Each of these things remains a unitary substance beyond its impact on others—and obviously, none of them is an ultimate tiny particle of matter from which all else is built. They are not ultimate materials, but autonomous *forms,* forms somehow coiled up or folded in the crevices of the world and exerting their power on all that approaches them. This is my definition of substance, a term well worth salvaging: an object or substance is a real thing considered apart from any of its relations with other such things.

What I am advocating is a reversal of the familiar social pattern in which everyone proves their adequate philosophical training by jabbing a few more daggers into the corpse of realism. From the flintiest analytic philosopher to the most dashing Francophone icon, philosophy today is united through a shared contempt for any probing of a real world in itself. Like all broad fashions of any era, this disdain begins to take on the character of an automatic reflex, and like all mental reflexes soon decays into compulsion. Given this atmosphere, it is widely supposed that substances are championed only by reactionaries living in an irrelevant past, while innovation seems to be on the side of relations and contexts, not individual things. On a related front, it is supposed to be the reactionaries who believe in substances independent of our perceptions, while the self-proclaimed avant-garde delights in bursting this final bubble of the true-believers—a tedious drama of canned iconoclasm playing out across the decades. The champions of wholes over parts and the doubters of independent realities can continue to mock the conservatism of their foes if they wish, but the fact is that they have now largely defeated those foes. Holism and antirealism, their days of novelty long past, have become the new philosophical dogmas of our time. The sole difference is that the old orthodoxies viewed their opponents as dangerous cutting-edge transgressors, while the new ones have so exhausted the field of critique and transgression that they are likely to view their challengers only as conservative throwbacks. Fortunately, the brand of realism defended in this book will be so unusual that no one is likely to take it for a rearguard action.

Object-oriented philosophy has a single basic tenet: the withdrawal of objects from all perceptual and causal relations. This immediately implies a single basic problem: how do relations occur? Despite the unsoundable depth of substances, their failure to express themselves fully even in physical collisions, objects *do* somehow manage to interact. These relations are the very carpentry of things, the joints and glue that hold the universe together. Given that objects never seem to enter into relations, what *does* enter into relations? If objects cannot affect one another directly, then perhaps they do so by means of *qualities*. The notion of free-floating qualities, stripped away from any underlying substance, is the central theme of a group of philosophers already termed the carnal phenomenologists. Following Husserl, they recognize that the objects aimed at by intentional acts never quite become visible. Nonetheless, we do not just float through a void, pointing sadly at the ineffable: we also live in the world as in a medium, enjoying juice and sunlight, suffering and dying from epidemics. We inhabit a sensual space in which, strictly speaking, objects cannot be present. Yet there are objects everywhere, like black holes or vacuums hidden from sight. By following the tension between these two moments of human perception, it may be possible to unlock the tensions found in the universe as a whole.

[2]

Two Borderlands of Intentionality

Martin Heidegger tells us that "the *Logical Investigations* occupied Husserl for more than twelve years . . . The intimate history of the genesis of this book is a story of constant despair, and does not belong here."[17] I have always regretted this act of discretion, just as I regret the robotic applause given to Heidegger's curt epigram, "Aristotle was born, worked, and died."[18] When we dismiss the biographer as a betrayer of secrets or a peddler of irrelevant gossip, a philosophical decision is made. The effort to protect philosophy from the cunning explanatory power of material circumstances may seem useful in its own way. Unfortunately, it also serves to protect these circumstances from philosophy. By walling off Husserl's books from personal despairs, from the cobbled streets of Halle and Göttingen, from the smokestacks, sunflowers, music, and ice storms of his day, we treat these things with implicit contempt.

This is unfortunate, given that Husserl's own philosophy did no such thing. The key to phenomenology is the notion of intentionality: the well-known axiom that consciousness is always conscious *of something*. In each instant, my attention is occupied by some specific reality. I fold a newspaper and am stunned by the deep blue tones of a lake; my tongue burns with curried chick peas; I feel electrical charges in the fur of a kitten, or inspect the damage to my shack after a tornado. The endless rejuvenating force of phenomenology lies in the philosophical dignity that it grants to such experiences. Never are they treated as some sort of frivolous anteroom to an ominous rumble of being. For phenomenology, the drama of the world plays itself out *within* specific appearances, not behind or beneath them. Moreover, intentionality is entirely democratic. Sacking the citadel of Troy and writing the history of being are intentional experiences, but so is watching a six-year-old crumple a piece of paper. To revive phenomenology means to restore our taste for the specific textures and overtones of concrete experience.

21

To this end, it is important to distinguish between two specific functions of intentionality. In one sense this concept works as an *adhesive*, a powerful glue cementing subject and object to such an extent that they no longer appear separable. For as Husserl puts it, "we do not experience the object and beside it the intentional experience directed upon it . . . only one thing is present, the intentional experience."[19] This is the side of intentionality that captures Heidegger's personal interest. While praising intentionality's bond between subject and object for eliminating all of the pseudo-problems of theory of knowledge,[20] he also condemns it for reducing the world to visible presence. Heidegger's departure from traditional phenomenology supposedly lies in his rejection of Husserl's lingering agreement with Brentano that "[intentions] are either presentations or founded upon presentations."[21] For beyond the tangible presentation of any entity lies its veiled *being*, a deeper reality that never comes fully to presence—which implies that phenomenology confines itself to a layer of surface-effects.

Along with the adhesive character of intentionality, there is what we might call its *selective* side. Conscious experience does more than perform a double gesture of binding subject and object while restricting both of them to the sphere of visible presentation. It also binds them in a very *specific* way, and even *defines* itself by what it experiences. Whenever I burn piles of garbage or go snorkeling in the Red Sea, these experiences define my life in this moment while shutting out other conceivable actions, such as the study of international law. We carve pumpkins, practice geometry, operate microbreweries, and detonate condemned buildings. This is our reality. Intentionality not only fuses subject with object in a single moment of presence—it also offers a very *specific* presence, a life that varies from moment to moment. Our fascination with distinct objects, colors, sounds, and flavors is not some sort of fallen absorption with shimmering zeroes. Instead, specific phenomena must be granted a positive place in the system of the world: the central categories of philosophy are deployed in the very midst of objects, not at a point outside of them. It is surely true that reality should not be reduced to its visible presence. But it is equally true that sunsets, greyhounds, bean fields, helicopters, witchcraft, and candles are not trivial or "ontic" distractions to be junked in favor of their underlying ground. In all their naiveté and elemental force, these objects fill up the cosmos. Husserl's patient focus on intentionality shows an intuitive respect for such phenomena, one that is lost by Heidegger's dismissal of individual beings.

We can safely assume that Heidegger the man knew all about the chiming of clocks, the soothing effect of green, the sting of pepper on the tongue, the barking of dogs, and the malevolent glare of inner demons. But Heidegger the philosopher left little space for these things, despite his sporadic analyses of jugs and bridges in later years. The primary role of sensuous appearance for Heidegger is simply to collapse beneath the onslaught of the deep and hidden; here, we see the grain of truth in Janicaud's outcry against the brooding, tunneling theologies of Heideggerian origin. Nonetheless, if the sensual concreteness of life is the place where philosophy must seek its fortune, it is equally important that we oppose the tedious, falsely progressive claim that philosophy must remain within the bounds of appearance. It might now seem like a case of wanting it both ways, as if this book were trying to claim the dual thrones of phenomenal surface and veiled underground at the same time. The solution to this paradox is bluntly cosmological: namely, the concreteness of intentionality will turn out to belong to *every possible layer of reality*, not only to human awareness. To remain concrete *does not* mean to remain confined within the human sphere. Eventually, this book will generate a model of the world featuring countless strata of reality: objects wrapped in objects sealed in objects frozen in objects, extending above, below, and within the theater of human consciousness.

The way to revive phenomenology is not through external rituals of compliance with Husserl's vocabulary, but by expanding the concept of intentionality to the point where it covers the entirety of the things themselves, thereby freeing us from the growing staleness of the philosophy of human access. As a first step down this path, we can examine a pair of intriguing fissures within the phenomenal world described in the *Logical Investigations*. Instead of maintaining the usual focus on categorical intuition, so favored by disciples of Heidegger, I propose that we examine the simple Husserlian distinction between *act* and *matter*.

A. Objectifying Acts

As noted in the previous section, phenomenology opposes all forms of naturalism. Any kind of explanatory theory about things must give way to a simple treatment of the things as they *show* themselves. The things themselves are regarded not as natural objects, but as *phenomena*, appearing in the orbit of human consciousness rather than exerting supposed causal effects on one another. With the physical world permanently closed off to intentionality, it settles down comfortably in the mental sphere. In practice, the mental turns out to be nothing more than the human, despite Heidegger's feeble treatment of animals[22] and Husserl's throwaway inclusion of the thinking creatures of other worlds.[23]

Brentano inspired the phenomenological movement by asserting that all consciousness is either a presentation or grounded in presentations. In *Logical Investigations* V, Husserl modifies this central role of presentations in conscious life. Weighing the arguments for and against his teacher's principle, Husserl concludes that sheer presentations are not dominant if these are meant to be *opposed* to wishes or fears or feelings of hatred—as if sheer presentations were one dominant form of mental act superior to others. This would imply that we first encounter neutral smears of color and sound, and then add a number of acts of judgment or moods to help shape a final mental product. Assessing this as a false picture of what happens, Husserl says that the world we confront is already articulated into *objects*, even if these never fully come to view. We do not perceive disconnected splotches of green and rumbling noises and later form judgments about them, but immediately recoil in fear from the swerving green truck as it rolls downhill. We do not taste scattered pixels of salt and peanut on our tongues, but savor the fresh cuisine of Lebanon. True enough, we never encounter a truck or falafel as a whole, but only flat, partial profiles of their total reality; there are always more sides of the truck to be seen, more depths of the food to be probed.

Nonetheless, if intentionality does not give us full-fledged objects, it also does not give us the mythical "raw sense data." What we encounter is a world already broken up into chunks—one in which we are always stationed far beyond whatever the senses seem to be explicitly telling us. This leads Husserl to a brilliant reformulation of his teacher's maxim. In his own words: "every intention is either an *objectifying act* or has its basis in such an act."[24] We are immersed in a world so fully carved up into specific slices that "qualities of other kinds are accordingly always founded on objectifying qualities; they can never be immediately associated with [perceptual] matter in their own right."[25] The objects of intentions need not really exist, as delusion and fantasy show: "a battle of centaurs"[26] dances before the mind in an objectifying act, presenting imaginary creatures rather than isolated colors and shapes. In short, the point of *Logical Investigations* V is not to *limit* the scope of phenomenal presentation, but to give it a broader sense than Husserl's neo-Kantian enemies would want to concede. With the concept of objectifying acts, what Husserl has identified is a paradoxical new medium, one made up neither of full-fledged objects nor raw, passive sensations. We do not really dwell amidst objects, because they forever surpass our explorations of them, remaining inaccessible to us. But neither do we live among brute sensory givens, since there is no such thing as sensuous matter without objectified form: a cacophony of random sound is already interpreted as a specific unit against its background, as are the minute colored points on computer screens. In short, we live in a strange medium located somewhere between substances and qualities, unable to touch either of them.

But alongside this deliberate paradox, there is another problem with Husserl's objectifying acts: the "objects" toward which they point are not very objective all. When the swerving truck is viewed by one person from the left side, by another from behind, and by another from a police heli-copter hovering overhead, Husserl fully realizes that none of these observers can exhaust the entire truck at a glance, since they only encounter specific *Abschattungen* or adumbrations of it. But when we pin down what he thinks the elusive single truck-object *really* is, the result is disappointing, though not surprising. It turns out not to be a real truck set loose in the world as an autonomous colleague and rival of other objects, since this could only rank as a superficial "empirical" understanding of it. Despite Husserl's claim that the object "is not [just] a reality in con-sciousness,"[27] he never allows himself to place it in an actual physical uni-verse, for fear of letting naturalism back into philosophy through the side door. The only remaining alternative is to praise the object as an "ideal" unity, one that lies outside any of its partial sensual profiles even while tying them all together, but one that also does not reside in the merely nat-ural world of causality.

This basic prejudice of phenomenology was later given lucid formula-tion by Jean-Paul Sartre: "The essence of an existent is no longer a prop-erty sunk in the cavity of this existent; it is the manifest law which presides over the succession of its appearances, it is the principle of the series . . . The phenomenal being . . . is nothing but the well connected series of its manifestations."[28] Stripped of its objectivity, though obviously more uni-fied than the separate appearances that announce it, the object is trapped in a difficult position. It is irreducible to its series of appearances, yet it exists outside of them only as an ideal principle, not as something truly independent. The supposed bonding of subject and object that takes place in intentionality is not enough to rescue phenomenology from idealism. There is still no place in Husserl's philosophy for a real fire with real infer-nal properties that allow it to destroy real pieces of paper. These matters are thrown to the scientists like bones to the dogs; meanwhile, the philoso-pher will merely describe how the burning piece of paper shows itself to consciousness.

But we can forget this criticism for now. To fault Husserl for his obses-sion with the sensuous presentability of intentional objects, to undercut his efforts with talk of a shadowy negative background that never comes to view, is to give the appearance of entering the camp of Heidegger and Derrida, whose armies are large enough as it is. Instead of joining their unsurprising campaigns against presence, we should instead try to salvage the more positive concept of phenomena that later trends in continental philosophy have tended to efface. Just before writing this paragraph, I was walking through the streets near my home, eating a bag of french fries, remembering my excited first reading of Husserl years ago, talking with an old friend, observing Arabic signs of every possible color, and enjoying the springlike breeze so typical of Cairo in February. From a Heideggerian standpoint, there is not much that can be done with these experiences: we can discuss the structures of Dasein that make our "absorption" with them possible, or we can poetize about the reclusive shadow of being that haunts them all. From a Derridean standpoint, there is no way to discuss this experience unless french fries and breezes happen to be mentioned in some "text" of James Joyce that can be twisted and punned to pieces, and perhaps vaguely connected with the politics of the day. And here we see the problem. The drama of philosophy for Heidegger and his heirs never lies *inside* specific concrete phenomena, but only inhabits the gap that separates these phenomena from us. For Husserl, the situation is quite different. The shimmering of waves on a pond, the arthritic pains in a fireman's knee, and a foaming mug of Dortmunder are all *philosophically worthy topics*, capturing our attention with their sensual facades even while pointing to the unified objects that exceed these facades.

B. The Blackbird

For Husserl, the field of consciousness is never an inarticulate sheet of sparkling perceptual data. Human awareness is riddled with *objectifying* acts that have already sliced up the world into separate pieces. Intentionality is not a matter of raw colors and sounds, but of the unified objects at which consciousness always aims but never reaches. The same object can manifest itself in countless different ways. Fifty thousand spectators view the same cricket match from different angles and distances, though it always remains the same event. Many people can cherish the same wish.[29] The converse is also true: the same sensory material can give rise to the most diverse articulations of objects. Husserl makes the somewhat droll point that the sight of a bird flying through a garden can support numerous possible expressions: "There flies a blackbird! . . . That is black! That is a black bird! There flies a black bird! There it soars!"[30] To this list we could add endless variations of our own: "Not that bird again!", "Thank God it's still alive!", "Kill it!", or "How the daffodils sway in its wake!" Someone might counter this excited observer with various possible responses: "I see four blackbirds, not one," "I see nothing but smoke," "But it is only a child's toy," or better yet, "I once knew a very special lady called 'Blackbird'. . . Would you care for a drink?" Husserl's point is simple but far-reaching: the real life of consciousness is occupied with objects, not with sense data. The material of the senses apparently serves as a constant anchor for our ceaseless ventures toward unified objects. But it is never itself the direct target of our awareness: "I do not see color-sensations but colored things, I do not hear tone-sensations but the singer's song, etc. etc."[31] Furthermore, if we try to focus on this supposed sense data, we will find that it is not really there. For what may have seemed at first like mere raw material for statements about blackbirds (for example: speeding dark thing, dusky cylinder, or silhouette with wing-shapes) are already objectively structured in their own right, split up into determinate forms from the start. I do not judge that I see a blackbird by putting together trillions of ultimate tiny pixels, but work at a more local level, by identifying widely known bird-elements that seem to be on the scene. At any rate, it is extremely difficult to say what is primitively "given" in our perception. The only reason we even speak of sensuality at all is that perception apparently cannot be made of intentional objects alone. For these objects always elude us, but life nonetheless unfolds in a dense carnal medium.

As is well known, Husserl draws a distinction between simple meaning-*intention* and direct meaning-*fulfillment*. I hear my uncle cry out that a blackbird flies in the garden, but am currently so bored and lazy that I take his word for it and never even look. As I reflect on what he says, my attention is directed toward the unseen blackbird, but only in a vague, emptily verbal sort of way. By contrast, my uncle seems to encounter the blackbird in its bodily reality by way of direct perception, a far more fulfilling intention than my own. Yet even my uncle only sees the bird from one specific angle, forever failing to grasp all of its features at a single glance. As we pass from me in my lazy state to my uncle in his alert and observant one, there does seem to be some sort of improvement—a closer approach to the blackbird itself. We pass from a lesser to a greater fulfillment of intentionality, though not to a perfect one, since there is still a "distinction . . . of a *provisional* and a *final fulfillment*. This final fulfillment represents an ideal of perfection."[32] The elusive ideal would require total overlap between what I intend and what I directly perceive: namely, "an *adequate* perception, one ascribing nothing to its objects that is not intuitively presented . . ."[33] In less perfect cases, the relative fullness of a presentation can be measured by "the sum total of properties pertaining to the presentation itself, through which it analogically gives presence to its object, or apprehends it as itself given."[34] Quite obviously, this ideal limit is beyond reach for any perceptual experience, since perception by its very nature gives us only specific surfaces and profiles of the things we encounter. Husserl does hold that perfect adequacy is possible in cases of introspection,[35] but this is unconvincing, since I do not coincide with myself in introspection any more than I coincide with the being of a crocodile when seeing it.

But at any rate, sheer empty intention and pure intuitive fulfillment share a single familiar structure: "both meaning-intentions and acts of meaning-fulfillment, acts of 'thought' and acts of intuition, belong to a single class of objectifying acts."[36] My life is adrift in a seductive environment of flavors and sounds. The supposed sheer sensory material that confronts me is actually already molded into distinct objects. When my uncle begins spouting off about something in the garden, I understand him to mean a blackbird soaring overhead. The bird now comes into my mind, whether as an actual image or a mere hazy concept. What occupies my mind at that moment is the intentional object "blackbird," not a random assortment of sounds and mental images. The object, whether seen or not, dominates the situation, bringing a wide range of qualities under its merciless yoke. But notice that even in a situation of perfect fulfillment, none of this would change. We might imagine what would happen if my uncle were to acquire the godlike power of seeing all inner and outer aspects of the blackbird simultaneously—a kind of messianic cubism through which the object would display every last one of its features to his eyes. Note that even under this dizzying scenario, the distinction between objects and sensory matter remains. Even here, my uncle's superhuman senses offer him not just a wild diversity of black-colored planes, but unify all of these views under the aegis of a single elusive object: the blackbird. In this way, we arrive at *a fundamental tension within Husserl's phenomena*. On the one hand, they have specific intuitive properties by which they are known; on the other hand, they are unified forms that cement these properties together as belonging to one distinct object.

This is why the case of *names* is so fascinating for Husserl. Expanding on his earlier modification of Brentano, Husserl declares that all objectifying acts are either nominal acts or grounded in such acts.[37] Echoing Aristotle and anticipating Saul Kripke, Husserl holds that names are "fixed appellations"[38] (cf. "rigid designators"[39]) referring directly to an underlying shadowy "this" rather than to any particular set of sensual-material qualities. "The meaning of a proper name lies accordingly in a direct reference-to-this-object, a reference that perception only *fulfills* . . . but which is not identical with these intuitive acts."[40] Intentional acts resemble proper names in aiming at objects that can never be presented in a wholly fulfilling manner. Perception can only *assist* our acts of meaning without being directly responsible for them, since these acts by definition go beyond the materials with which they work. In other words, the blackbird in the garden can only be named as "that thing there," not as any particular set of visible qualities. Certainly, we can try to zero in on it by making lists of increasingly detailed attributes, such as "that black winged creature with a beak and two eyes that is now flying in the air." But Husserl notes that these properties only help us *identify* the blackbird; they are not quite enough to *name* it, since there is always much more to the blackbird than any list of sensual traits we might produce. It may even turn out that some of them are incorrect: as Kripke would observe, the bird might have lost one of its eyes without my uncle knowing it, and might even be a grackle or a crow instead of a blackbird—not to mention a bat or an experimental CIA drone. For phenomenology, to name an object is to point to some kind of unifying *form* that binds together many distinct properties; a name is never just a shorthand alias for the total list of these properties. Sensual qualities are always qualities *of an object*, even when we fail to distinguish these objects correctly amidst all the confusions of the senses.

C. Objects and Qualities

We already know that Husserl departs radically from traditional realism, shutting out the existence of the natural world altogether and letting phenomena rule the cosmos. But even within this limited phenomenal sphere, we encounter a classical problem of philosophy that marks a central theme of the present book: *the deep-seated tension between a single object and its manifold qualities.*[41] Aristotle famously states that "being one is being *indivisible,* just exactly what it is to be a *this . . .*"[42] The paradox here, as identified in Leibniz's *Monadology,* is that "the monad, which we shall discuss here, is nothing but a simple substance that enters into composites—simple, that is, without parts," and yet "monads must have some qualities, otherwise they would not even be beings."[43] Although Husserl departs from classical philosophy in several obvious ways, this is not one of them. We will need to discover how these dual layers of the world weave through one another, resisting or penetrating each other.

But the beginning of this section already hinted at a *second* version of the problem of the one and the many in phenomenology. It stems from a passage cited above, to the effect that "there are . . . not two things present in experience, we do not experience the object and beside it the intentional experience directed upon it, there are not even two things present in the sense of a part and a whole which contains it: only one thing is present, the intentional experience . . ."[44] We are not talking about two previously separate entities called "self" and "object" forced into a shotgun marriage, but about a single encompassing reality: intentional experience. Given the collapse of separate subjective and objective spheres for Husserl, this is clear enough. But it is only half true. Intentionality is not just the unreserved union of subject and object, but also contains *separate* objects as specific contents, including myself insofar as I am not identical with what I intend. This is why intentionality has been known since medieval times as "intentional *in*existence," and why Husserl continues to refer to it as "immanent objectivity." As Brentano puts it, "each mental phenomenon contains something as object in itself . . ."[45] However strong the bond between myself and the things, this bond has also decomposed into particular elements that have not fused together like metals in a furnace—not

at all, since the supposed intentional whole remains broken into portions
from the start. Not only do numerous distinct phenomena populate the
same intentional act, but even perceiver and perceived remain somehow
distinct. I do not melt unconsciously into the image of the green apple as
if we were truly the same thing, but am fascinated by the apple, letting it
work its magic as a specific terminal point of my consciousness. I am not
dissolved along with objects into some sort of global purée, but must deal
with them, whether by bowing before their might or reducing them to
dust. Nor are the different objects in my awareness dissolved into each
other. Although in one respect the intentional act is a seamless fabric without parts, in another respect it is riddled with numerous interior objects
that hypnotize me, that absorb my attention as I enjoy their sensuous
facades and aim my attention at the elusive objects lurking beneath them.
In short, *the unified intentional experience is already a descent into its own
particles*.[46] When Husserl insists that parts are not "really" in their
whole,[47] this disclaimer applies only to the old-fashioned *physical* sense of
part and whole. Have no doubt about it: the intentional whole is swarming with parts.

The problem of the one and the many has now arisen in two different
ways. In Husserl's phenomenology, it is both: (a) the enmity between a
unified intentional object and its particular sensuous features, and (b) the
discord between an intentional act's unity and its multiple interior contents. In the first case, this red ball before me is not *just* a bare featureless
"this," but also red and round and cheap and made of plastic and origi-
nated from a Pacific Rim sweatshop. In the second case, the red ball and I
are cemented together in a single unified relation, though at the same time
the ball and its neighboring objects are still quite distinct from me. These
two divisions mark the two central paradoxes of intentional existence. By
gradually transforming these paradoxes into a full-blown metaphysics of
objects, the present book will revive and extend the basic principles of phenomenology. While some readers might wonder whether this theory of
two dualisms is too eccentric a lesson to draw from Husserl, others will
have noticed the intimate connection between these oppositions and the
famous Husserlian reductions: eidetic and phenomenological.

The *eidetic* reduction tries to arrive at the essential kernel of a thing by
varying its modes of appearance and stripping away the more transient features until we gain direct intuition into its essence. But notice why this is
necessary in the first place: only because of the tension we have already
described between the elusive intentional object itself and its particular
sensuous manifestations. If the donkey-object and pineapple-object
appeared in adequate perception from the start, no eidetic reduction
would be necessary, since everything would lie spread before us like
sparkling pearls. Hence, the eidetic reduction is a sharp instrument for

probing the strife between the essence of a thing and the specific concreteness in which it always becomes manifest. And as Husserl recognizes, this strife is insurmountable—even my uncle, with his shaman-like visionary powers, cannot obliterate the difference between the unified blackbird and its innumerable qualities, contours, adumbrations, and profiles.

Meanwhile, the *phenomenological* reduction places in suspension any talk of the external reality of what we perceive, flattening everything onto a single intentional plane where subject and object are united. But note once again that this reduction is necessary only because the appearances and I are in some sense clearly *not* the same. If intentionality were truly a global placid lake, I would be so intimately fused with the objects of my experience that I could never notice them at all. We would have sheer unity à la Parmenides and Zeno, a global intentionality without organs. In other words, the phenomenological reduction is needed only because the objects eternally *flaunt their otherness in my face*, as they emit blinding colors, nourish me, or wound me with poisonous spikes. The phenomenological reduction, then, points to a strife between the unity and duality of human experience—the simultaneous sameness and otherness of objects.

Since this is not a book about Husserl, there is no need to offer a fuller analysis of the reductions. I mention them here only to indicate that the aforementioned double dualism in intentionality lies at the heart of Husserl's system, and is not some bizarre curiosity scraped up from the swamps.

D. Two Borderlands

We have seen that phenomenology begins by fencing off two wild borderlands from the realm of philosophy. The first of these is scientific naturalism. By bracketing the question of an object's independent physical existence, the object is reduced to the series of its appearances, or rather to an ideal principle that strings through these appearances and unifies them. The opening section of this book was designed to salvage something of the natural world. Although Janicaud and the theologians seem to be bitter opponents, their root assumption was identical: plurality exists only in phenomena, not in real objects. In opposition to both camps, I argue for a plurality of the depths, a cosmos of multiple autonomous actors irreducible to their phenomenal appearance.

The second patch of wilderness shunned by phenomenology is that of raw sensation. *Logical Investigations* V established that intentionality is made up of objectifying acts. Humans do not encounter raw sense data and then impose a grid of solid entities onto the rawness; our conscious acts always aim far beyond the exaggerated, ramshackle facades that are presented to us, and stretch toward the elusive objects that unify these facades. We have seen that these objects never become present in sensation, since even if it were possible for some superhuman consciousness to see all sides or properties of an object at once, the object would still be more than the sheer sum of these qualities. But at the same time, it seems that no sensation is possible without objectifying acts. Even if we tried to read Husserl's later notion of raw "hyletic data"[48] as a kind of backtracking from the fifth investigation, this would only prove the case further—sheer sensory matter is initially banished from phenomenology to such an extent that special rescue operations are needed later to address it. But the purpose of this book is not to defend raw sense data; Husserl's theme of objectifying acts is perfectly compelling as it is. The purpose, instead, is to ask how sensory properties can exist at all.

If all intentionality is object related, it clearly cannot be *only* object-related. For objects are forever inaccessible. In the simplest possible terms: if there were nothing but objects in intentionality, the world would remain invisible. While the first section asked that we salvage naturalism, the current section means to say that we must rehabilitate some form of sensationalism as well. Even if it remains impossible to encounter formless sensation unattached to any objectifying act, there must still be a side of sensation that is sheer formless enjoyment, quality without substance. There must be an ether or solar wind of loose sensual materials if the world is to be visible in the first place.

The cumulative lesson of this book so far is that phenomenology is caught at the midpoint of two intersections: (1) On the one hand, we deal only with objects, since sheer formless sense data are never encountered; on the other hand, an "objects-only" world could not be tangible or experienceable in any way, since objects always elude us. (2) On the one hand, phenomena are united with our consciousness in a single intentional act, while on the other hand they are clearly separate, since they fascinate us as end points of awareness rather then melting indistinguishably into us.

Combining these two problems, we have arrived at a turbulent structure of objects. First, they are both immanent and transcendent. Second, they are both austerely unified and sparkling with qualities as numerous as the stars. This structure of dual axes lies at the center of phenomenology, barely mapped, like an untapped vein of silver or a hidden oil reserve. But to work out its hidden dynamics requires that we go beyond the mere description of phenomena and return to the abandoned regions of metaphysics, despite all warnings of its dangers.

[3]

Bathing in the Ether

A knife cuts through a melon, opening its juicy interior to the light of the sun. Edmund Husserl is in attendance, and reflects on what he has just seen: the flash of the gleaming knife at noon, the reddish pulp and mottled black seeds freed from the prison of the rind. Forever alert to the sensual contours of things, phenomenology makes room for the pursuit of objects in their carnal, seductive character. For those who hope to revive the concreteness of philosophy, this can only be a good thing.

Nonetheless, I have already made two complaints about Husserl's way of dealing with melons and suns. First, these things are treated as phenomena rather than as objects, which means that they are not allowed to interact with each other except when chaperoned by a thinking human subject. Husserl and his various descendants are concerned only with the profiles and contours that knives emit toward humans, not with the mutual contact of knives and fruit, which they tend to write off as scientific naturalism. Second, it is left unclear what the sensual medium of our experience really is. We know that it is not made up of objects, since objects always withdraw from view and never become carnally present. But neither is it made of preobjective raw data, since no such data exists without having already taken on objective form. The world of the senses is somehow both objective and raw, both noun and adjective, in a way that has not been sufficiently clarified.

The first of these complaints entails a somewhat lonely struggle, since the contemporary atmosphere in philosophy is still too pleased by its surpassing of old-fashioned realism to be very interested in any *new* brand of it. If there is a sense in which Heidegger can be read as a realist corrective to Husserl,[49] even Heidegger does not see the collision of inanimate things as philosophically meaningful. But the second battle is not a solitary quest at all, since an entire school of phenomenology aims precisely at clarifying the status of the sensual realm. Beginning with the works of Levinas and Merleau-Ponty, we discover the carnal phenomenology that

33

continues today in the haunted prose of Alphonso Lingis. This new tradition is concerned not with objectifying acts aimed at abstract intentional unities, but with the translucent mist of qualities and signals in which our lives are stationed. Instead of rushing past sensual surfaces toward the ideal object or executant tool lying beneath them, *les charnalistes* bathe in an ether of the senses. In the calming works of Emmanuel Levinas, our relation to this ether is described as enjoyment. We can use the section on this theme in *Totality and Infinity* to anchor our discussion.

A. Passivity

Let it be granted that intentionality aims at objects that never fully appear, rushing past whatever is directly given. Let it be granted that the human use of objects is always entangled in a vast network of complicated references, thereby pushing us beyond the naive isolation of individual substances. Even so, none of this tells us more than half of the story. We do not solely rush away from the here-and-now or continually vanish into some ever-deferred "elsewhere." We always stand *somewhere*, in some concrete zone of sensuous realities and no other. The present book hinges on defining this "somewhere" and describing its features—a purpose in which Levinas can be of some assistance. Although his own philosophy ultimately aspires toward an Otherness that would *escape* the concreteness of any specific moment, he starts out with a more intimate description of such moments than most authors provide. "I eat bread, listen to music, follow the course of my ideas."[50] It is in this bewitching world of bread and music that we will now set up camp.

En route to this zone of earthly nourishments, Levinas makes a highly misleading claim about Husserlian phenomenology: "The thesis that every intentionality is either a representation or founded on a representation dominates the [*Logical Investigations*] and returns as an obsession in all of Husserl's subsequent work."[51] In this view, Husserl privileges "intelligibility, characterized by clarity, [which] is a total adequation of the thinker with what is thought, in the precise sense of a mastery exercised by the thinker upon what is thought in which the object's resistance as an exterior being vanishes."[52] Like Descartes's clear and distinct ideas, intentionality is "entirely present, without anything clandestine . . . [it is] the disappearance of what could shock."[53] Levinas will offer his own philosophy as an alternative to this Husserlian regime of oppressive light, so devoid of all concealment and surprise.

But with this gesture, Levinas unfairly mixes two distinct phenomenological themes. For in one sense, it is not true at all that Husserl grants privilege to representation. As we have seen, *Logical Investigations* V established that intentionality is essentially object oriented, not representational. In this respect it is unjust to claim that Husserl reduces perception to something luminous and intelligible, since our mental acts aim at inaccessible unities that lie deeper than what is given. In fact, we have seen that Husserl's fixation on these objective intentional unities is so intense that he actually has very little to say about what the representations of the senses really are—which is precisely why the carnal phenomenologists are able to break fresh ground with their various remarks on colors, sexuality, and food. In this first respect, then, there is not too much sensory presentation in Husserl, but too little.

There is a second sense, of course, in which Levinas is right. In order to overcome scientific naturalism, Husserl strips from the things their character as autonomous agents at work in the cosmos, restricting them to the phenomenal silhouettes that they present to the human gaze, or at best to the ideal principle of these silhouettes. But it should also be noted that Levinas himself has an ambiguous track record on this point. We are all familiar with his hymns to the otherness of things, to the untamed substantiality of rock or metal that resist being shaped into axes and knives. But every such example in Levinas is outweighed by perhaps a dozen announcements that the world in itself is a single anonymous rumble, and that only human being can hypostatize individual existents from amidst the monotonous drone of a unified *apeiron*.[54] If intentionality is enough to make Husserl an idealist, then this theory of hypostasis surely ought to be enough to qualify Levinas for the club. Both thinkers are equally bored by the inner life of inanimate objects, and circulate primarily in the restricted homeland of human perception.

Regardless of whether Levinas is in any position to call Husserl an idealist, he does push this criticism in an interesting direction. We have already heard his lament that "representation is a pure present."[55] Put somewhat differently, "representation involves no passivity."[56] Although the phenomena we encounter lie outside us in some way, there is another sense in which intentionality claims to determine them completely, leaving no residue outside the relation itself. It is precisely through "passivity" that Levinas hopes to escape the trap of the single instant and begin contact with the Other—a future that surprises the crystalline stasis of the here and now. In short, Levinas is making use of a familiar distinction between intelligibility and sensibility. While this has the potential to focus phenomenology on the sensual world to a greater extent than before, it is a disaster in all other respects. For the great advance of *Logical Investigations* V was to advance beyond a simplistic two-storied universe of passive sense data and active intelligible mental acts. For Levinas, intelligibility is in one place, and sensibility in another, whereas for Husserl, the distinction between them occurs at every possible layer of perception—already a more sophisticated model.

Against the activity of mental representation, Levinas praises the passivity of enjoyment and the vulnerability of corporeal existence. Our body's "indigence—its needs—affirm 'exteriority' as non-constituted, prior to all affirmation."[57] Rooted in the world, we depend on a surplus of reality that comes from beyond the sphere of intelligible meaning: a surplus that Levinas terms alimentation or nourishment. The lucid and dignified human consciousness is replaced by a needy or lascivious body immersed in rewards, disasters, and feasts. "To doubt, to labor, to destroy, to kill— these negating acts *assume* objective exteriority rather than constitute it. To assume exteriority is to enter into a relation in which the same determines the other while [also] being determined by it."[58] Our lives are so thoroughly shadowed by this passively received netherworld that even the consumption of meals takes on ontological weight: "[the] sinking of one's teeth into the things which the act of eating involves above all measures the surplus of the reality of the aliment over every represented reality . . ."[59] In this way, we are denied the mighty sovereign power of which we might have dreamed. I do not constitute the world, but rather "the world I constitute nourishes me and bathes me. It is aliment and 'medium.'"[60] Although it is regrettable that Levinas chooses to fix this medium at a single site, rather than scattering it into numerous levels as Husserl tries to do, this aliment or medium is precisely the sort of concept we are looking for.

B. Quality without Substance

According to Levinas, all of our dealings with things emerge from a milieu of *enjoyment*. This means that the things are independent of any use I make of them, and also means that they are individual units not fully absorbed into the system of the world. "In enjoyment the things are not absorbed in the technical finality that organizes them into a system."[61] The target here is obviously Heidegger's global contexture of equipment, which Levinas replaces with a model of autonomous finalities. The world does not dissolve into a total empire, but confronts me with certain individual characters: "the crust of bread, the flame in the fireplace, the cigarette— offer themselves to enjoyment."[62] And again, "furnishings, the home, food, clothing are not [equipment] in the proper sense of the term . . . we enjoy them or suffer from them; they are ends. Tools themselves, which are in view of [something], become objects of enjoyment."[63] To enjoy something is to bask in its tactile contours, to encounter it in its independence apart from all use I might make of it: "Enjoyment—an ultimate relation with the substantial plenitude of being, with its materiality—embraces all relations with things."[64] This is a constant experience, not an intermittent one. Levinas does not contend that enjoyment kicks in during holidays and

vanishes amidst stress and trauma. Enjoyment is simply one side of experience, one that is always accompanied by the system of functions that it
works to counter. It is not true that I simply enjoy bread and flame without ulterior purposes, since those references are always present in the
things as well. I can never simply enjoy; I simultaneously objectify.

The medium in which enjoyment occurs is termed *the element.* "In
enjoyment, the things revert to their elemental qualities."[65] It is impossible to use the elemental medium for any practical aims, or even to grasp it
directly: "one is steeped in it; I am always within the element,"[66] and "the
adequate relation with the element is precisely *bathing.*"[67] It comes from
nowhere and takes on no shape, "as though we were in the bowels of
being."[68] This latter phrase has only a figurative meaning for Levinas, since
he is aware that enjoyment actually freezes me in my own sphere and never
reaches the depth of the elusive Other. For although the element is a "wave
that engulfs and submerges and drowns . . . a total contact without fissure
nor gap,"[69] although it consists of publicly available water and sky that
belong to no one, there is still a sense in which it is *my* element, since the
Other always lies somewhere beyond. "In enjoyment I am absolutely for
myself . . . Not against the Others . . . but entirely deaf to the Other, outside of all communication and all refusal to communicate—without ears,
like a hungry stomach."[70] Sensation is no more infinite than intelligibility,
even if it is more apt to take the things on their own autonomous terms.
In fact, the element occupies a strange middle ground: it is neither a dis-
tinctly formed object that could be catalogued and manipulated, nor a slice
of concealed reality. That is to say, "it lies outside the distinction between
the finite and the infinite."[71] The element is that which is completely
nonobjective. It is neither the manipulable object of human experience,
nor some metaphysical object-in-itself; yet all objects emerge from it and
sink back into it.

It needs to be determined just what this ether or elemental medium is.
We already know that it lacks any determinate shape: "The element has no
forms containing it; it is content without form."[72] And although Levinas
has already told us that eating is a relation to the inner substantial plenitude of things, this does not mean that the element is *itself* substantial.
After all, the fact that it is tangibly accessible to us rather than hidden
murkily in the depths already rules it out as a candidate for objecthood,
and assigns it to the place of sheer quality: "The pure quality of the element does not cling to a substance that would support it."[73] It is not like
a solid, but rather like a liquid, one which "manifests its liquidity, its qualities without support, its adjectives without substantive, to the immersion
of the bather."[74] And again, "it is not a question of a *something*, an existent manifesting itself as refractory to qualitative determination. Quality
manifests itself in the element as determining nothing."[75] Here already, we

have a full determination of what the elemental is supposed to be: an ether of loose quality not attached to any substance. It can never be grasped in the form of individual objects, and is also not a direct incarnation of reality itself, since the Other will always exceed any selfish enjoyment of the elemental. Whatever other questions may need to be asked about the ether, this is a good starting point.

Another name that Levinas gives to the elemental is "sensibility," already signaling his deep bond with Merleau-Ponty. Not surprisingly, Levinas condemns the rationalist tradition that views sensation as a confused mode of thought, a poor man's reason. Instead, the sensual realm has to be taken on its own terms: "This situation is not reducible to a representation, not even an inarticulate representation; it belongs to sensibility, which is the *mode* of enjoyment."[76] Forever bathing in the sensory ether, I am not a detached mind passing judgments on my surroundings: "One does not *know*, one *lives* sensible qualities: the green of these leaves, the red of this sunset."[77] Furthermore, we already know that sensation does not entirely point beyond itself toward some series of ulterior references. Sensation "does not even experience [infinite regression]. It finds itself immediately at the term; it concludes, it finishes without referring to the infinite."[78] In this way, sensation is an end in itself. Finally, and perhaps most importantly, sensation differs from thought in not standing in aloof remove from the things it confronts. Sensation bathes so fully in its milieu that its very nature "is to be within, to be inside of."[79] This point will be of crucial and unusual significance a bit later.

But there are already some important unsolved difficulties in this model of the substanceless ether. In the first place, Levinas never defines precisely *where* enjoyment takes place, or even *what* it enjoys. Most relevantly, does our enjoyment unfold only in a single sensual ether that remains constant at all times, or can we actually enjoy specific objects in specific ways? Levinas seems to lean toward the former option, but surely the latter is closer to the truth. To enjoy bread is not to enjoy atoms, or raw wheat, or flour, or bread dough, or even the wind and sea that envelop me as I eat it—but *bread*. At one moment I can enjoy the bread, at the next moment enjoy the spectacle of my entire plate of food, and at the next shift my enjoyment to the breakfast or seaside as a whole. It seems clear that in each of these cases, the character of the enjoyment changes. But this seems to run counter to Levinas's own instincts, since he prefers to confine the elemental to vaguely defined sites of meteorology: "It is wind, earth, sea, sky, air."[80] There is no valid reason to shift immediately into this sort of nature poetry, and of course Levinas himself recognizes that we also enjoy cities, streets, "fine cars," and "fine cigarette lighters."[81] In fact, he seems to recognize quite explicitly that enjoyment is never separable from the specific things to which it ought to be opposed: "For in fact the sensible objects we enjoy have already undergone labor. The sensible quality already clings to a substance. And we shall have to analyze further the signification of the sensible object qua thing."[82] This last sentence already concedes a significant change in the theory, since we can no longer confine the ether to some sort of vague national park of refreshing breezes and bubbling waters. The elemental is itself shaped and refigured by the inaccessible things that it shadows, whether these be fine sunsets, fine grapes, or fine snowmobiles. To this extent, Levinas is forced to recover Husserl's insight from *Logical Investigations* V that there is no absolute boundary between passively received sensation and actively formed objects. There is no dualism, as if once and for all, between sensation and thought, but only a ubiquitous schism between the thing as a unit and the myriad sensual facets by which it appears. Levinas does focus his theoretical interest on sensibility in a way that Husserl does not, and for that he deserves our full praise. However, this tends to happen only by means of a relapse into the absolute gulf between sensibility and understanding that Husserl had already discredited.

To conclude this section, it should be added that Levinas is too one-sided in his treatment of sensual naiveté. Specifically, he states that "sensibility, essentially naive, suffices to itself in a world insufficient for thought. The objects of the world, which for thought lie in the void, for sensibility—or for life—spread forth on a horizon which entirely hides that void. The sensibility touches the reverse, without wondering about the obverse; this is produced precisely in contentment."[83] Here, Levinas contrasts the sincerity of sensual enjoyment with the purported cynicism of our relation to objects, since the latter are said to take the form of sheer manipulable property. But this is just a typical case of trying to segregate the entire world into two zones by means of a structure that actually spreads freely throughout *both* of those zones. It is certainly true that I do not rise above the murmuring sensuality of the world in which I bathe; my relation to this ether is entirely sincere. But it is equally true that my relation to *specific* things is sincere: to purchase or barter melons, to use them as targets for archery, to poison them and offer them to the enemy, are actions every bit as "sincere" as any aimless basking in the shapeless qualities of the earth. In all of these cases my life expends itself in dealing with the melons, listening closely to their strengths, limitations, and possibilities as I come to terms with their reality.

C. Satisfied with Appearance

Along with the theme of sensibility and its exact structure, this book has also been concerned with the status of the reality of the world. We should now ask whether Levinas fully takes the measure of the world's autonomy, or whether he remains confined to the sphere of human access. The evidence on this question is ambiguous. In one sense, Levinas clearly holds that there is a reality to the world that exceeds our grasp of it at any given moment. The centering of his philosophy as a whole in the notion of the "Other" is already an overwhelming indication of this. The same holds for his innate sympathy for the independent substantial plenitude of things, as revealed when we sink our teeth into a piece of corn or feel a cold evening wind. Whereas "a thing only offers itself to us by way of a side,"[84] it must be said that "enjoyment, as interiorization, runs up against the very strangeness of the earth."[85] Phrased in Heideggerian terms, Levinas has no sympathy for the presence-at-hand of things. The strangeness confronted by our enjoyment cannot possibly be overcome, since "what the side of the element that is turned toward me conceals is not a 'something' susceptible of being revealed, but an ever-new depth of absence."[86] And in an emphatic piece of new terminology, we hear that "this way of existing without revealing itself, outside of being and the world, must be called *mythical*. The nocturnal prolongation of the element is the reign of mythical gods."[87]

But Levinas's account of the nocturnal, unapparent, and mythical realm suffers from the same bias as his treatment of the sincerity of enjoyment. Those who are familiar with his earlier career will not be surprised by an apparent return of the "*il y a*" of *Existence and Existents*. In that brilliant early treatise, Levinas openly asserted that the world itself is an impersonal anonymous rumbling, not inherently broken up into specific beings. Only a human *hypostasis* of objects was considered capable of allowing the emergence of specific existents in the heart of impersonal existence. This theory of the impersonality of the world is not abandoned in the period of *Totality and Infinity*, but openly defended. As Levinas continues to put it in the later work, the mythical is "an existence without existents, the impersonal par excellence."[88] As the absolutely Other, it is the ever-surprising "future." But despite Levinas's appeal to mythical gods in the plural, the future is always only one: "we have described this nocturnal dimension of the future [in *Existence and Existents*] under the title *il y a*."[89] And it is no surprise when we hear that "the element extends into the *il y a*,"[90] since Levinas allows neither of these terms to have any *specific* personality. All concrete features are to be restricted to the zone of things regarded as visible spectacles for humans, and are forbidden amidst the vague ambient wealth of wind and sea—to say nothing of the hidden mythical depth.

This is perhaps my least favorite aspect of the philosophy of Levinas. We have already seen that his account of enjoyment tries to confine the elemental to a single layer of sensual passivity, even though it actually recurs in different forms on all possible layers of experience, including highly sophisticated ones. To enjoy India is to enjoy *India*, to enjoy riddles is to enjoy *riddles*, and to enjoy the study of Arabic grammar is to enjoy this field of study itself—not just the wind and the sea. It is not the case that entities become specific only on some derivative level of reason and possessiveness; in each object, sensual enjoyment is already incarnated quite differently, and remains opposed to the elusive total object itself, which remains absent. The same is true of the mythical night of the *il y a*. There is not some global totality of the world, revealed in insomnia, that only human beings are capable of splitting apart into fragments. If we enter a strange room containing a chair, an electric drill, a bottle of wine, and a tank of tropical fish, there is not just a single "ever-new depth of absence" into which all of these entities vanish. Instead, each of them has its *own* ever-new depth.

Perhaps we should concede that Levinas's ever-absent Otherness[91] of the depths at least points to a minimal trace of realism in his thought. But no sooner does he show his minimal realist colors than he instantly denies them by an alternate route. While praising Descartes and Kant for noticing the inscrutable darkness and passivity of sense perception,[92] he prefers not to leave much of anything to be kept in this autonomous darkness. In a grudging remark about Kant, Levinas gripes faintly that "in postulating things in themselves so as to avoid the absurdity of apparitions without there being anything that is appearing, Kant does indeed go beyond the phenomenology of the sensible."[93] This is clearly not meant as a compliment, as emphasized by the rescue effort of the next sentence: "But at least he does recognize thereby that of itself the sensible is an apparition without there being anything that appears."[94]

Phenomenology as a movement, like most recent movements in philosophy, tends to be deeply uncomfortable with metaphysical issues. Probably for this reason, it exhibits wild mood-swings in its discussions of the reality of the world. When fighting psychologism, it hoists the banner of realism, denying that objects are internal psychological data and insisting that they are independent of our mental acts. When fighting natural science, it takes the opposite tack, and tries to rescue objects from physical causation by placing them in a purely "ideal" realm. Whenever it is *forced* to take a stand on this question, it generally claims that the whole problem is actually a "pseudo-problem" generated by sloppy traditional categories. It is asserted in shaky tones that phenomenology has overcome the entire question of reality, which only tradition-bound hacks could ever take seriously. But the reduction of problems to pseudo-problems is one of the most overrated philosophical stratagems of our age, one that often serves only to get authors off the hook when there are problems that they are unable to clarify. It is the "what difference does it make?" approach to philosophy, too often accompanied by contorted facial expressions, and too often aimed at those who have labored subtly and patiently for years at issues that critics take only a few seconds to dismiss. In fact, the question of whether the world is real or not for phenomenology makes a *huge* difference, since it bears directly on the internal structure of phenomena themselves. The middle-ground position of claiming that "it makes no sense to ask" is not as neutral as it appears, for it entails a *de facto* reduction of objects to phenomena. Those who try to remain agnostics about the reality of any extraphenomenal realm still do not hesitate to strip such a realm of its philosophical role. The question of whether phenomenology deals with realities or only with human access determines whether philosophy can range freely over the whole of the world, or whether it will remain restricted to self-reflexive remarks about human language and cognition. The fate of two utterly different styles of philosophical thought hinge on this decision: a choice separating Leibniz from Frege, Whitehead from Husserl, or Bruno Latour from the more deserving targets of the 1996 "Social Text" hoax.[95]

A simple litmus test can be used to pin down the difference. Of any philosophy we encounter, it can be asked whether it has anything at all to tell us about the impact of inanimate objects upon one another, apart from any human awareness of this fact. If the answer is "yes," then we have a philosophy of objects. This does not require a model of solid cinder blocks existing in a vacuum without context, but only a standpoint equally capable of treating human and inhuman entities on an equal footing. If the answer is "no," then we have the philosophy of access, which for all practical purposes is idealism, even if no explicit denial is made of a world outside of human cognition. To remain "neutral" on this question is to condemn philosophy to operate only as a reflexive meta-critique of the conditions of knowledge. It is to trim the hair of Samson while he sleeps, imprisoning philosophy in the human realm while stripping it of the power to conduct nocturnal raids on trees, boulders, lizards, and stars. For all the fertility of his descriptions, Levinas fails this litmus test no less than Husserl does.

D. The Ether

Regardless of whether phenomenology ever brushes up against a real world, it is important to ask what it tells us about the structure of perception. This problem lies at the center of Husserl's works, since intentional acts are always objectifying, but objects are only ideal limits and never directly accessible. Hence, there must be more to consciousness than aiming at intentional objects—some sort of penumbra of qualities-without-objects floating in its midst. For Husserl, this penumbra is *not* a single layer of passive given data, as shown by his critique of the neo-Kantians. Sensuality occurs on every level of the world, in the form of countless shadows of countless layers of objects. It is not confined to a level of passive reception from the otherworld, a level that he does not believe exists. Yet Husserl is so concerned with the objectifying structure of intentionality that he pays little attention to the carnal or sensual ether with which all phenomena are accompanied. Levinas, along with Merleau-Ponty, was the first to make this ether of vague perfumes and flavors into an explicit philosophical theme. For Levinas, there is a single formless element from which the things of our lives emerge. But I have already claimed that this model has several key theoretical weaknesses:

1. It is confined to a *single* passive or receptive layer of reality, and refuses to become entangled in all the manifold layers of objects. Strictly speaking, this would mean that enjoyment is always the *same* enjoyment, whether I am enjoying a foreign city, a bowl of pasta, a coniferous forest, or the friendship of a loyal pet donkey. But if we view the world as passively given sensuality that is then shaped after the fact by human viewpoints, we will have relapsed into a position that Husserl attacked quite effectively. In other words, Levinas does a better job than Husserl of exploring the blank space on the philosophical map known as carnality. However, he tries to do this by means of a conceptual tool that Husserl has already rendered obsolete.

2. For Levinas, the ether of enjoyment does extend directly into the depths of reality itself. But this depth turns out to be nothing but a single anonymous rumbling without parts. Ultimately, Levinas seems to deny that there is a *plurality* of things themselves in autonomous isolation from one another. In this respect he resembles Parmenides and Heraclitus, with their shared assertion that all is one from the standpoint of *logos*, and that only human senses and *doxa* generate a plurality.[96]

3. Finally, and more importantly than it might now seem, Levinas misunderstands his own notion of the sincerity of consciousness. It is not just when feeling the wind and the sea that I am naively absorbed in my actions, but also when I handle carpenter's equipment, critique the stupidity of mass media, denounce all truths as arbitrary, or defraud the local waterworks. While bathing in the sensory ether is certainly an act of sincerity, the same is true of an objectifying intentional act. Sincerity is not located at a single pampered point in reality, but spreads everywhere like a vapor or a drifting rain.

To his credit, there are times when Levinas seems to recognize this. Every object, for him, is actually *compressed* from an elemental medium that threatens to reemerge at any moment: "[the] identity of things remains unstable and does not close off the return of things to the element. A thing exists in the midst of its wastes."[97] Levinas then makes use of the sorts of traditional terms at which Heidegger tends to sneer, concluding that "in things the distinction between matter and form is essential, as also the dissolution of form in the matter."[98] Intriguingly, Levinas views aesthetics as a major site where this duality plays out: "The aesthetic orientation man gives to the whole of his world represents a return to enjoyment and to the elemental on a higher plane. The world of things calls for art, in which intellectual accession to being moves into enjoyment, in which the Infinity of the idea is idolized in the finite, but sufficient, image."[99] I will return to the theme of art in chapter 8.

We are now in full contact with the central theme of this book. In *Tool-Being*, I focused on objects as withdrawn unities that never come to presence. In the present book, what interests me is the cloud of gaseous qualities that *are* present, in which objects do take form and become manifest. This is nothing other than sensuality, as described in the works of the carnal school of phenomenology—the branch of phenomenology that deals with actual experiences such as smoking and weaving, rather than continued tiresome studies of language and negativity.

[4]

The Style of Things

One of the weaknesses of certain forms of contemporary philosophy is a fondness for especially arid prose. Rather than unfairly singling out any particular author, we can make use of a random internet generator designed to capture the very philosophical style to which I refer. On the very first try (as on the dozens that followed) the computer provides a devastating sample. The "author" of the following random passage is the nonexistent Andreas J. La Fournier, employed by an all too existent major university:

> It could be said that the subject is interpolated into a textual precapitalist theory that includes consciousness as a totality. Sartre uses the term 'realism' to denote the paradigm of textual society. However, Lacan's analysis of postcapitalist theory holds that sexuality is intrinsically a legal fiction. The subject is contextualized into a structural paradigm of discourse that includes narrativity as a whole.[100]

In its familiarity and its vagueness, such prose risks nothing. It returns home not with spices, rhesus monkeys, and myrrh, nor even with ghost stories and bullet wounds, but only with *success*—and not of the honorable kind.

One of the most appealing features of the carnal phenomenologists, the badge of honor that identifies them even at a distance, is their genetic resistance to pedantry of the aforementioned kind. The majestic style for which they are known is not an incidental ornament, like ribbons on a cat's tail. It is really the sole language appropriate to the strange layer of sensuous reality that they have unearthed. As Nietzsche once wrote, the only way to improve one's style is to improve one's thoughts;[101] more generally, to alter one's style would be to alter one's thoughts. By this measure alone, it seems that something new must be happening in the writings of Merleau-Ponty. There is something faintly chilling about his descriptions,

as numerous readers have witnessed over the years. With uncanny alert-
ness to the subtlest workings of our minds, he invokes "the city whose
temper I recognize in the attitude of a policeman or the style of a public
building."[102] He calls our attention to "an ashtray or a violin,"[103] and
seems at times to encourage narcotic experiments.[104] Magicians and
haunted houses enter his books, as do meteorites and devils, while schiz-
ophrenics stroll past chestnut vendors and mountain ranges. Images seen
with only one eye are said to have no real place in the world, since they
"are swallowed up in it, as ghosts, at daybreak, repair to the rift in the earth
which let them forth."[105] He extends bizarre but touching praise to carpet
for its ability to resist sound,[106] and is surely the only philosopher ever to
ask "what, finally, is lighting?"[107] Obsessed with the darkest colors, he
speaks of "the secret blackness of milk,"[108] while insisting of the fountain
pen's black that "[it] is less the sensible quality of blackness than a somber
power which radiates from the object . . . and it is visible only in the sense
in which moral blackness is visible."[109] He observes, somewhat ominously,
that "[a] church can be burnt down, [a] street and pencil destroyed, and .
. . all the scores of the Ninth Symphony and all musical instruments . . .
reduced to ashes."[110] In his later years, he concludes that "like crystal, like
metal, and many other substances, I am a sonorous being . . . I hear myself
with my throat."[111] The troubling vibrations that emanate from passages
of this kind bear witness to one primary fact: Merleau-Ponty's citizenship
in a world where objects are not the obtuse material blocks of traditional
realism. Instead, they are equal parts angel and monster, shrouded at all
times with colors, rumors, and lingering smells.

A. Sensation

As we have seen, there was already something mysterious about the status
of sensory qualities for Husserl. They are utterly overshadowed by the
objects at which consciousness always aims, but are nonetheless required in
order to make these objects visible. Merleau-Ponty agrees that the issue is
puzzling. "Perception," his major work begins, "seems immediate and
obvious: I have a sensation of redness or blueness, of hot or cold. It will,
however, be seen that nothing could in fact be more confused, and that
. . . traditional analyses missed the phenomenon of perception."[112] While
intentionality always aims at unified ideal objects, "it is [the] pre-objective
realm that we have to explore in ourselves if we wish to understand sense
experience."[113] This perplexity before the riddle of perception is the basic
stylistic trait of Merleau-Ponty as a thinker and writer. The sheer poetry of
sense experience rings in his ears to the end of his life: "this red under my
eyes is not, as is always said, a *quale*, a pellicle of being without thickness

. . . [but] emerges from a less precise, more general redness, in which my gaze was caught, into which it sank, before—as we put it so aptly—*fixing* it."[114]

The first step in clarifying the mystery is to endorse the lesson of Husserl's fifth investigation, and dismiss any notion of raw sensation that would then get molded by the human mind after the fact. Merleau-Ponty is well aware that "the notion of sensation distorts any analysis of perception. Already a 'figure' on a 'background' contains . . . much more than the qualities present at a given time."[115] Perception is always already an interpretation, and once this is recognized, "sensation, which provided a starting-point, is finally superseded, for all perceptual consciousness is already beyond it."[116] It is clear to him that what we perceive is *objects*, not uncooked neutral sensibilia. In this way he avoids the mistake of Levinas in *Totality and Infinity*, who asserts that objectifying acts display "Husserl's excessive attachment to theoretical consciousness," and that they lead to "transcendental philosophy, to the affirmation . . . that the object of consciousness, while distinct from consciousness, is as it were a product of consciousness."[117] We have seen that Levinas worries about the idealistic tendencies of *any* kind of objectification, and that in this way he paints himself into a corner. He is left with nothing but a formless elemental matter, passively received by humans prior to having any inherent form. Merleau-Ponty dismisses this possibility outright. As he puts it, with more than usual thoroughness: "There is no *hyle*, no sensation which is not in communication with other sensations or the sensations of other people, and *for this very reason* there is no *morphe*, no apprehension or apperception, the office of which is to give significance to a matter that has none, and to ensure the *a priori* unity of my experience, and experience shared with others."[118] Matter is not a specific place on a map, a place to be found in wind and stars as opposed to organized armies and large-scale industrial machines. Instead, it is intertwined with form in every portion of the cosmos, as Husserl already implied.

Another insight retained from Husserl, again quite justifiably, is that qualities belong to objects themselves rather than to our consciousness of them. Far from appearing as contents of my mind, qualities are already attached to things, even as these things recede from me. For example, "color in living perception is a way into the thing. We must rid ourselves of the illusion, encouraged by physics, that the perceived world is made up of color qualities."[119] More generally, "it is absolutely necessarily the case that the thing, if it is to be a thing, should have sides of itself hidden from me,"[120] and "the real lends itself to unending exploration; it is inexhaustible."[121] To perceive is always and everywhere to perceive *things*, not mere sense data arbitrarily molded by humans into objects. Forever denouncing the idea that "vision can be reduced to the mere presumption of seeing . . . as the contemplation of a shifting and anchorless *quale*,"[122] Merleau-Ponty ends his career with the lovely remark that a quality most often has a merely "atmospheric existence . . . bound up with a certain wooly, metallic, or porous configuration or texture, and the *quale* itself counts for very little compared with these participations."[123] As he observes further in some truly luscious passages, the qualities are permanently subordinated to the things: "an object is an organism of colors, smells, sounds, and tactile appearances"[124] and on the same note, "the sensory 'properties' of a thing together constitute one and the same thing, just as my gaze, my touch and all my other senses are together the powers of one and the same body integrated into one and the same action."[125]

B. The Body

As we fix our attention on objects, numerous fluctuations of sound and light occur in our vicinity, threatening to confuse our access to the world. There is "a working together on the part of partial stimuli and a collaboration of the sensory with the motor system which, in a variable physical constellation, keeps sensation constant."[126] Bodily organs and artificial limbs work like quivering tentacles to maintain a constant focus on the entities in our field of action. Things do not sit around as inert targets for my thoughts, but summon my entire body:

> [Insofar] as my hand knows hardness and softness, and my gaze knows the moon's light, it is as a certain way of linking up with the phenomenon and communicating with it. Hardness and softness, roughness and smoothness, moonlight and sunlight, present themselves in our recollection . . . [as] certain ways the outside has of invading us and certain ways we have of meeting this invasion . . .[127]

Nor is this true only of our own natural body parts. For instance, an organ-player "settles into the organ as one settles into a house."[128] It is my body rather than my mind which judges the relative size of things, and we all know that this innate sense extends even to a car, when we "feel" whether or not it can squeeze into the parking space ahead of us.[129] The tapping of the blind man's stick gives him a new layer of perception: "the stick is no longer an object perceived by the blind man, but an instrument *with* which he perceives. It is a bodily auxiliary, an extension of the bodily synthesis."[130]

Through our physical bodies and their extension in the form of tools, we are folded into the world in almost lascivious fashion. Our physical bodies represent "a communication with the world more ancient than thought."[131] My physical body is a universal translation tool, "a general power of inhabiting all the environments which the world contains,"[132] the power to explore mountains, dungeons, ice-storms, illnesses, wars, and religious conversions. "In short, my body is not only an object among all other objects . . . but an object which is *sensitive to* all the rest, which reverberates to all sounds, vibrates to all colors."[133] This openness through the body also closes me off in my own physical constitution. Too tall to be a jockey, too soft to be a Special Forces commando, too male to give birth, too restless to stay in the village, too contemporary to live as a knight or centurion or Czar, too foreign to become Hindu or Druze, too poor and contemplative to be a reckless playboy, too untalented to become a chess champion, too human to climb walls or eat grass, and too fragile to drift through outer space like a comet—I am condemned by my own inherent limits to choose from a restricted range of possibilities for exploring the vastness of the universe. In this way, says Merleau-Ponty, my physical constitution resembles a powerful psychic trauma that cannot be overcome. For just as a trauma is "a manner of being,"[134] "so it can be said that my organism, as a prepersonal cleaving to the general form of the world, as an anonymous and general existence, plays . . . the part of an inborn complex."[135] Our bodies are the ultimate form of sincerity. Even the most pompous cynic, scoffing at governments and at the ignorance of his colleagues, rarely mocks his own arms, or sneers at the heartbeat within.

C. The In-Itself-for-Us

Knowing already that sensation and the body are open to the world, we still want to know whether this world has an autonomous reality outside of our perception. Like his fellow phenomenologists, Merleau-Ponty oscillates here between two deeply opposed intuitions. In one sense, he happily admits that the world we explore is something that exceeds us, and which needs to be approached on its own terms if it is ever to yield up its secrets. In the preface to the *Phenomenology of Perception*, Merleau-Ponty already shows a keen sense for the innate resistance of the world: "the real is a closely woven fabric . . . [that] does not await our judgment before incorporating the most surprising phenomena, or before rejecting the most plausible figments of our imagination."[136] In other words, the essences spoken of by phenomenology are not just "meanings" for human consciousness. They are realities. Although our encounter with things illuminates them only to the degree that they are significant for us, this merely proves that we are not attentive enough to "the non-human element which lies hidden in them."[137] As he puts it, "to 'live' a thing is not to coincide with it, nor fully to embrace it in thought." The gap between perceiver and perceived ultimately seems unbridgeable, and one author is singled out, somewhat unfairly, for not recognizing this: "Bergson's mistake consists in believing that the thinking subject can be fused with the object thought about."[138] All of this suggests that Merleau-Ponty is the champion of a world distinct from human experience.

But as usual with all phenomenologists, we also sense pangs of guilt in Merleau-Ponty about pushing this too far and slipping into some sort of naive version of scientific realism. The foregoing statements about the independence of the world are immediately contradicted by statements of an *opposite* character. For ultimately, Merleau-Ponty remains a philosopher of perception rather than of objects, and he has little patience for those who "do not see that the return to perceptual experience . . . puts out of court all forms of realism."[139] Although he knows that the thing resists my efforts to probe it, he simultaneously holds that "the thing is inseparable from a person perceiving it, and can never be actually *in itself* because its articulations are those of its very existence."[140] In more provocative terms, "the very experience of transcendent things is possible only provided that their project is borne . . . within myself."[141] In other words, the subject "extracts [the things round about it] from its own core."[142] Which is to say that "unless thought itself had put into things what it subsequently finds in them, it would have no hold upon things, would not think of them."[143] Nor does this trace of idealism disappear in the later work. In *The Visible and the Invisible* Merleau-Ponty states quite clearly that "[the notion] that the world could pre-exist my consciousness of the world is out of the question."[144] On the same page, he praises the destruction of certain pseudo-problems "once one has admitted the ideality of the world."[145] Though these later passages are mixed with various concessions as to the *reality* of the world, it is granted such reality only "as an intelligible structure,"[146] not as a real event.

Faced with this contradiction, Merleau-Ponty begins to develop what might be called a metaphysics of relations.[147] If an object is not reducible to my perspective on it, and yet is also not a real entity outside of this perspective, then there is still another option: namely, perhaps an object is the focal point of *many* perspectives. Merleau-Ponty formulates this doctrine in numerous passages. For instance, he observes that a house is always seen from one specific angle, "but it would be seen differently from the right bank of the Seine, or from the inside, or again from an airplane: the house itself *is* none of these appearances."[148] Instead of concluding from this that the house is something nonperspectival, he pieces it together by amassing all of the perspectives of it that can possibly be imagined. As he puts it, "the house itself is not the house seen from nowhere, but the house seen from *everywhere*."[149] In passages strikingly reminiscent of Whitehead, Merleau-Ponty begins by telling us that "every object is the mirror of all others."[150] He now stands on the verge of a full-blown cosmological theory, proclaiming that "when I look at the lamp on my table, I attribute to it not only the qualities visible from where I am, but also those which the chimney, the walls, the table can 'see'; but the back of my lamp is nothing but the face which it 'shows' to the chimney."[151] The scare quotes cannot hide what amounts to a radical philosophical claim: that the reality of a thing is defined by the sum total of perspectives by which other things perceive it. Continuing down the same path, he concludes that "the completed object is translucent, being shot through from all sides by an infinite number of present scrutinies which intersect in its depths *leaving nothing hidden*."[152] In a final renunciation of realism, he announces that "taken in itself . . . the object has nothing cryptic about it; it is completely displayed and its parts co-exist while our gaze runs from one to another."[153] In the most general terms, "our body as a point of view upon things, and things as abstract elements of one single world, form a system in which each moment is immediately expressive of every other,"[154] and "it is of the nature of the real to compress into each of its instants an *infinity* of relations."[155]

These are not words of agnostic caution, but a full-blown manifesto for a philosophy in which the old substances of realism are incinerated, replaced by a universal house of mirrors in which each thing reflects all the rest. On this basis, Merleau-Ponty claims "to have united extreme subjectivism and extreme objectivism."[156] But in fact, he holds that this was *already* one of the great achievements of phenomenology, which established that I am "open to phenomena which transcend me, and which nevertheless exist only to the extent that I take them up and live them."[157] In order to overcome the endless debates about subject and object, Merleau-Ponty proposes that "we must discover the origin of the object at the very center of our experience . . . [and] must understand how, paradoxically, there is *for us* an *in-itself*."[158] This catchy but paradoxical formula lies at the heart of his entire philosophical position. Stated differently: "One cannot, as we have said, conceive any perceived thing without someone to perceive it. But the fact remains that the thing presents itself to the person who perceives it as a thing in itself, and thus poses the problem of a genuine *in-itself-for-us*."[159]

The germ of this in-itself-for-us can already be found in Husserl's notion of intentional objects, which are never reducible to *specific* perspectives but also cannot be thought of as parts of nature existing outside of any *possible* perspective. What makes Merleau-Ponty different here is the extreme form he gives to the mirror-theory. Instead of the chair being nothing more than an ideal principle unifying all the ways in which the chair can appear to me over time, Merleau-Ponty seems to regard the chair as the sum total of the way it is "perceived" by me, the chimney, the candle, the grandfather clock, and the dog—"perceived" is put in quotation marks simply to show that he is no animist. With this, it seems that he is moving a step away from Husserl and a step toward Whitehead and Leibniz, toward a world in which the things really do perceive each other. But it is still hard to see how this can happen if all of these entities are merely in themselves *for us*—namely, how there can be any relation between chair and chimney apart from my having some hand in that relation.

And in fact, it turns out that for Merleau-Ponty there is *not* any real relation between chairs, chimneys, and clocks when humans are not on the scene. In the hall of mirrors, not all mirrors are equal: indeed, the mirror known as I myself turns out to be responsible for the existence of all the others. For just like Levinas, Merleau-Ponty contends that the world itself is a plenum packed full without parts, a kind of undifferentiated *apeiron* that is shattered into fragments only by the labor of human consciousness. It takes no subtle work of reading to make this evident; the claim is present everywhere in his works. For instance, he insists that *"looking at the things themselves*, the melting of the snows and what results from this are not successive events, or rather the very notion of event has no place in the objective world."[160] By this he means, quite explicitly, that the world is a vast homogeneous totality until humans burst onto the scene. For events are "shapes cut out by a finite observer from the spatio-temporal totality of the objective world. But on the other hand, if I consider the world itself, there is simply one indivisible and changeless being in it."[161] The calm and measured prose masks a sweeping philosophical claim as radical as those of the pre-Socratics. But the source of Merleau-Ponty's dogma appears to be Bergson rather than Parmenides, as can be gathered from the claim that "the objective world is too much of a plenum for there to be time."[162] If all humans were struck dead instantly, the dissolving of sugar in a glass would no longer have real *durée*, and might as well occur in an instant as in a century, since time and space are a plenum until an observer splits them up into lived segments. Obviously, this entails a thoroughly antirealist position. "For what," he asks rhetorically, "is meant by saying that the world existed before any human consciousness? . . . Nothing will ever bring home to my comprehension what a nebula that no one sees could possibly be."[163]

This serves to emphasize the way in which Merleau-Ponty's hall-of-mirrors cosmology *differs* from that of the daring Whitehead. For the great English philosopher, the relations chair/myself and chair/chimney are only different in degree. Although there are moments when Merleau-Ponty also seems on the verge of such a theory, his heart is not really in it, and he eventually retains all of the antimetaphysical bias that typifies phenomenology as a whole. Everything that he will say about the intertwining of the chair with its parts, or the chair with the chimney and the candle, will turn out to hold only when I myself am interacting with these things. In this respect Merleau-Ponty, so often an innovator, is no more than a product of his age.

D. Flesh

With his concept of the in-itself-for-us, Merleau-Ponty artificially limits the scope of the cosmos to that of human awareness. But he continues his analysis of this perspectivism in an interesting way: in the end, it comes to be known as "flesh." This concept becomes especially clear in *The Visible and the Invisible*, though it was already hinted at in the earlier *Phenomenology of Perception*. Right from the start, the analysis of flesh shows us both the strengths and limitations of Merleau-Ponty's position. For in one sense, he alerts us skillfully to a zone in which things are not strictly isolated from one another, but bleed into one another. Here it is not yet called flesh, but simply "depth," defined as "the dimension in which things or elements of things envelop each other."[164] This suggests a promising theory of the overlapping negotiations between the things of the world, as they unfurl all of their powers and defects before us and before one another. But Merleau-Ponty steps back yet again from the cosmological implications of his breakthroughs, and confines himself to the narrowly human side of perception. Endorsing yet again the notion that the prehuman world is devoid of any specific things, he blames all the defects of philosophy on inanimate objects. For "we have to rediscover beneath depth as a relation between things . . . a primordial depth . . . which is the thickness of a medium devoid of any thing."[165] His discussion of the concept of flesh will be tainted by this same bias.

Merleau-Ponty has high hopes for this concept, "and one knows there is no name in traditional philosophy to designate it."[166] If not for his early death, he would probably have given us a systematic philosophy of the flesh, of that ether or solar wind in which the things and I bathe in each other's glow. For Descartes and his successors, the gap between soul and world was so wide as to be bridgeable only by God as the occasional cause. For Merleau-Ponty, it is the flesh of the world that serves as a sort of medium or occasional cause, as a molten plasma through which the things and I transmit messages to one another. He asks (with the answer "yes" already on his lips) "whether every relation between me and Being, even vision, even speech, is not a carnal relation, with the flesh of the world."[167] To have a body is already to be folded into the things rather than to stand at a distance from them: "the thickness of the body . . . [is] the sole means I have to go unto the heart of the things, by making myself a world and by making them flesh."[168]

Flesh is the intertwining, interlacing, interfacing of I myself with the sensible world: "the presence of the world is precisely the presence of its flesh to my flesh."[169]

Whatever we might think of Merleau-Ponty's relation to realism, he does insist on a distinction between the visible and invisible realms. For as he puts it, with typically seductive prose, the visible thing is "a quality pregnant with a texture, the surface of a depth, a cross section upon a massive being, a grain or corpuscle borne by a massive wave of being."[170] The total reality of the visible, as Husserl already knew, always lies outside those of its appearances that are directly manifest to us. For Merleau-Ponty, the flesh is the medium through which the visible and the invisible, or the visible and the tangible, pass over into each other and melt back into one another. The world is "a whole architecture, a whole complex of phenomena 'in tiers,' a whole series of 'levels of being'."[171] This concept of the levels of being will resurface in the next chapter. For Merleau-Ponty, it is the flesh alone that links each of these levels to the next. It is a kind of conducting fluid or radio frequency linking all entities with their neighbors. Or in his own, more poetic terms: "Between the alleged colors and visibles, we would find anew the tissue that lines them, sustains them, nourishes them, and which for its part is not a thing, but a possibility, a latency, and a *flesh* of things."[172]

Lodged amidst this flesh, I as human have a double role. I am not only a viewer casting my eyes over the landscape, but a hooded figure whose body is lashed by the wind and rain. I must consider "myself seen from without, such as another would see me, installed in the midst of the visible, occupied in considering it from a certain spot."[173] Here again, Merleau-Ponty seems to be on the verge of a bold cosmological step, stripping away the usual privilege of human being and announcing a world filled with symmetrical relations between human and nonhuman alike. There would seem to be a democracy among all such entities, since "if I who see [a] cube also belong to the visible, I am visible from elsewhere, and if I and the cube are together caught up in one same 'element' . . . this cohesion, this visibility by principle, prevails over every momentary discordance."[174] But the reversibility Merleau-Ponty has in mind is one in which only *human* reality presents any paradox. As was baldly stated in his first major book: "There are two modes of being, and two only: being in itself, which is that of objects arrayed in space, and being for itself, which is that of consciousness."[175] And the pitiful cube is summoned to the scene once again to learn its lowly place in the scheme of things: "the cube is not for itself, since it is an object."[176] My own view is that Merleau-Ponty shows naked bias with this restriction. There is nothing specifically human about the flesh, which functions as a general communications medium rather than as a narrowly perceptual one. Flesh cannot be absent when two pieces of plywood, abandoned in a ghost town, smack into each other in a windstorm. Even for these stupefied objects there is an intertwining of the visible and the invisible, given that they fail to exhaust each other's depths through their causal interaction.

E. Style

I once knew an arrogant sculptor who snapped at some remarks about artistic style that were made in his presence. It was proposed during a conversation that one might design a computer capable of generating countless new works in the style of an already known author or musician. The sculptor objected to this notion, not in the manner of a luddite, but that of someone quite confident in a specific philosophical position: "there is no such thing as a style apart from the sum total of works an artist has produced." Whatever the merits of this position, they are opposed by the entire phenomenological tradition, and in my view rightly so. A style is actually *not* a mere concept abstracted from numerous singular cases, but an actual reality that none of its manifestations can exhaust. One can hear a newly discovered Charlie Parker recording and immediately recognize the style; one can and will say that "that solo is really classic Bird," even though up till now it was not part of the known Parker oeuvre. We sense that a certain person does not really belong in Brooklyn or in the military just by their general style, without being able to pinpoint any disqualifying factors. In this sense, styles are no different from intentional objects as defined by Husserl, which lie beyond any of their current profiles and even any of their possible profiles. We can say of any object that it is not a bundle of specific qualities, nor a bare unitary substratum, but rather a *style*. And although style is not often seen as one of Merleau-Ponty's key technical terms, I would suggest that it may be the most important of them all—just as his personal style of seeing the world is surely his most lasting contribution to philosophy.

In several memorable pages, Merleau-Ponty tries to pin down the reality of artworks, which he openly asserts are not reducible to a list of qualities. "Any analysis of Cézanne's work, if I have not seen his paintings, leaves me with a choice between several possible Cézannes, and it is the sight of the pictures which provides me with the only existing Cézanne, and therein the analyses find their full meaning."[177] Even if an infinite intellect were to describe Cézanne's painting by way of an endless descriptive list, we would not yet have the Cézanne style in its living unity, which exceeds such descriptions. A style is never visibly present, but enters the world like a concealed emperor and dominates certain regions of our perception. "It is well known that a poem, though it has a superficial meaning translatable into prose, leads, in the reader's mind, a further existence which makes it a poem."[178] A certain Paul Verlaine poem begins, "In the ennui unending/of the flat land,/the vague snow descending/shines like sand."[179] Verlaine's whimsical music is not translatable into a literal statement of its content, as if he were merely saying "this area is a dull, flat plain with heavy winter snow that sometimes sparkles as it falls." This explains the unsatisfying, even *annoying* effect that occurs when people quote poems and song lyrics for *content*, as though they were translatable into statements of prosaic wisdom. In fact, poets have less in common with oracles than with the voluptuous sorcery of drummers or chefs, and are just as difficult to quote out of context as cymbals or wine. In any case, the animating style of the artwork makes it analogous to the human body, so central to Merleau-Ponty's thought: each of these is "a nexus of living meanings, not the law for a certain number of covariant terms."[180] Indeed, the ability to grasp the style of things beyond any of their particular appearances is so central to human existence that Merleau-Ponty concludes that only mental patients begin to lack this ability.[181] Even philosophy, he holds, is less a set of arguments than an animating impulse by which a thinker sees the world in a unique fashion: "only the central theme of a philosophy, once understood, endows the philosopher's writings with the value of adequate signs."[182] And even an "as yet imperfectly understood piece of philosophical writing discloses to me at least a certain 'style'— either a Spinozist, critical, or phenomenological one—which is the first draft of its meaning."[183]

But not just artworks and human bodies are animated by a style. Objects in general are stylish, and are grasped in each case as unitary postures that exceed any of their specific profiles. An object is not merely a sound and light show, but a stylistic unit. Or as Merleau-Ponty puts it, things are a certain behavior, not a set of properties: "It is not I who recognize, in each of the points and instants passed through, the same bird defined by explicit characteristics, it is the bird in flight which constitutes the unity of its movement, which changes its place, it is this flurry of plumage still here, which is already therein a kind of ubiquity, like the comet with its tail."[184] And despite the fact that our eye ought to grasp only colors and shapes, there is a sense in which "one sees the hardness and brittleness of glass . . . the springiness of steel, the ductility of red-hot steel, the hardness of a plane blade, the softness of shavings."[185] In the end "each color, in its inmost depths, is nothing but the inner structure of the thing overtly revealed."[186] And though an object exceeds all of its visible contours, it is not some underlying featureless lump. It is not a "bare particular," but a *specific* invisible style. As Merleau-Ponty describes it so wonderfully, "the brittleness, hardness, transparency and crystal ring of glass all translate a single manner of being."[187] That single manner of being is the reality of the thing. He continues, in one of those passages that we should all wish to have written ourselves: "If a sick man sees the devil, he sees at the same time his smell, his flames and smoke, because the significant unity 'devil' is precisely that acrid, fire-and-brimstone essence."[188]

On a humbler level than the acrid devil-essence, "it is impossible to completely describe the color of the carpet without saying that it is a carpet, made of wool, and without implying in this color a certain tactile value, a certain weight and a certain resistance to sound."[189] What we see in the style of an object is a certain kind of behavior or way of dealing with situations, just as in the case of humans. To become acquainted with a new person or new city is to make a series of initial conclusions based on surface-effects, before gradually reaching an unspoken assessment as to the underlying mode of being of this person or city, though surprises will always still occur. The unity of a style is that of "a symbolism in the thing which links each sensible quality to the rest."[190] Just as our body is a symbolic medium that translates actual volcanoes and Spanish coins into forms perceivable by our senses, so does the style of a thing animate its multitude of distinct and isolable qualities.

This same sense of style also lies at the heart of *The Visible and the Invisible*, famously uncompleted at the time of Merleau-Ponty's death. Here too, there is a style of things in which "the thin pellicle of the *quale*, the surface of the visible, is doubled up over its whole extension with an invisible reserve."[191] It is a style "allusive and elliptical like every style, but like every style inimitable, inalienable, an interior horizon and an exterior horizon between which the actual visible is a provisional partitioning."[192] And in a series of passages too magnificent not to quote in full, he observes that

> This pebble and this shell are things, in the sense that beyond what I see of them, what I touch of them, beyond their grating contact with my fingers or with my tongue, the noise they make in falling on my table, there is in them one unique foundation of these 'properties'. . . The power of this principle is not a factual power: I know very well that the pebble, the shell, can be crushed at once by what surrounds them. It is, so to speak, a power *de jure*, a legitimacy: beyond a certain range of their changes, they would cease to be this pebble or this shell, they would even cease to be a pebble or a shell.[193]

For the moment, he leaves open the question of what the permissible range of changes may be. More important for now is simply that *some* range of changes is possible. The thing, as a style, remains what it is despite numerous possible oscillations and modulations in its properties, even if there are certain vaguely sensed limits that it must not transgress. And if artworks aspire to generate such styles, philosophy seeks to map them: it "interrogates the world and the thing, it revives, repeats, or imitates their crystallization before us."[194]

In the end, Merleau-Ponty even proposes that the world itself is not a physical cosmos, but simply the grandest of all possible styles: "I am a field of experience where there is only sketched out the family of material things and other families and the world as their common style."[195] Despite the repeated occurrence of the word "family" in these passages, there is no question here of defining styles as "family resemblances," a theory favored by contemporary nominalists who like to deny any unifying force above and beyond qualities themselves. For Merleau-Ponty, the style is a real force that animates the qualities; it is not qualities that piece together a style. But it is noteworthy that the world as a whole is to be regarded as a style. For if the world is flesh, it must also be seen that "the flesh is not matter, is not mind, is not substance."[196] Merleau-Ponty enters the vicinity of Levinas when he adds that "to designate [the flesh], we should need the old term 'element,' in the sense it was used to speak of water, air, earth, and fire, that is, the sense of a *general thing*, midway between the spatiotemporal individual and the idea, a sort of incarnate principle that brings a style of being wherever there is a fragment of being. The flesh is in this sense an 'element' of being."[197] The world is flesh or element, an electrified medium in which all entities, as elusive *styles*, generate surfaces of qualities that fuse together or signal messages to one another. In other words, the world is not *just* made of substances, objects, or styles: it is made up of such styles *and* of the flesh by means of which they come into contact, and which thereby serves as the only causal medium between them. For one object cannot engage another directly, outside the mediation of the worldly flesh. Just as the seventeenth century employed God as the medium of causation, Merleau-Ponty gives this role to the flesh of the world, despite his frequent suspicions that there are no independent individual things. Objects are unifying styles rather than sets of properties, and hence never appear. If the world as a whole is a style, then this is only insofar as it too never fully appears. What *does* appear is the element of flesh— the very carnal medium that we are trying to pin down.

[5]

The Levels

In the preface to his remarkable book *The Imperative*, Alphonso Lingis inserts the following summary of his argument:

> The book elaborates two theses: it shows sensibility, sensuality, and perception to be not reactions to physical causality nor adjustments to physical pressures, nor free and spontaneous impositions of order on amorphous data, but responses to directives. And, resisting all forms of holism, it holds that the directives we find in the night, the elements, the home, the alien spaces, the carpentry of things, the halos and reflections of things, the faces of fellow humans, and death have to be described separately.[198]

This soft-spoken declaration contains something old and something new, though even the old is spiced with novelty.

In one sense, Lingis preserves the basic phenomenological analysis of sensation described in the preceding chapters. As the preeminent early translator of Levinas and Merleau-Ponty, he fused and assimilated the insights of both authors—not by giving scholarly reports on their work, but by reenacting their insights and extending them into strange domains. In this sense, he is the legitimate heir of the carnal phenomenologists. Indeed, it is Lingis alone who has shown the intimate bond between Levinas and Merleau-Ponty as philosophers of the imperative, of the summoning lure that stretches beyond any given sensory perception. The ethical demand of the Other exceeds any of its particular claims on us, just as the style of things is an elusive power that compels the behavior of our body. Moreover, Lingis extends the ethical imperative well beyond its usual scope. He refuses to limit imperative force to the human or divine Other, and actually fragments it to a degree bordering on animism: our whole environment is saturated with imperatives. As he memorably puts it, we "instinctively turn away from the one who with air conditioning and electric lighting freely chooses his own climate when outside the tropical rain

is dancing over the dry dormant earth and over the laughing birds and children."[199] And further: "The agency of welcome and summons could well
be other animals. The summons could come from plants . . . But the alien
and the exotic also summon us imperatively. The open roads, the oceanic,
the stormy skies summon us. We know the summons of music that soars
off to ancient courts, or the shadows that summon us to the realm of spir-
its and death."[200] Though the spirit of Emmanuel Levinas lingers here, the
letter is drastically modified.

But perhaps the key to Lingis's most systematic book is its second
major theme: the critique of holism. "When our look sweeps over the landscape, surveying resources and envisioning tools, we also see the fields rip-
pling with the meaningless hum of insects, the rhythmic flow of the green
hills, the sky speckled with birds veering and reversing. The carpenter's
hammering goes smoothly, by itself."[201] The roots of his antiholism lie
clearly enough in the Levinasian critique of Heidegger's tool-analysis. But
there is a difference between the positions of Levinas and Lingis, and it is
crucial. We have seen that for Levinas, the existence of individual things is
the result of a human hypostasis. In itself, the world is merely a single
anonymous rumble—a universal *il y a* that oppresses the sleepless, an ominous Being devoid of parts. The individual objects of Lingis, by contrast,
are not the products of human consciousness—they are tribes of omens
always already set loose to practice their dark and noble crafts in the world.
The autonomy of stars and coral reefs is *real* for Lingis, no less than the
independence of electric eels, cinemas, sunflower fields, snowflakes, and
molten ores buried deep in the moon. When he offers fruit salad to his pet
toucans, their beaks clapping in triumph, this is not a human hypostasis:
the toucans, bananas, grapes, and cubes of pineapple are genuine sovereign
agents that resist and cajole each other at every step. This simple step is
enough to distance Lingis from the entire phenomenological tradition,
which has always valued wholes over parts. It separates him to an equal
degree from deconstruction, hermeneutics, most recent analytic philosophy, and the ultra-holism of process metaphysics. In the kingdom of
autonomous carnal entities, Lingis has few real compatriots. Given that he
is not as well known as the other figures described in this book, some background information may be useful.

Lingis occupies a strange position as an author, being widely known
but also strangely limited in his direct philosophical influence. Few would
deny that he is the most colorful personality in continental philosophy
today, with memorable eccentricities marking his bizarrely equipped home
and his general persona, and with a lifestyle notable for its ceaseless pil-
grimage through foreign nations. If any book had been written in the past
three decades about cult academic celebrities in American college towns,
Lingis would surely have been one of the stars of that volume: State

College, Pennsylvania has been reduced to a shadow of its former self since his recent departure, at least in the eyes of the student population. Just as few would deny that he is the most gifted prose stylist in continental thought, with a unique and somewhat unearthly voice that has earned the admiration of a number of literary superstars. Moreover, his general philosophical position is already clear enough even in those books that have a more anthropological flavor; in *The Imperative*, the originality of this position is displayed in systematic form. And finally, Lingis would probably have to count as the most *prolific* phenomenologist of all time in any nation: the startling descriptions that appear as flashes of fire in better-known authors occur in nearly every paragraph of Lingis's books, with sometimes vertiginous effect.

Yet for all of this, the impact of his work upon contemporary continental philosophy has been significantly less than these factors would suggest. Two reasons for this asymmetry immediately come to mind. *First*, continental philosophy in the English-speaking world has taken a turn that could hardly be less congenial to Lingisian themes. Where he is engaged with the flesh and pulp of the universe, contemporary fashions have turned primarily to the interpretation and deconstruction of written texts. Where he offers concrete phenomenologies of far-flung misty temples, others prefer Husserl's technical language to his concern with the things themselves. And where Lingis offers a lascivious multiculturalism of endangered birds and transvestite dancers, the dominant brand of multiculturalism is now a gloomy, sanitized discourse of linguistic oppression and imperial encodings. The common ground between these approaches does not exist, and perhaps *should not* exist—why build bridges between the rain forest and Party Headquarters? *Second*, for all the flamboyance of his character and the notoriety it has brought him, Lingis is not an especially adept self-promoter. His reserves of energy are rarely spent even on defending his ideas, much less proselytizing for them. In general he is surprisingly noncombative in philosophical matters, and tends to introduce his most interesting ideas in the quietest possible tones.

Just as his books are filled with alien cultures and abandoned ideas, his home offers refuge to wasp colonies and Asian pheasants. This exotic atmosphere has made him a citizen of remote but fertile islands, both personally and professionally. A friend of mine once expressed this situation with lucid California vulgarity: "Lingis is in his own world a lot, but it's a big-ass world."[202] The child of Baltic immigrants, his alien obsessions serve as camouflage for what is in some ways the most deeply American personality I have ever encountered. I refer not to the protesters' America of banks and oil companies, but the mutating America of Huckleberry Finn, White Fang, Captain Ahab, Jack Kerouac, the Voyager probe, and other utopians-in-motion. It is impossible to imagine a French or German

Lingis, or even, despite his cultural affinities, a Brazilian Lingis. But it is easy enough to imagine him visiting other planets.

A. Imperative Objects

What makes *The Imperative* such a challenging book is its tendency to cut against the grain of the usual mission of the intellectual. The philosopher is supposed to be a champion of critique, and more generally of freedom; the genuine thinker is the one who rejects the naive pieties of the ignorant, shaking off all external constraint. And yet Lingis, who seems in his own life to be a model transgressor of social norms, whose books take place in the erotic pageants and libertine carnivals of the Third World, begins his book with an explicit assault on this model of thinking: "There are in our cultures today those who in all things seek to set forth their freedom. For them humans are the free animals; freedom is not only distinctive to humans, but is their supreme and sole value."[203] The counterpunch comes two paragraphs later:

> But how many people are there who in everything they think, do, and feel respond to directives! For craftsmen there is a right way to make some thing and a right way to use each thing. Hang gliders learn from the winds and the thermals and from the materials the right way to make and to fly a hang glider, as the composer learns from the symphony emerging before him which are not yet the right notes.[204]

This has broader implications than might be imagined. In the first place, the imperative is not designed to punish us by restricting our freedom; few who know the books or person of Lingis would worry that he is trying to introduce some sort of stifling universal ethical code. The imperative actually has an ontological character even more than an ethical one. Its target is the dreary tendency to split the world into two mutually incompatible zones, one of them a mechanistic causal chain of objects blindly assaulting one another, and the other an arbitrary space of human freedom that imposes subjective values on a mindless grid of neutral materials. As Lingis puts it, "the philosophy of mind has failed to recognize the way perception *responds to directives.* The proliferation of new models to understand our relationship with our environments continues to invoke only the two opposites of physical determinism or a freedom exercised in choice and in the positing of values and prescriptions."[205] In a sentence that would fit perfectly in Husserl's fifth investigation, Lingis remarks critically that "the philosophy of mind still maintains the notion that a properly untendentious description of our perceived environment would not mention any directives, that what guides our sensibility and perception as directives is in fact imposed or projected onto our surroundings."[206]

Although the latter chapters of his book offer a serious reading of Kant's ethical imperative, Lingis has already refused to restrict his imperative to matters of human morality. His real motive force is the phenomenological insight into the gap between perception and those dark crystals of reality that lurk just beyond it, which emit facades and lures into our vicinity, demanding to be approached in a very specific way if we are to unlock their secrets. For "every sensualist knows that there is a right way to savor the wine and the smells of a tropical town, a right way to move in the rain forest and see the hummingbird dance and the night come upon the mountain town."[207] And condemning those inept bunglers who ruin the greatest scenes on earth, he asks: "do we not avert our steps from the one whose ears are scabbed with a Walkman when the winter arrives tinkling in on snowflakes, when the petals of the cherry trees of the Silver Pavilion of Kyoto fall in frail music, when the down of a white bird intones the skies over Irian Jaya?"[208] Admittedly, we might dream up bizarre scenarios in which use of a Walkman might be the ethical act *par excellence* in such cases. But this is less interesting than the fact that some imperative speaks to us in every situation, even if we choose to flout it: "We do have the power to crush the penguin chick and knock over the sunflower with a blow, as we may block and muddy the river, but our cruelty and our disdain feel the panic of the chick and the vertical aspiration of the sunflower."[209] Critics may object that an imperative equally present in all ethical and unethical acts is a useless concept. This is not the case. What it does is simply eliminate the notion that we meet a world of raw sense data with arbitrary behavioral choices. What we actually do is listen and respond to the weakness of the bird and the frailty of the flower, and ratchet our tenderness or viciousness up to the appropriate level needed to comfort or destroy these creatures.

B. The Senses under Command

But Lingis goes another step further. He does not stop with unifying our ethical responses to humans, dogs, hammerhead sharks, and Maltese temples, in which we stand tactfully before the contours of these things before responding to them. For Lingis, the very *perception* of things has an imperative structure—and this is what links him most closely with the theory of intentional acts described so far. What Lingis's book offers, without explicitly declaring it, is a unified field theory of ethics and the phenomenology of perception, a perfect fusion of Levinas and Merleau-Ponty. For the merest perception of objects requires that we respond to the directives of a signaling but inaccessible unit that is able to seduce us only with its various limited facades. Much of this was already clear in the early days of the phenomenological school, a tradition to which Lingis remains deeply sympathetic. As he emphasizes, what we perceive are things and not just inarticulate smears of sensation. "Things finalize our sensibility and make it into perception."[210] We do not project subjective readings onto neutral puncta of stimuli, but explore a world broken up into objects and districts by its very nature. As Lingis notes, "we feel the real warmth or coldness of things through the medium that varies. Ice cream feels as cold on a warm day as on a cold day; a person feels as warm when felt under the bedcovers and in the warm water of a pool . . . We hear the real sound of a person through the blanket that muffles or the telephone that distorts his or her voice."[211] And in a strangely disturbing example, "the weight of a thing is felt to be constant whether it is laid on top of our hand or lifted with one finger, whether we lift it with one hand or both, whether we lift it with our hands or feet or teeth, and whether it is laid on our stomach or forehead which we normally rarely or never use to feel the weights of things."[212] Feeling a thirty pound weight on one's forehead or one's kneecap, it is clear that the physical sensations in each case will be utterly different. The weight never becomes directly tangible in some sort of pure medium free of sensual effects, yet it still manifests itself as something constant, as an imperative, a unified crystallized reality lurking like the Sphinx beneath all of its specific impacts on various parts of our bodies. Aristotle already noticed that our memory is composed of things, not our perceptions of those things.[213] We do not remember the minuscule distortions of sunrays on the famous river as we crossed it years ago, but the river itself.

Stated in programmatic form: "Thought is obedience. The freedom of thought makes this obedience possible. Thought subjects itself to the order of what is, what was and shall be, what must be and may be. Though our eyes and hands are free to wander unhindered in the environment, they do not shape a drifting mass of tints and tones; things become visible and tangible as tasks and summons for sight and touch."[214] The key role is played not by human freedom, but by the commanding voices of the things. "As we are led to the real color and shape of the statue in the park through its transitional appearances, so anyone can be led."[215] The object is neither a mere nickname for some set of encountered properties, nor a Christmas present that eventually gets unwrapped—but more like an unknown Halloween visitor hidden permanently behind countless masks and robes. The objects commands us to approach its depths endlessly: "our sensibility is drawn into these depths beyond the profiles of things, summoned by them."[216] As he puts it in a memorable passage: "The key, the inner formula of a mango, a willow tree, or a flat smooth stone, is never grasped; the real thing is before our perception as a task for an exploration."[217] Just as the bottle of wine from a famous vineyard in Burgundy remains a task, one to be savored on just the right occasion and in just the right mood, so too is there a right way to squint one's eyes to see the beloved person approaching from three blocks away, and just the right volume of voice with which to call out to them. Recalling Merleau-Ponty, Lingis observes that the imperative of the thing is answered less often with concepts than with minute bodily adjustments that bring the thing closer to us: "When we look at the sequoias, our eyes follow the upward thrust of their towering trunks touching the sky and their sparse branches fingering the mist. We comprehend this . . . not with a concept-generating faculty of our mind but with the uprighting aspiration in our vertebrate organism which they awaken."[218]

And yet Lingis quickly shows us the other side of the coin, just as the earlier phenomenologists compelled us to see it. For insofar as objects signal to us as a hidden summons or lure, we are never in direct contact with them. Along with the imperative objects themselves, there is a sensual medium in which the thing emanates its forces and qualities. This subject matter feels so elusive that Lingis first approaches it by a kind of metaphoric approximation. Apart from the concealed objects that confront us with directives, "sounds also dematerialize the substance of the things they resounded . . . They drift off things and link up with one another and we hear a Morse code or jazz of sounds ricocheting in the free space."[219] The contrast is as central to Lingis's view of objects as to the views of the other carnal phenomenologists. On the one hand, "the things that are really stabilized as things in our environment . . . lie at rest there, substances kept in reserve."[220] But by the same stroke, "the furnishings of our home also spread about themselves auras and patinas, shadows and densities. When we sink back into our wicker chair as it whispers again marshland murmurs, the patterns of the room vibrate off the layout and shapes of appliances, cabinets, and lamps."[221] We are never quite at home with substances, which always tempt us beyond the point where we are now. The place that we occupy now can never be a substance, but only a specific *level* of the world, one defined by a Morse code or jazz of sensual qualities broken free from any underlying objects. And with his discussion of the levels of the world, Lingis gives us perhaps the most important expression of his philosophical standpoint.

C. Levels of the World

It is through his discussion of the levels that Lingis tacitly breaks with the phenomenology of perception. For Lingis, "the holism and figure-ground presuppositions of the phenomenology of perception have to be discarded.

A field of perceived things is not the basic form of our sentient contact with our environment. We must elaborate a phenomenology of the levels upon which things take form . . ."[222] What holism and the figure-ground model have in common is a lingering assumption that the transcending free human is the source of all significance in the universe. If we consider the world itself, we will find that it is already broken up into shards of glass, bulky towers, land animals, dolphins, and neutrons. To say that the world is first a *whole*, and only later broken up into specific things, is to betray a human-centered bias in philosophy, since it is really the practical world of an individual human life that unifies all objects into a selfish whole. But in the imperatival world, the point is that the world as we know it is never complete, but summons us toward the flickering depths of the things themselves, responding to each in its own language and with a different movement of our mind and body. The same holds for the figure-ground model of perception, which treats the things as though they were nothing but visible finalities spread out before our view, when in fact they are hidden lures that emerge toward us in a kind of windy and starry space—the very space that Lingis calls a level, a space made up neither of objects nor of formless qualities, but of something still undefined. Approaching an outdoor cafe at nighttime, "we see a volume of amber-hued glow. When we enter it, our gaze is filled with the light. We begin to make out forms discolored with an amber wash, like fish seen through troubled waters."[223] When the individual things finally come into focus from out of this amber-colored mist, we find that "the tone of light has become a level about which the colors of things and faces surface according to the intensity and density of their contrast with this level."[224] The background is the carnal medium in which we stand at each moment, a shower of qualities freed from the elusive substances to which they presumably must belong. We can say, with Lingis, that "a level is neither a purely intelligible order, nor a positive form given to a pure a priori intuition; it is a sensory phenomenon."[225] The levels "emerge from the sensory elements, as directives that summon. By following them, a field unfolds."[226]

What unifies a cafe or a city or the life of a philosopher is not a list of facts or a total whole of meaning, but rather a *style* that defines the proper level of activity in question, and which exceeds any current set of particulars; "we recognize the style of a city [even when] all the things in it are rearranged and replaced."[227] We can try to imagine the life of Nietzsche transposed into England or Florida, can think up events that might have occurred to us in these places, and are able to reject certain possibilities as not having quite the right style to be credible. We can ponder how Sade might have portrayed heroes of gluttony or sloth rather than homicidal lust, and if we are skillful enough the results will not be merely arbitrary. Style is a reality exceeding all of the particular facts of any given situation, and just as individual things have a style that exceeds our grasp, so too does any given level. And "a style is not something that we conceive but something we catch on to and that captivates us."[228] We use our bodies to enter the style of any environment, and ultimately into the style of any given thing we find there. We find that a level is not organized into a system by a single all-encompassing purpose, but is thoroughly peopled with "free and nonteleological energies": trade winds, storms, radiation, continental plates, chattering birds.[229] More relevantly, there are qualities so free and nonteleological that they no longer even belong to specific things: "The yellow does not materialize the substance of the plant stalks; it spreads in an ether where green shadows flow about it."[230] This ether or level of qualities is the very environment that this book has been seeking. It is the place where we always stand, and where we must stand in order for any objects to be able to entice us into their depths at all.

With the concept of the levels, Lingis begins to exit the founding dogmas of continental philosophy, with its deeply holistic and antimetaphysical biases. What is most characteristic of Lingis's levels is that they are *not* a feature of human perception that follows us around wherever we go, but a feature of reality itself. The human being merely explores them, without being responsible for generating them. True enough, the level defined by Paris is different for a scientist, a child, and a seagull, yet all of them explore the contours of the same city, observing the same street or entering ever more deeply into the same urban spectacles. But we need to go beyond the poignant drama undergone by living creatures, and see that the levels as well as the imperative objects that signal into them are relevant here. For it must be noted that a level is a place from which objects are physically *absent*, but into which they phosphoresce all of their qualities, and by means of which they communicate with one another. And this happens between clouds and tungsten filaments just as between humans and monkeys. Without a sensual level of qualities on which such objects could come into contact, there would be no causal efficacy at all.

Of the three carnal phenomenologists discussed in this book, Lingis is the only one with any degree of realist instincts. Levinas does a fine job defending individual substances against the apparent human-centered holism of Heidegger's tool-analysis, yet in the end he requires these substances to be hypostatized by human being from amidst the anonymous rumble of the *il y a*. Merleau-Ponty beautifully describes the flesh of the world, and takes pains to note that the objects look at me just as I look at them—but what is lacking is any sense in his works that the objects look at each other too. Lingis follows a different intuition, and for this reason his book can have a mesmerizing strangeness even for those who are thoroughly familiar with his forerunners. As is typical, we find Lingis making an audacious claim buried in the midst of one of his chapters:

> We can never make into a real possibility the notion that as soon as we turn
> away from the tree it lapses into the inaccessible metaphysical apeiron of the
> Kantian in-itself. The tree falling in the depths of the rain forest night is heard
> by innumerable animal ears of which our own are an ephemeral variant. The
> deep-sea coral reefs and the Antarctic icescapes are not visions our own eyes
> create; they are reliefs on levels of visibility visible in general.[231]

A lazy reading of this passage would zero in on its apparent dismissal of the
Kantian in-itself, as though Lingis were simply the nine hundredth contemporary author to join in the ceremonial public beating of any reality
principle in philosophy—as if he were simply chiming in redundant agreement with Žižek, Rorty, or Davidson. Yet the passage above is clearly aimed
not against the world-in-itself, but only at the doctrine of a formless *apeiron*. For Lingis, the tree falling in a depopulated forest results not in the
silence imagined by Bishop Berkeley, nor even in a dismissal of the question
as meaningless—it results in the tree being heard by innumerable animal
ears. And in the Antarctic icescapes where even most insects and germs have
frozen to death, Lingis speaks of "reliefs on levels of visibility visible in general." What is present in Lingis that is so frustratingly lacking in Merleau-
Ponty is precisely this intuition. The glaciers of the South Pole and the
currents of water jetting from and toward the glaciers are themselves fleshly
to one another, "visible in general," even in the absence of all humans. They
encounter one another not as stupid inanimate bulks working with mechanical torpor, but as topographical bulges in the world, as imperative objects
never fully manifest to each other but communicating with one another
through the levels that bring their qualities into communion.

If Lingis is a phenomenologist by training, he is a cosmologist by tem-
perament, perhaps less attuned to the mannerisms of the human salon than
Merleau-Ponty, but more alert to the chattering of birds and the cracking
of ice-shelves and the drifting of meteors in distant space. In *The
Imperative* one finds the ingenious dualism that has given the present book
its inspiration: the world is made entirely of imperatives and of levels, or of
objects and sensations. The imperatives are always objects, demanding our
respect for their ungraspable inner integrity. We are never directly
acquainted with objects, but only with the windy ether or plasma into
which their living qualities are released, and which alone form a tangible
environment. The level is not primarily a human phenomenon, or even an
animal phenomenon, but a *relational* one. We have already seen that the
imperative threatens the usual concept of freedom. It turns out to be
equally threatening for the usual picture of physical causation accepted by
philosophers.

Without a trace of irony, Lingis writes that "the table itself is not so
many impressions imprinted on our surfaces nor the sum of its functional

uses; it is contained in itself, exists beyond all we could ever itemize of it."[232] The thinghood of the thing is impossible to define, but is presupposed by all of our exploratory perceptions. Lingis observes that we have no real "concept" of a grapefruit, but circle about its reality in attempting to approach it in stages.[233] "The task [that things] present to us designate *themselves* as the accomplishment."[234] But neither is it the case that the world is made up entirely of substances or objects. This would leave us with a bland cosmos indeed, since these substances never become present to us at all. We do not cry desperately in a colorless void, begging for the distant objects to approach us, but always stand *somewhere*, feeling the breezes from Mumbai and hearing the sounds of tabla drummers or gasoline pumps. This is the reality of a level, with its disembodied sensual effects which Lingis is always at his finest in describing: "But the colors also disengage from the things to play off one another . . . The sounds depart from the things to link up with other sounds and lead our hearing away from things . . ."[235] Or even more bewitchingly, "the things exist in a movement which does not only project their integral essences down the tracks of practicable reality; across a wave of duration they refract off masks, veils, simulacra, shadows, and omens."[236] This contrast between the density of hidden substances and the sensual taunts of their facades becomes especially evident in unfamiliar surroundings, as the nomadic Lingis knows better than anyone: "In a foreign city the pagoda, the parks, and the colors and designs of the shantytown crystallize into ensembles which present us with unknown shapes and substances dense with imperatives for oblivion-seekers."[237] There is no systematic derangement of the senses here; we are not speaking of a chaos of isolated data. But rather, "painters, musicians, haute-cuisiniers, and perfumers will represent the visual, the sonorous, the gustatory, and the olfactory in layouts that do not simply represent, as signs, the things."[238] It is from this level of sensory superfluity that we launch our raids on objects, like divers reaching for pearls. And "the unattached colors, the rebounding tones, the tangible engulfing our touch draw our whole sensibility into impracticable spaces full and complete in themselves."[239]

And yet I will insist that this sensual realm of objectless qualities is not simply a playground for human perception. Objects by their very nature are self-contained units, withdrawn from each other as much as from us. The vibrant flesh that lies between humans and objects also lies between objects and other objects. Merleau-Ponty had already noted that the things see us just as we see them. But for Lingis, the things actually seem to enter into negotiations and duels with one another: "A thing arises as a relief on the levels of the site which extends about it and harbors other things . . . The levels extend the layout as a system *where the things witness one another* and each contributes to the consistency and coherence of all."[240] He does not confine this eerie grain of realism to a stray remark here and there; it recurs throughout his discussion of the status of things in the world. We read, for instance, that "things have to not exhibit all their sides and aspects, have to compress them behind the faces they turn to us, have to tilt back their sides in depth, have to not occupy all the field, *because they have to coexist in a field with one another*, and that field has to coexist with the fields of other possible things."[241] And in a passage of almost terrifying classicism, Lingis sings a cosmic poem to "the strong colloidal forces in nature that maintain separate beings, seabirds and women and not a chaos of atoms in collision and disintegration,"[242] as if to call for the return of the old substantial forms from the coffin where they now unfairly reside. In the most general possible terms, beings collide with one another in a field, in a series of levels that connect them with one another. These objects can never be fully deployed in any single level, since their nature is never to manifest themselves entirely in any interaction at all. But insofar as entities interact at all, they share some common language of charm or brute force by which they are able to persuade or annihilate one another. The language they share is, in each case, a level of the world. With the carnival of levels extending throughout the cosmos, carnal phenomenology has put its finger on an intermediate zone through which objects signal to one another, and transfer energies for the benefit or destruction of one another. It is the medium through which objects *are* able to interfere with one another. And this is what we are seeking.

PART TWO

Setting the Table

"*Every attempt to dislodge ingenuousness from the universe is in vain. Because, in a word, there is nothing other than sublime ingenuousness, that is to say, reality.*"

—JOSÉ ORTEGA Y GASSET
"Preface for Germans"

[6]

Objects

The present work is designed as both a sequel and a counterpoint to the previously published *Tool-Being*. While the goal in that book was to reestablish some sense of a depth of objects apart from all relations, the current book is concerned with *nothing but* these relations. Let it be granted that the object in its inner life is never touched by any of the entities that bump, crush, meddle, or carouse with it. Even so, objects do affect one another, do enter into causal relations with each other, do somehow nurture or damage each other in every instant. To resolve this paradox is the second mission of object-oriented philosophy—the first mission having been to establish the autonomy of objects. Now, if the substantial core of objects lies completely apart from all relations, then these relations obviously must occur by means of something grafted onto that core, something that serves as a deputy for the shadowy master-object concealed in its inner sanctum. If the object can never be touched, at least its qualities seem tangible; indeed, it seems likely that qualities somehow contain the key to the problem. This is why the current book began with a long meditation on the carnal phenomenologists, whose work is largely concerned with an ether or solar wind of qualities detached from any substance. But it soon became impossible to remain within the sphere of phenomenology, for the tension in reality plays out constantly at innumerable *nonphenomenal* levels at which objects massage or hunt down other objects. The drama of the world is never confined to that single layer where human consciousness happens to be located at any given moment. The phenomenal sphere fails to exhaust the riches of reality itself, and for this reason falls short of defining the full scope of philosophy, which of all human pursuits deserves the fewest geographical restrictions.

Nonetheless, human things are what we know best, and which often provide a useful starting point to philosophical puzzles that exceed our immediate human experience. In this second part of the book I will search the human terrain of metaphor and humor for an initial key to the main difficulties faced by a metaphysics of objects. This first step should lead us toward a theory of relationality in general. In turn, this seems likely to push us up against the boundaries of those cosmological outposts abandoned by philosophy several centuries ago.

The book *Tool-Being* followed Heidegger's famous analysis of equipment in a way that yielded unexpected results. Rather than giving us merely a description of the practical activity of human Dasein, the tool-analysis pushes us toward a theory of objects themselves. Contrary to the most typical reading of Heidegger, the tool-being of objects cannot be its unconscious usefulness for humans in opposition to its conscious visibility. After all, human praxis is no less guilty than explicit human perception of reducing its objects to a mere caricature of their total reality. To use a hammer and to stare at it explicitly are both distortions of the very reality of that hammer as it goes about just being itself, unleashed in the world like a wild animal. An airport is certainly something deeper than its color and shape, but it is also much more than its current usefulness, and even more than all *possible* uses of it. Any sort of human relation to objects will inevitably fail to grasp them as they are. Even to use something unconsciously is still to reduce it to mere presence-at-hand, even if obliviously so. This was the starting point for the argument of *Tool-Being*.

But the argument went another step further. For it is not only human practical and theoretical deeds that reduce things to mere caricatures of themselves. *Relationality in general does this.* A police officer eating a banana reduces this fruit to a present-at-hand profile of its elusive depth, as do a monkey eating the same banana, a parasite infecting it, or a gust of wind blowing it from a tree. Banana-being is a genuine reality in the world, a reality never exhausted by any relation to it by humans or other entities. The basic dualism in the world lies not between spirit and nature, or phenomenon and noumenon, but between things in their intimate reality and things as confronted by other things. With this single conceptual step, metaphysics is freed from its recent pariah status in philosophy—supplanting all phenomenologies, hermeneutic circles, textual disseminations, linguistic turns, and other philosophies of access, and thereby regaining something of its former status as queen of the sciences. There is no question here of reviving the old style of metaphysics of presence criticized so vehemently by Heidegger, Derrida, and their various heirs. After all, the implication of the tool-analysis is that objects *never* become present—not even by means of some sort of gradual, asymptotic approach. All that really needs to be abandoned in the Heideggerian position is his unspoken assumption that the gap between Dasein and the world is the sole philosophically significant rift, the single chasm across which all of the problems of philosophy unfold. This assumption stems most directly from Husserl's rejection of all naturalism, but is ultimately grounded in the Copernican

Revolution of Kant. However, if we push the tool-analysis to its limt, we actually find that all relations in the cosmos, whether it be the perceptual clearing between humans and world, the corrosive effect of acid on lime-stone, or a slap-fight between orangutans in Borneo, are on precisely the same philosophical footing.

For this reason, it becomes necessary to follow Whitehead's lead and seek new models in the high speculative tradition of the seventeenth century, a period which has always fascinated present-day students, but which since Kant has been reduced to a kind of precritical museum exhibit. In the year 2005, it is still possible to be a relatively orthodox Kantian or Hegelian and nonetheless earn promotion through the ranks of Western academia. Yet few people outside of Internet chatrooms would be able to get away with proclaiming their belief in the existence of harmonized monads, a global deity with infinite attributes of which only two are knowable, an infinite matter laced with enfolded potential forms, or a causality made up entirely of miracles or divinely ordained illusions. Continental philosophy would hardly accept wild speculative gambits like these; the same goes without saying for the analytic camp, despite the increasingly larger stature of metaphysics on that side of the fence. Like all events of shattering genius, the Kantian Revolution is so victorious that it is now taken for granted. And in fact, the pre-Kantian systems cannot be resurrected in their original form, since many of the criticisms of them do strike home: with rare exceptions, only cranks or showboats would claim to believe straightforwardly in the sorts of philosophical theories that were dominant prior to the *Critique of Pure Reason*. But there is one extremely powerful hidden force working in favor of a guerrilla metaphysics: namely, the fact that the generally educated public secretly hungers for its triumph, or the triumph of something like it. Nobody outside of the professional guilds feels much enthusiasm for the arid and narrowly self-reflexive style of much philosophical discourse today. I refer not only to the fussy, penny-pinching style of philosophy dominant in the Ivy League, but just as much to my own family of continental philosophers, whose rakish berets and lugubrious Black Forest climbs cannot mask a fundamental bookishness—one that makes little contact with the world itself.

In any case, the model I developed in *Tool-Being* was one of objects receding from all relations, always having an existence that perception or sheer causation can never adequately measure. An object is like a wishing-well where rocks and coins never strike bottom. From this model there resulted several pressing difficulties that I will review in some detail in the following chapter. But what is important for the present book is that the secret inner life of tool-beings can never be more than a *half-truth*, since objects still have a public life as well. The object-oriented model begins by providing us with a world of ghostly realities that never come into contact with each other, a universe packed full of elusive substances stuffed into mutually exclusive vacuums. Neither I nor the monkeys outside my hotel room can ever see, touch, or consume a pineapple in its subterranean reality. Pushed to its logical extreme, this would make relations of any kind strictly impossible. Yet this is clearly an exaggeration, as it gives no explanation of how one object communicates with another, let alone annihilates another.

But notice that this theme is already addressed by the carnal phenomenologists, however obliquely. These authors already spoke of an ether formed of qualities-without-substance, a sensual world from which all objects are irretrievably absent. But though these objects do remain absent, life somehow unfolds nonetheless. The world is filled with roulette tables, electrical grids, and the smell of freshly picked berries or buckets of ammonia; meteorites incinerate forests and gouge craters in villages near our homes. While Heidegger led us toward a cryptic underground of hermetically sealed tool-beings, the carnal phenomenologists invite us into a medium of sensual delights that, by definition, *never* recedes. There is truth and falsity in both extremes. To crossbreed their virtues demands painstaking attention and the careful piecing together of a system that would clarify the duel between objects. The subtitle of the present book is meant to invoke the materials for constructing such a system: the joints and glue, the tenons, pipes, tunnels, and crawl spaces, the copper cable, luminous fibers, and smoke signals that link withdrawn objects to one another *despite* their permanent seclusion in private vacuum-sealed cells. A metaphysics of objects necessarily begins as a theory of the carpentry of things.

The basic elements of this theory are roughly as follows. There are objects or tool-beings, withdrawn absolutely from all relation, but there is also a ubiquitous ether of qualities through which these objects interact, and whose mechanisms still need to be elucidated. To these principles, there are two crucial addenda. First, the term "objects" does not refer to some pampered set of "natural kinds" at the expense of other realities. Anything that is real can be regarded as an object, in a sense of reality that needs more exact determination. No privilege is to be granted to objects over against mere aggregates, as though atoms were real and baseball leagues only derivative, or individual soldiers real and armies only derivative. What must be avoided is any initial dogma at all as to whether there are ultimate building blocks of the cosmos from which everything else is constructed. The important thing is that any object, at any level of the world, has a reality that can be endlessly explored and viewed from numberless perspectives without ever being exhausted by the sum of these perspectives. And this is true of all objects, not just some limited set of physical microparticles. Lake Michigan confronts me as Lake Michigan, and must be reckoned with as such: considered qua lake, it is not just trillions of atoms slapped together, but something much bigger than its parts. Second, it follows that objects at *all* levels are linked by the aforementioned ether of qualities; it is not just humans and the world that are linked in this way, even if there may be special features found in human perception and not in geological collision. Hence, the carnal phenomenologists offer us not just a phenomenology of perception, but also the outlines of a general theory of the translation of forces between objects. In this sense, among all contemporary philosophers it is the inventive Bruno Latour who is probably the closest to the position that I will defend. As described above, carnal phenomenology is attuned to a gap between the intentional object that never appears and the raw sensuality that also never appears, and as a result it inhabits only the middle ground between these two spheres. But in fact, this was only half of the story.

The gap between the invisible intentional object and its palpable sensual profiles is not the only rift in the world. There is also a gap between intentional objects and real ones, since the target of an intentional act is not *itself* the object to which it refers. That is to say, the banana aimed at in my objectifying act is merely an ideal principle unifying a series of appearances, while the banana as a reality grows in the sun and harbors nutrients beneath its skin. Husserl's deep-seated idealism is what prevented his seeing the insuperable difference between these two realities. In the sensual sphere, there is a difference between the banana as a single intentional object and the banana as a set of sensuous qualities. But there is also a lower floor of being, where we find a difference between the *real* banana as a single private reality, and that same real banana considered as a multitude of real attributes, quite apart from any relation that other entities may have with it. Leibniz held that the monad in itself is purely one, and that only the different *relations* each of them has with other entities saves all monads from being purely identical. (The fact that they are regarded as internal relations lodged inside the monads by God, rather than real external interactions between them, is irrelevant here.)

I maintain that this is not true: no quality can be added to a thing by way of relations if that thing began as a simple lump of unity. The qualities of the monad belong to it just as much as its unity does, and quite apart from any mirror-like reflecting of other things. What we have in every interaction are two layers of being, the dog itself and the dog as caricatured by the relation; in turn, each of these realms is split in half by a further division between the dog as a single system and the dog as a system of features or traits. In *Tool-Being* I suggested that this is the meaning of Heidegger's notoriously opaque fourfold, though further discussion of this theme will be of interest mostly to fans of Heidegger and is best developed elsewhere. The discussion in the present book will be limited to developing this quadruple structure in systematic independence, ignoring for now any possible links with the well-known quadruple theories of Heidegger, Aristotle, Plato, or the McLuhan family.[1] The fourfold structure may seem bizarre, but only in the sense that *all* metaphysics has come to seem bizarre. Considered in itself, it is simply the automatic result of crossbreeding two utterly classical distinctions: (1) the difference between substance and relation, and (2) the difference between the unity of a thing and its plurality of features, between its existence and essence, or analogously between its *tode ti* and *ti esti.*

It will now be useful to offer a final summary of *Tool-Being* in light of the tasks of the current book. Although the origin of these ideas lies in a specific reading of the philosophy of Heidegger, I will not refer to his works here, since any interested reader can easily consult the earlier book.

A. The Revival of Substance

A burning warehouse can be approached from many different sides while still remaining the same warehouse. This is not merely the naive assumption of common sense. It is the faith of our bodies, which attempt to gain a new perspective on the fire by circling the police roadblocks, squinting, using binoculars, loading Internet news reports, or questioning survivors as they flee the scene. It is also the experience of our minds, which successively misinterpret various aspects of the fire and are forced by the weight of reality to adjust themselves to it. The burning warehouse is an object to which no viewpoint does justice. I see no good reason to avoid calling it a *substance*, as long as we remember that this term does not refer to rock-hard billiard balls or other underlying physical lumps. The nature of substance remains a mystery, and not only to humans: for it is not only we who distort the burning warehouse with our gaze. The same is true of the fire, which does not spread through the building with infinite speed, but faces different levels of resistance from its interior walls and sprinkler systems, and fails to grasp any aspects of the building that are more subtle than its flammability. Its earth-colored ceiling, its *Jugendstil* entryway, its dreary and stagnant smell: the fire is far too stupid to grasp any of these features of the building, just as humans were too limited to detect the frayed wiring throughout the walls until it was too late. An object is a box of surprises, never fully catalogued by the other objects of the world. As soon as one accepts that there are multiple relations to the same things, and that neither animate nor inanimate actors are able to sound the depths of their neighbors, the standpoint of object-oriented philosophy has already been established. What lies behind all events are inscrutable tool-beings or substances lying in some sort of still-undetermined vacuum. And somehow, the vacuums must manage to communicate with one another. This is guerrilla metaphysics.

There is nothing inherently "naive" in saying that something lies behind appearance. There may well be a naiveté associated with certain theories as to the *character* of the real world. For example, it might turn out to be shaky to hold that there is a hidden world made up of monads, or fire and water, or metal and wood, or ghosts, or quarks. It might be altogether flawed to suggest that one specific layer of pampered entities explains all of the rest. There are good reasons to follow Heidegger and Derrida in criticizing "ontotheology," in which the structure of reality in itself is used as a mandate to privilege certain specific entities at the expense of others: as when someone says that all humans are thrown out into nothingness, but *especially* Germans, or philosophers, or poets. But the solution is to cease using the infinitely withdrawn things themselves as the measuring stick for what we do experience, not to deny that there are such withdrawn things at all. To abhor the hidden at all costs is a strange attitude, one that rejects the very breakthrough of Heidegger's tool-analysis, with its implicit undermining of all the various perceptual and physical impacts of the hammer in favor of the hammer in its underground reality.

The theme of metaphysics is objects and their interactions, whatever these objects may turn out to be. To concede the existence of autonomous objects is to have a metaphysics. Even not to believe in objects, to be a remorseless solipsist or a philosopher of pure events, is to be a metaphysician. Even the natural sciences can be described as a form of metaphysics, one that contends that reality is made up of atoms or other tiny corpuscles whose character ultimately explains the character of all else in the world, and which regards physical causation as the only kind there is, whether through direct impact, fields of force, or other physical means. The theory defended in this book opposes these others by holding that there is an absolute difference between perceptions and objects, that the sum total of events does not exhaust the reality of objects, that there is no privileged layer of tiny parts that explains all else, and that physical efficient causation is only a special case of metaphysical formal causation.

This may be a good place to comment in general terms on the nature of dogmatic crackdowns in philosophy. One of the labor-saving devices of the human mind is that we rarely consider questions as independent themes, but approach them instead from an already established intellectual standpoint. Most of us are not rattled by the occasional reports of sea serpents or bleeding tombstones, because we have educated ourselves into a world in which these do not exist, in which they belong only to the superstitions of peasants and the lies of urban charlatans. Any conservative senator is likely to react skeptically to evidence of global warming, no matter how ironclad; any Vietnam-era liberal will be almost impossible to convince that military action is justified, no matter how compelling the case. No disciple of Gottlob Frege is likely to give a sympathetic reading to the arguments of Spinoza, and I have yet to hear a kind word about the great John Locke from any continental philosopher but one. This phenomenon resembles what is sometimes called a "paradigm."

Beginners in any field generally lack such paradigms, which is why they often strike us as lost or confused, and also why they are often more difficult opponents in debate than trained experts, since experience provides us with a rapid but predictable organizing mechanism for what we learn. But those who freeze rigidly into any such mechanism often strike us as somehow robotic, as dogmatic enforcers of the familiar. Note that this can be just as true of cutting-edge literary theorists as of Bible-thumping authoritarians. Hollow dogma can be found in any party at any time, and is equally paralyzing no matter where it occurs—for which reason it is always more interesting to meet explosive minds who oppose us wildly rather than cookie-cutter ideologues who happen to adhere to the usual views of our particular tribe. It is both a reward and a punishment for victorious models of the world when they finally gain the upper hand, since their victory comes at a price: that of having to support an entire bureaucracy of detectives and enforcers who crack down on all hints of dissent. Everyone is familiar with this depressing process, which it would be cruel to describe in too much detail.

But we ought to ask just what the detectives and enforcers are working for in continental philosophy these days. Surely, the reigning assumption now consists in a communal disdain for any form of substance or essence, anything lying behind the actual permutations of appearance as they occur in any particular moment. There is a kind of fraternity initiation rite in which we prove our intellectual acuity by debunking the naive beliefs of others in anything hidden. Since it is often difficult to find an actual living human to serve as a suitable target for this critical onslaught, a mental image of the gullible, oppressive reactionary is often brought before the mind: his lips trembling angrily as progressive free-thinkers assault his crumbling pieties.

In all fairness, this attitude seems to be grounded not in any sort of brutal unfairness to opposing positions, but simply in the understandable human urge to avoid backtracking of any kind. There is a near-universal hatred of repeating work that was regarded as already done. Everyone reacts with something like rage to being forced to drive back home to pick up the forgotten document, to reclean the apartment after the landlord threatens to withhold the deposit, to rewrite pages that we thought were finished, to clean the beach yet again after the garbage barge sinks offshore. For similar reasons, no one wants to imagine that what seems to be a present-day fiesta of free critical thought might be betrayed once again to the metaphysicians—the decrepit palace restored, and the king returned to the throne as the Jacobins weep.

But the history of philosophy has always been less progressive than *periodic.* The reappearance of an ancient concept in contemporary philosophy need not mean the sad revival of a pulverized nullity, but possibly the appearance of a genuinely new form of thought. No chemist, upon encountering the element known as argon, folds her arms skeptically or slams down a clipboard and shouts: "We've just done neon, and now you want to go back and bring us *another* inert gas? I thought we were beyond that!" It would be stupid to say that krypton, xenon, and radon are "reactionary" merely because their outer valence shell is just as complete as helium's already was; no scientist dismisses them as "retrograde" elements and fashionably prefers lithium or potassium as more progressive. In the same sense, we might think of Nietzsche as simply a more complicated version of Empedocles with extra protons, a revival of madness and eternal return in the heart of contemporary philosophy. By the same token, it is quite possible that philosophy will someday once again be dominated by the problem of universals, the theory of monads, neo-Platonist cosmologies, or proofs for the existence of God, though presumably always in a more red-blooded contemporary form. No one can say for sure. My point is that a return to substance is no more inherently reactionary than Foucault's retrieval of "power" from Thrasymachus. If there were dejected sighs when compact discs suddenly replaced cassettes, this was surely for reasons of cost, and not because anyone was annoyed to see the disc-shape regain preeminence. I have made this point at some length because experience shows that it is often a *mental image* of what constitutes intellectual progress, rather than any inherently weighty arguments, that explains why the antiessentialist, antisubstance, philosophy-of-access viewpoint enjoys such apparently unshakable prestige in continental philosophy today.

B. Vacuums Everywhere

If there are objects, then they must exist in some sort of vacuum-like state, since no relation fully deploys them. The recent philosophical tendency is to celebrate holistic interrelations endlessly, and to decry the notion of anything that could exist in isolation from all else. Yet this is precisely what an object does. An object may drift into events and unleash its forces there, but no such event is capable of putting the object fully into play. Its neighboring objects will always react to some of its features while remaining blind to the rest. The objects in an event are somehow always elsewhere, in a site divorced from all relations. To anticipate the usual criticisms of relationless solid objects made by many philosophers, note that the vacuum in question is not physical, but *metaphysical*. I am not speaking of some preexistent lump of atoms that remains the same despite all external changes: to be physical in this sense is already to be stationed in a world, to occupy a distinct space, and thereby to take up a definite stance toward other such spaces and the entities that occupy them. Spatial objects are to some extent always relational, whereas objects simply are not. To say that the world is filled with objects is to say that it is filled with countless tiny vacuums, like those bubbles that the Pythagoreans thought had been inhaled by the universe itself. What guerrilla metaphysics seeks is the vacuous actuality of things.

The great recent opponent of any ontological vacuum in philosophy is the marvelous Whitehead, who uses "vacuous actuality" as a term of contempt. For Whitehead's philosophy of organism, any attempt to refer to an actual entity apart from its complex of relations with other such entities is a cardinal philosophical error. Despite my undying admiration for Whitehead's speculative boldness, I find it necessary to start on the opposite foot on this issue, and to counter the contemporary reflex that opposes all attempts to view anything out of context. To say that everything is related to everything else is not quite as liberating as it sounds, and for two distinct reasons.

The first defect is that the relational theory is too reminiscent of a house of mirrors. Consider the case of ten thousand different entities, each with a different perspective on the same volcano. Whitehead is not one of those arch-nominalists who assert that there is no underlying volcano but only external family resemblances among the ten thousand different perceptions. No, for Whitehead there is definitely an actual entity "volcano," a real force to be reckoned with and not just a number of similar sensations linked by an arbitrary name. Yet if we try to determine just what this volcano is for Whitehead, it turns out to be nothing more than its perceptions of *other* entities. These entities, in turn, are made up of still further perceptions. The hot potato is passed on down the line, and we never reach any reality that would be able to anchor the various perceptions of it.

The second defect is that no relational theory such as Whitehead's is able to give a sufficient explanation of change. If the volcano holds nothing in reserve beyond its current relations to all entities in the universe, if it has no currently unexpressed properties, there is no reason to see how anything new can ever emerge. In a strict sense, there would be no actual volcano, but just a series of perceptions of it and by it.

Leibniz would object to the theory of vacuous actuality on similar grounds. He would claim that, stripped of all relations, objects would end up as nothing but featureless units. The vacuums would be filled with "bare particulars," and because of the principle of the identity of indiscernibles, they would actually all be the same object. This is why his monads have to be packed with relations from the start, since without a unique individual set of relations they would be nothing distinct at all. Certainly, given that Leibniz's monads have no windows, there is a sense in which he too is defending a theory of vacuous substance. But although the relations of his monads to other monads are entirely *internal*, they are still relations pointing outside of the monad itself, and not qualities belonging to the monad in a non-relational way. Take away all relations, Leibniz holds, and the monad would be a bare lump of unity.[2] The response of object-oriented philosophy is simply to deny that relations and qualities are the same thing. The specificity of the monad cannot possibly come from relations, since this leads us into the same house of mirrors as with Whitehead. That is to say, if we start out with an army of featureless monads, we cannot possibly give them concrete personality by injecting them with numerous relations to other monads that are equally indistinct and featureless, equally parasitical in their dependence on relationships for any identity. The right way to see the situation is that the object in its relationless vacuum is *not* devoid of character at the outset. The thing apart from its relations is actually not an empty bare particular, but remains torn apart in its private vacuum between its irreducible unity and its colorful particularity.

Finally, we can never repeat enough that the difference between an object and its relations is a difference that permeates the entire cosmos, and not some sort of poignant psychic feature found only in human beings. It is not the tender particularities of the human soul that first put a flaw in the cosmic jewel, cutting reality apart into substance and relation. Quite the opposite: there is no object at all, whether animal, floral, or mineral, capable of caressing the skin of another object so perfectly as to become identical with it or otherwise mirror it perfectly. When a gale hammers a seaside cliff, when stellar rays penetrate a newspaper, these objects are no less guilty than humans of reducing entities to mere shadows of their full selves. To repeat, the gap between object and relation is inherent in the nature of things, and not first generated by the peculiarities of the human mind. The fact that humans seem to have more cognitive power than shale or cantaloupe does not justify grounding this difference in a basic ontological dualism.

But by the same token, it is equally invalid to draw vitalist conclusions, and to conclude that because humans and rocks both enter into relations, rocks must already have human cognitive powers in germinal form. This does not follow in the least. There is a fallacy shared by both the human-centered and vitalist models of relation. Namely, there is a common obsession with the special magic of human knowledge, which in both cases is made into the centerpiece of the cosmos, whether jealously hoarded for people alone, or scattered through the world like pixie dust. In one case, human knowing is regarded as an absolutely unique source of transcendence and negativity. In the other, it is taken to be always already present even in lobsters, millet seeds, cornflower crayons, and moon rock. Neither of these alternatives is convincing. Human knowledge may indeed be something quite special, but this does not mean that it is something philosophically basic that creates a vast gap between humans and nonhumans, any more than noteworthy objects such as backbones and glass create such a gap between themselves and other things. No ontologist would ever dream of dividing the world into objects with spines and those without (though for zoology this might be illuminating). If we shift to the case of glass, the human-centered philosopher is like someone who says that the difference between glass and nonglass is ontologically fundamental, while the vitalist is like someone who says that everything in the world is actually already glass, though perhaps in a "weaker" form than windows. What is lacking is the most sensible alternative, which is to say that human knowledge, just like glass, backbones, reptiles, music, and mushrooms, arises at a certain point in the history of the universe, but without necessarily forming some sort of root metaphysical dualism in the world. I see no convincing reason to regard human knowledge as of such pivotal importance in the universe. For this reason, I do not accept the panpsychist criticism of *Tool-Being* made by David Skrbina, despite the continued refreshing quality of all panpsychism.[3]

C. The Wheel of Objects and Relations

Object-oriented philosophy makes no distinction between anything like primary and secondary qualities, or between certain privileged realities that are always substances and secondhand derivative ones that are always relations. One of the objections made against theories of substance is that they pamper some elite layer of explanatory things—subatomic particles for the sciences, or everyday specimens like horses and trees for Aristotle—while explaining away all more complex entities as secondary products of the combination of simple parts. Either everything is made of atoms, and moods are explained away as the by-product of brain chemicals; or machines are viewed as artificial composites with no reality of their own. But whereas Leibniz would hold that a soldier is real and an army is not, Locke already grasps that an individual soldier is no less complicated than an entire army.[4] I would only disagree with Locke that such substances ought to be defined as "powers." To call an army a certain power to overwhelm cities may be a good way of pointing it out amidst a crowd of entities or of predicting its future impact. But this power is not the same as the reality of the army itself. We can certainly ask, "How will this army respond if forced to fight in desert conditions?" but this does not mean that the army is reducible to its potential to fight in any particular conditions, or even in all imaginable conditions, since no such conditions can exhaust the reality of the army. The same holds true for individual soldiers, for the nations they serve, and for each soldier's teeth, legs, eyes, helmets, munitions, and the molecules and atoms that make all of these possible. None of these things is inherently more or less complicated than the others. And none is more or less an object or substance than the others.

The point is as follows. If someone asks where substances are located in reality, it is impossible to single out an elite cadre of substances at the expense of all other entities. We find substance neither in the really, really tiny things, nor in the really, really natural things, nor in the really, really divine things. Substances are *everywhere*. What we have is not a universe split between aristocratic natural kinds and miserable, pauper-like accidents. Instead, we have a universe made up of objects wrapped in objects wrapped in objects wrapped in objects. The reason we call these objects "substances" is not because they are ultimate or indestructible, but simply because none of them can be identified with any (or even *all*) of their relations with other entities. None of them is a pristine kernel of substantial unity unspoiled by interior parts. We never reach some final layer of tiny components that explains everything else, but enter instead into an indefinite regress of parts and wholes. Every object is both a substance and a complex of relations.

But if every object can also be considered as a set of relations between its parts or qualities, it is equally true that *any relation must count as a substance*. When two objects enter into genuine relation, even if they do not permanently fuse together, they generate a reality that has all of the features that we require of an object. Through their mere relation, they create something that has not existed before, and which is truly *one*. When the sun and the moon join in a lunar eclipse, this eclipse has an identity and a depth that belongs to neither of its parts, and which is also irreducible to all of its current effects on other entities, or to the knowledge we may have of it. It is a reality stretching far beyond its current manifestations, one that may have effects not currently registered anywhere in the environment. Granted, a relation between two objects may last only a brief while. But the same is true of objects that are obviously substances, such as mayflies or the fleeting chemical element of californium. Durability is not a requirement for objecthood, just as being part of nature or having an exceptionally tiny size is not. Substances are filled with relations; relations become substances. The wheel of substance and relation throws everything in the cosmos sometimes into one of these roles, sometimes the other. Or rather, an object always plays both roles simultaneously, and it is only our reflection on them that places it more emphatically in one light or another.

I have already noted the way in which object-oriented philosophy distances itself from those features identified as harmful in the so-called metaphysics of presence. In the first place, the objects I have described in this theory never become present at all, so that the relevant insult here would actually be "metaphysics of *absence*." By definition, objects are withheld from any attempt to relate to them. It is not even possible to get "closer" to the things in such a way that presence could provide some sort of measuring stick for how nearly we have approached reality. The relation that a wasp or the moon has to the sun, my own loose understanding of how the sun functions, a Stone Age shaman's worship of it, and an astrophysicist's deep grasp of solar reality are certainly quite distinct from one another. The last-mentioned form is perhaps the best of them all, the one toward which I and the shaman and the wasp and the moon should wish to strive. Nonetheless, even the astrophysicist has no better chance of coming in contact with the sun-object than do the wasp and the moon. No such contact is possible at all—which is emphatically *not* to say that there *is* no true sun. The *inaccessibility* of the subterranean depth of the sun does not entail its nonexistence.

D. The Quintessence

The purpose of this chapter has been to summarize the main features of the theory of objects sketched in *Tool-Being*. So far, we have seen that the world is filled with objects that withdraw from all relation, and which inhabit private vacuums of their own. Furthermore, objects are not confined to one level of reality, but exist in all sizes and in all natural and unnatural places. We cannot point to one part of the world and claim it is filled with objects, and point to another part and claim it is made up solely of relations. To put it somewhat paradoxically, the world is packed full with mutually isolated vacuums, crowded together more tightly than drops of water in a drum.

But it was also necessary to refer to another, more elusive theme in the theory of objects. Along with the gulf between the object and its relational effect upon other objects, we have a second gap between the object and itself. We already saw that for Husserl, the intentional object is not identical with any of its manifested properties, but always exceeds them. Yet he rightly insists that the *intentional* object is not the real object of scientific naturalism, but only an ideal principle of unity. Hence, even within the ideal sphere alone the intentional object is creviced by a division between the thing as a unity and the thing as a plurality.

But in the meantime, the present book has already rejected the *de facto* antirealism of most phenomenology. The monkey itself is real, and is *really* one monkey, not merely an ideal unity aimed at by intentional acts. What we have, in other words, are two separate axes of division. First, there is the central distinction developed in *Tool-Being* between a thing and its relations. Second, there is the difference between a single object and its specific qualities, notes, features, traits. The object is divided in two both in itself, and in its relation to others, yielding *four poles* that must somehow be unified. Whatever holds them together can be considered as a fifth term that links these poles as belonging somehow to the same object. To use a traditional term, we could call it the *quintessence* of the thing.

Roughly speaking, these were the main features of the model of reality introduced in *Tool-Being*. But at the end of that book, it was noted that there were a number of interesting problems that arise from the model of object-oriented philosophy.

[7]

The Problem of Objects

It has become almost a cliché to say that questions are more important than solutions in philosophy, and that problems are never really solved. But while I do not quite believe this, I also do not believe that a philosophical system justifies its existence primarily through its ability to solve whatever random questions those who happen to pass it on the sidewalk might throw at it. The need to be able to defeat all comers, to be impregnable to all objections, is more a social desire than a strictly intellectual one; the most aggressive arguers we know are seldom the most interesting thinkers. Any great philosophy remains haunted by numerous difficulties that it never quite solves, and that someone with even minimal training can easily spot. Lacking such problems, its principle of motion would disappear, and it would wither to nothing. When tackled effectively by a philosopher's successors, these problems are neither settled for the ages nor left in dolorous mystery. What really happens is that they are translated into new and more interesting problems, perhaps broader ones—and a new style of translation is what we call a new philosophical standpoint.[5] Intellectual stagnation results not from unsolved problems in the mind (these are never absent) but from a waning capacity to displace familiar problems into unfamiliar ones. Whereas great periods of philosophy funnel their assembled problems through newly constructed canals and other watercourses, the more rigid periods treat these problems with suffocating binary flip-flops around a stale shared consensus. This is fundamentally no different from the process whereby daily routines begin to wear us down, hometowns become prisons, old jobs become insufferable, and psychic compulsions arise from the inelasticity of desire. Intellectual health, no less than emotional balance, seems to require a certain principle of variation.

Needless to say, the standpoint presented in this book is not presented as an answer to all ills, an oracle among theories. It is simply an attempt to push one idea as far as it can go, so as to examine both the breakthroughs and the impasses that arise from that idea. But these impasses are the very subject matter that we aim to study. They are not instant derailments that reduce the whole of guerrilla metaphysics to zero. What lies at the center of this book is not a set of answers to problems, but a single new concept: that of an object that both withdraws from all relation and yet somehow does enter into relation. Object-oriented philosophy is not designed as a magic cudgel able to pulverize all possible counterarguments in advance, but more as a kind of Suez or Panama through which phenomenology is obliged to transit, without knowing all of the consequences in advance. It is a series of initial translations of Heidegger's tool-analysis, displacements that I find both compelling and inevitable, and whose end-point remains almost as unknown to me as to the reader. At the close of *Tool-Being* I already sketched out the key problems through which it will be necessary to pass. In this chapter I will review these problems, hoping to condense them into more graspable and memorable form. From there, we can try to push them several steps further than in the previous book. What has been invoked repeatedly is a world in which objects withdraw from one another into the darkness, unable to affect each other directly. Objects, tool-beings, substances, or things (the names are used interchangeably) inhabit some sort of vacuum free of all relations, though it is still unclear where this vacuum is located, and even whether it is spatial at all. Moreover, the difference between objects and relations is not a difference between two specific types of things, but between two moments in *each* thing, since a carnival tent sometimes acts as an object and at other times as a sheer aggregate of *multiple* objects. Finally, it was seen that there is not only a duality between an object and its relational effects on other things, but also a second duality in the heart of the object itself based on the internal tension between its existence as a unified thing and its possession of specific qualities.

The basic difficulties that arise from this model are not difficult to grasp once they are pointed out. The most general problem is that if objects cannot touch each other, we need to know how they interact at all (section A). The second problem is how a unified object is related both to its own qualities and to the smaller objects that are its parts, and whether the qualities and the parts of a thing are the same (section B). The third problem is this: if objects always withdraw from one another, and every reality's true essence is defined by its withdrawal, then we hardly know where the world of events and occurrences is located, since a universe of total withdrawal could only lead to a static darkness (section C). Fourth, if all relations can immediately be defined as objects in their own right, then there seems to be nothing to stop every possible bizarre combination of things from forming a new substance. In other words, it needs to be shown how it is possible for there to be aggregates that are not automatically new substances. It needs to be discovered what the firewalls are that prevent everything from affecting everything else, so that we can avoid the paranoia of absolute holism (section D).

A. Vicarious Cause

The most pivotal issue for object-oriented philosophy is vicarious causation, a concept introduced as a modification of the long-discredited notion of *occasional* cause. If objects exceed any of their perceptual or causal relations with other objects, if they inhabit some still undefined vacuous space of reality, the question immediately arises as to how they interact at all. More concisely: we have the problem of nonrelating objects that somehow relate. Since no causation between them can be direct, it clearly can only be *vicarious*, taking place by means of some unspecified intermediary. Whatever this third term may be, it already seems clear that it has something to do with the shower of loose qualities that captured the interest of the carnal phenomenologists.

As we saw, Husserl had already noticed that intentional objects are never directly accessible. But objectless sensuality is also not directly accessible, so that we find ourselves immersed in something midway between the two. Levinas and Merleau-Ponty paid special attention to this ether of qualities without objects in which humans forever bathe. Lingis pushed things in a slightly different direction with his discussion of the levels, hinting at a certain realist twist to carnal phenomenology: the level is not something permanently fixed between humans and world, but there are varying levels *within* the world. Human consciousness is not what establishes these levels, as if it alone introduced a sensual medium into the world—instead, it simply navigates the levels like a freelance submarine or zeppelin. In this way, the fleshly medium of loose qualities is placed *everywhere* in the world. It is allowed to spread between *all* of the objects of the world rather than being confined to the single tear-jerking rift that separates people from all that is not people, as still tends to happen in Levinas and Merleau-Ponty. For this reason, Lingis is probably also the *last* of the carnal phenomenologists, since his levels already push us beyond the human-centered limits of this school.

What Lingis calls a level, I will also refer to as a "medium." A medium is any space in which two objects interact, whether the human mind be one of these objects or not. Human sense experience is only one particular zone or medium of the world, and possibly not even the most interesting one. The medium between objects is the glue that makes possible the entire carpentry of things—without it, the world would remain a set of noncommunicating crystalline spheres sleeping away in private vacuums. If substances cannot communicate directly, then there still must be some way

in which they allow their traits to break free and act as couriers and emis-
saries, entering the world of relations as if into an illegal dance club.

The problem of causation by way of deputies rather than through substances themselves already dominated one of the great eras of systematic
philosophy, the seventeenth and early eighteenth centuries in Europe. At
an earlier time it had also played a pivotal role in Islamic theology. In
Europe, what really links the so-called Rationalists and Empiricists is their
shared puzzlement over the problem of communication, which initially
seems so hopeless between the separate zones of the world. In the former
group, God is invoked to serve as the link between disparate real substances; in the latter, the human mind is the medium that links together
disparate qualities in the *hypothesis* of an underlying substance. In both
cases, the problem is how autonomous zones of the world manage to fuse
together. Although the final Kantian settlement is sometimes viewed as a
good compromise between the two alternatives, it actually comes down
rather heavy-handedly on the side of the Empiricists: any sort of communication between substances that does not involve human beings is banished to an unknowable, barely mentionable place. Kant simply has far less
to say about the collision of rocks than Bruno, Descartes, or Leibniz. The
single remaining gap between human and world banishes any more general treatment of causation, which is now left entirely to the physicists.

In keeping with its Kantian heritage, contemporary philosophy is still
obsessed with the problem of communication, though it is now reduced to
the single theme of the gap between appearance and whatever might lie
beyond. In cases where every "beyond" is dismissed, we still see privileged
gaps between humans and the withdrawal of being, or humans and negative traces, or humans and excess. Although I generally prefer salvaging traditional philosophical terms over coining neologisms, an exception really
must be made for the term "occasional cause," a term that arouses such
consistent ridicule among contemporary philosophers that any attempt to
revive it would be in vain. This is not entirely the fault of those who
ridicule it. Historically, the doctrine of occasional cause always brashly
appeals to an all-powerful divine force that, *somehow, someway*, has sufficient power to correlate uncommunicating substances with one another.
By allowing the theme of causation to coincide with the Divine Mystery,
causation was allowed to take permanent sanctuary in the asylum of ignorance. While there may be strong religious grounds for ascribing ubiquitous causal power to God, we can hardly blame the majority of
philosophers who find this theory unsatisfying to the point of comedy.
Obviously, one should also clarify *how* God manages to make objects touch
each other. The term "vicarious cause" has been coined as a way of keeping our focus on how isolated substances might communicate, without
dredging up any of the historic debates between theologians and skeptics.

But there is another fascinating dimension to the problem of vicarious causation, one that seems to have barely been noticed in the past. For occasionalism is not just a question of how two *separate* objects are able to affect each other without directly touching. The same puzzle is already found *within* individual objects: note that a substance is also the vicarious cause of its qualities, since it brings them together in a single whole, even while they remain distinct and affect each other only *through* the substance itself. Consider an apple. Its sweetness and fragrance and color and price and nutritional value are to a large extent distinct. Yet somehow all of these qualities are unified in a single thing, despite their relative inability to interfere with one another.

On a related note, there is one sense in which a substance is not affected by its qualities at all, since it can lose some of them while remaining itself, but another sense in which it depends on them utterly. But this means that the union of an object *with its own essence* requires vicarious bonding no less than the bond between one thing and another. This delightful little paradox was already glimpsed to some extent by Leibniz, since for him God must inject the bare *unity* of a monad with all of its relational *qualities*—and this unity and these qualities, without God's intervention, would have nothing to do with one another in his philosophy. At any rate, we need to know both how distinct traits are bonded together in one object, and also how they ever become liberated from that object.

The implications are as simple as they are mysterious. We have already noted a quadruple structure of objects formed by the intersection of two distinct axes. What is now so fascinating is that the problem of vicarious cause (a.k.a. occasional cause) is actually present along *both* axes. As just mentioned, there is a communication problem not only *between* separate objects, but also *inside* of objects. Communication seems to have broken down across the entire universe. Whatever vicarious causation may be, it is called upon to serve as the glue of the universe, the cement that binds macrocosm and microcosm alike. And this leads us to the second problem that arose from the model of objects I developed in *Tool-Being*.

B. Whole and Part

The question here concerns the relation that any object has to its own parts. This question might refer either to the traits of a thing's inner consistency, *or* to the actual component substances from which it is pieced together. At the same time, there is also a sense in which no substance has any parts at all.[6] To give an example, it cannot really be said that windmills are made of ladders, pumps, rotating blades, and wire-mesh crow's nests. Or rather, it is made of these things only in a derivative, material sense.

Although the windmill needs these smaller parts in order to exist, it never fully deploys these objects in their total reality, but makes use of them only by reducing them to useful caricatures. That is to say, a windmill does not fully sound the depths of its own pieces any more than a human observer does. It merely siphons away the needed qualities from these objects, just as animal stomachs reduce the sparkling allure of fruits to brutal, one-dimensional fuels. To reverse an old cliché, there is a sense in which *the sum of parts is always greater than the whole.* The whole is always an oversimplification of its parts. The windmill caricatures the ladder and the pump, ignoring their full reality by harnessing them to a specific formal task.

It is somewhat different when we speak of the windmill-substance as possessing *qualities*, such as solidity, ability to pump water, squeakiness during the night, and so forth. In one sense, it is true that the windmill is a stark monadic unity that endures (within certain limits) even when these qualities are altered. But in another sense, it also really *possesses* these qualities as genuine moments. The result is clear: the question of wholes and parts is just a variant of the more general problem of vicarious cause. That is to say, the single windmill must somehow link up both with the plurality of its notes, and also with those physical parts that it so desperately needs but which Aristotle was right to exclude from its substance. But this is just another way of stating a rather simple point: an object must relate both to other objects and to itself, and *both relations must occur vicariously.* The medium in which this occurs is the third problem that arose at the end of *Tool-Being.*

C. Worlds Inside of Vacuums

The question here concerns the space in which reality unfolds—the very location of the world. Objects are now said to exist in their own private vacuums, remote from all possibility of being probed. Yet the world as we know it is an active arena in which events *do* unfold, in which objects melt or regenerate each other, transform or fuse into one another. It remains unclear where this happens—we seem to know nothing but objects, and objects seem to be impenetrable crystalline shells, devoid of interactive drama or motion. The vicarious medium in which objects interact with one other and with their own qualities must also provide the space where all the events of the world unfold. If every object is a vacuum, it is equally true that every vacuum must contain a world—a medium in which distinct qualities interact or at least float side-by-side in some sort of charged ether. But since it has already been suggested that every relation must be regarded as a substance in its own right, the loose relation of objects or qualities caressing one another is also a relation that occurs on the *inside of a substance.* When two rocks smash together, what occurs is not some impossible fusion of two substances, but rather a marriage of two caricatures, two limited sets of features siphoned by the rocks from one another: and this means nothing else than the features of a new unified *collision-substance*, as will be discussed later. This is important, because it raises the possibility that there is not a single medium of interaction between things, but rather just as many media as there are objects: separate media housed like molten plasma at the burning central cores of things. In astrophysics, Lee Smolin has theorized that every black hole contains an entire universe of its own. By analogy, we might say that every object is not only protected by a vacuous shield from the things that lie outside it, but also harbors and nurses an erupting infernal universe within. The object is a black box, black hole, or internal combustion engine releasing its power and exhaust fumes into the world.

These problems cry out for the additional clarification that will be attempted in Part Three below. But one important aspect of the situation should already be clear. The three problems we have just discussed–vicarious cause, the relation between wholes and parts, and the place where relations occur—are unified in a single concept. They are linked together in the medium of ethereal qualities, which always exists in the core of a substance and nowhere else. The carnal phenomenologists began to explore this medium beautifully, but with the exception of Lingis they tend to limit it to a single point of intersection between human and world. The ultimate aim of guerrilla metaphysics would be to clarify the mechanisms of this ether to such an extent that it unleashes a gold rush of further speculations, a Wild West of philosophy to replace the constricted, tedious, human-centered mandate of contemporary thought.

So far, the first three problems cited in *Tool-Being* have boiled down to a single central problem: that of the medium between qualities or things. This leaves only one final major problem, but it turns out to have a different and even opposite character from the others.

D. Firewalls

All philosophies of substance known to me have drawn some sort of distinction between substances and mere aggregates. In most versions of the theory, substances are sought in naturally occurring wholes (trees, camels, souls), while aggregates are viewed merely as extrinsic combinations of inherently unrelated parts (cities, or bags of Christmas candy). It is easy to view a horse as a substance, but harder to regard a stable of six hundred horses as a substance. There would be no problem at all, of course, if substance were merely a word, an arbitrary agreement that we shall all agree to *declare* such and such a group of elements to be called a single substance. It would then be simply a matter of analyzing the procedures by which various tribes of humans come to a rough consensus as to what counts as substance and what does not. But I have been arguing that substances are real—that when they are real they occur quite apart from any human declaration of this fact, and even from any ability of the nonhuman environment to register their existence. Furthermore, I have also stated that any relation immediately becomes a new substance—which makes it seem as if there were no such thing as aggregates at all. The question obviously arises as to whether there is any difference between a substance with its manifold qualities, and an aggregate strung together from random shards strewn about in the street.

If I specify some bizarre chain of entities, such as an oilcan, the Dead Sea, and a specific mallard duck, this trio immediately strikes us as an absurd candidate for substancehood. But if we imagine some twisted anecdote that involves these three objects acting in perfect unison (I will leave it to the reader to invent the details) then it suddenly seems a bit more plausible that certain theories of substance might accept this motley union into the ranks of genuine objects. But there is a big problem with having recourse to such an anecdote, even though such strange unions occur all the time. Namely, we now seem to be defining substances by their *external effect* on the outer world ("the duck was placed in the Dead Sea and fished the oilcan from the water, leading to a prize-winning photograph for a lucky journalist"), even though we began with precisely the opposite supposition. Pragmatic impact on the outer world cannot be the yardstick by which to judge the reality of objects whose very nature is supposedly to hide in a vacuum. Nor can we use physical proximity or shared motion as criteria of substance, since plenty of counterexamples can be imagined for both of these standards. We obviously need a formal criterion of substance, not a material one. All of these questions can be termed the problem of *firewalls*, because it is the question of what prevents any arbitrarily weird assortment of things from becoming a substance merely by human decree. We need to know what firewalls a substance contains to prevent it from being penetrated by just any old relation to any old entity.

The preceding three problems eventually boiled down to the single question of what a relation really is. We often overlook that there is a certain degree of paradox to any relation, since it involves a multiplicity that is also somehow one. But the question of firewalls is obviously different. It apparently has nothing to do with relations at all, since it concerns only the thing itself, what makes it tenable, what allows it to fend off everything not pertinent to it. In a sense, this is just a further displacement of the ageless question of being, since what it asks is simply this: in what does the being of a thing consist? This may be one of the many questions that can never fully be answered, but only transmuted into new and unexpected forms. If the first three problems ask about the nature of relations, this last problem asks what it really means for a substance to exist in a vacuum. Heidegger began with a negative approach to his own question of being, with the profound initial insight that being cannot be thought of as presence-at-hand. I would give it an even more general twist, and say that being cannot be conceived in terms of any relations at all. This is a useful negative starting-point, but still tells us too little about what vacuous tool-being really is. Among other things, we will need to ask if an object is located in the world or somewhere outside it.

The remainder of this book now has a manageable set of problems, albeit a very difficult set. At the center of everything there lies a world of elusive objects torn apart in two directions by two separate rifts in being. A thing is divided from all presentations of itself, but is also divided between its own unity and multiplicity. In all directions, some sort of vicarious causation is required, and the mechanisms of such causation have not yet been mapped. We now have a kind of nuclear philosophy in which the basic atom of reality—the object—is occasionally blown apart into fragments that might be studied in some detail. What we need most of all is a way to cross from one quadrant of reality to another, so that we are not left with an impossible universe of nontransmitting, noncommunicating, isolated poles.

Admittedly, we have now gone a good deal off the beaten track of contemporary philosophy, and will be investing our time in problems that do not occupy many others for the moment. But let it be remembered that we have reached this point through simple pursuit of the unstated implications of tool-being. Once it was conceded that the world is made up of withdrawn objects, utterly sealed in private vacuums but also unleashing forces upon one another, all of the other strange-sounding problems follow in quick succession. Let anyone who does not agree with the strategies of guerrilla metaphysics specify clearly which of its initial steps is invalid. Let there be no smug appeals to Occam's Razor, appeals which always seem to defend current orthodoxies rather than pushing toward any *new* form of "parsimony." The system sketched in this book was not dreamed up for poetry's sake, even if its poetic aspects provide a deep satisfaction. As soon as the shift is made from the philosophy of access to the philosophy of objects, it seems to me that the problems raised here become uncircumventible. All of the problems that were raised have now been reduced to two basic puzzles: (1) the mechanisms of vicarious causation, and (2) the nature of the vacuous life that defines every object. Perhaps these problems will be unified in turn, or perhaps they will resist all further integration.

Although neither of these problems is easy, it is the structure of the vacuum that seems like the more inscrutable of the two. For this reason, we should begin by trying instead to find some entryway into the problem of vicarious cause: the communication that occurs through all the various girders, freight tunnels, shafts, and pulleys of the world. This is why Part One addressed the sensual realm, and we ought to remain there until we have more fully charted its mechanisms. This having been done, it may prove easier than before to blast our way into the inner corridors of objects, like those benevolent destroyers who design particle accelerators and scanning/tunneling microscopes, or like strongmen splitting quartz and geodes at a county fair.

The closest point of approach to objects turns out to be through *metaphor*. In a little-known but brilliant essay,[7] José Ortega y Gasset gives a vivid account of the metaphoric relation that meshes perfectly with the credo of object-oriented philosophy. Indeed, it was this very essay that opened the doors for me to such a philosophy, many years ago. Ortega draws an absolute distinction between the object in its executant reality and the object as represented, a distinction that this book accepts without reservation. Ortega holds that in the metaphoric relation, two separate poles of the object seem to interfere with one another—precisely the sort of event we are looking for, since we seek the mechanisms of all forms of interference between the loneliest poles of the world. If metaphor can shed any light on the communication between the different poles of being, then it may provide a kind of skeleton key to unlock the other relations in the heart of the world. The case of metaphor is the subject of chapter 8.

In chapter 9, a second point of access is provided by the unlikely theme of *humor*. In Bergson's famous essay on laughter, we find yet another theory that sheds light on the interference between two separate poles of being, and which also displays a stunning convergence of philosophical views with Ortega's theory of metaphor. Humor, like metaphor, plays out solely on the level of representation rather than that of the things themselves. Nonetheless, both may provide useful hints about the communication between separate poles of reality *in general*, far beyond the merely human level.

In this context, some new terminology may prove helpful. Since there will now be repeated discussions of the three different sorts of relation between isolated poles, it will be better to have specific terms for each of them so as to avoid the continued use of elliptical phrases. When we speak of the things themselves, the duality between their sheer unity and their plurality of traits, let's refer to these as *physical* relations. The physical realm here refers not to "physical" in the sense of the laws governing inanimate bodies, but in the sense employed by Xavier Zubiri, surely the most innovative ontologist of the past half-century in the continental tradition. For Zubiri, "physical" refers to the Greek sense of *physis*, as pertaining to all that belongs intrinsically to any object. When speaking of the physical world, this book is concerned not with the fate of inert material mass, but with the inner reality of substantial forms.

When we speak of the relation within the heart of things as perceived, let's refer to *sensual* relations, in keeping with the discoveries of the carnal phenomenologists. We have seen that in the senses there lies a dualism between the unified object that evades us and the multitude of properties that it exhibits: neither of these poles is ever accessible in its own right. Phenomenologists know that the intentional object can never become present in the flesh, but they also know that there is no purely given sense data free from the specter of intentional objects. At each moment we are trapped in a middle kingdom that has been described loosely as the ether or plasma or medium of the world. The phenomenology of perception plays out only on this sensual level, making no claim to drive into physical reality itself—indeed, in its abhorrence of all naturalism it even tends to deny the very existence of a physical realm, and certainly holds it at arm's length from philosophy. For the moment, I will also behave as though *human* perception gave an exhaustive description of the sensual realm. It can be decided a bit later whether this dualism between intentional objects and sensual qualities can also be found in the lower animals and insensate minerals, or whether it belongs to some entities and not others. This will be a question for Part Three. We now have *physical* and *sensual* relations as two separate themes. Let the double entendres roll . . . Let them roll for three or four minutes, and no longer.

And finally, when we speak of the interaction between separate objects, let's refer to *causal* relations. It should be remembered that there is no question here of brute efficient causation between masses slamming into one another or mutually influenced through electromagnetic and gravitational fields. Rather, we are speaking of a kind of formal causation between metaphysical substances, one whose nature has not yet been exactly determined. Additionally, we do not yet have to decide whether there is only one kind of causal relation or many. That is to say, it will be determined only later in this book whether the unity of a physical thing generates the unity of a sensual object, or the plural traits of a real thing generate its plurality in the sensual sphere—or whether neither of these things happens, or some combination of them. All of this belongs in chapter 10.

For now, we can simply try to complete the picture of sensual reality begun by the carnal phenomenologists. This can be done through an examination of metaphor and humor.

[8]

Metaphor

We need to shake up the majestic solitude in which each of the four poles of being holds itself aloof from the others. In the world as we know it, a kind of splitting of the ontological atom occurs ceaselessly. Objects collide with each other—triggering events, forming new objects, releasing qualities into the many breezes of the world. Having already identified the four poles of objects, we need to describe the space in which they meet: a space that is already a *fait accompli*, given that relations clearly do occur. To shift scientific metaphors, what we need is a sort of chemical technique that shows the mechanisms by which objects break apart or melt together.

For reasons that I hope will become clear, metaphor and humor seem like ideal test cases for us. Although these may seem like strange topics for a book on metaphysics, they share several promising features. Both have been recognized since ancient times as distinctive human talents—whether in Aristotle's remark that metaphor is the unteachable gift that belongs to humans and especially to those of genius, or in the age-old definition of the human being as the laughing animal.

Now as always, poetic gifts and a sense of humor are valued among the most important traits of our companions. Both themes also shed light on the relative abilities of humans and animals. For even if metaphor and humor seem to belong primarily to humans, they also seem to be present to some degree in higher birds and mammals, who employ metaphors in the form of tools or delight us with their pranks. Additionally, metaphor and humor both shed crucial light on any philosophical debate concerning gradual change versus quantum leaps, since these phenomena display both aspects. For in one sense it is true that individual metaphors and jokes do not work equally well for everyone, and that some are more beautiful or funnier than others. But just the same, at any given moment *they either work or not*. Perhaps I could be induced by some genius of the absurd to laugh at the red pen on my desk, but at the moment it is simply not humorous at all—unhumorous to an *absolute* degree. It will turn out that the same holds true for unskilled or worn-out metaphors, which contrary to postmodernist attempts to bleach over the distinction between live and dead metaphor, simply do not work at all.

Furthermore, experience shows that the themes of metaphor and jokes are surprisingly able to provoke opinionated reactions to a greater degree than almost any other philosophical topic. I have had numerous calm and open-minded discussions about controversial subjects such as politics and the fate of the soul after death, but almost never a mild conversation about the apparently harmless themes of poetry and comedy. Indeed, I have been snapped at several times when discussing these topics with people I had regarded as friendly acquaintances. This suggests that both topics speak so intimately to the private core of each of us that we sense that no theory is capable of doing them justice—or at least no theory proposed by someone else. Finally, both metaphor and humor are directly related to the theory of objects developed in this book. In the current chapter, I will show that metaphor generates tangible interference between two of the isolated poles of a thing; in the next chapter, we will see that humor does something similar.

Metaphors and jokes are only useful equipment for this book, not the central topic of inquiry. For this reason, there will be neither opportunity nor need to present a full survey of everything that has ever been written about these two universally fascinating themes.For the current discussion, I will limit myself mostly to Ortega's neglected gem of an essay, cited by virtually no one. This essay deals *explicitly* with the tension between a thing's underground reality and its sensual profile, making it unusually useful for our purposes. I will also speak briefly of some related notions from Max Black,[8] and offer several criticisms of Derrida's celebrated "White Mythology,"[9] cited here because its shortcomings shed light on what is most wrong with the rejection of metaphysics in continental philosophy. I will also have a few words to say about Donald Davidson.

A. Execution versus Presentation

Ortega's theory of metaphor is presented only in a single early work, originally the preface to a book of poems by one Moreno Villa. Now known as "An Essay in Esthetics by Way of a Preface,"[10] it appeared in 1914 when Ortega was thirty-one years old, and raised themes that were never fully developed during the author's distinguished career. Although fully compatible with the rest of his philosophy of vital reason, the essay is unique in his oeuvre for its ontological claims about the inner life of inanimate objects. Rather than offering a full aesthetic theory, Ortega limits himself to a treatment of metaphor, which he terms "the beautiful cell"[11]—the root material or alpha factor from which beauty emerges.

Conveniently for us, everything hinges for Ortega on a fundamental contrast between two modes of being that he terms *execution* and *image*. Departing somewhat from his examples, let's consider the case of a headache. When a migraine arises within me once every few years, my life is delivered over to its power. My very existence is deployed in the act of enduring its nearly crippling pain. Sleep eludes me; powerful pharmaceuticals are the only escape hatch, and even these need time to purchase and to take effect. Now contrast this experience with that of observing a friend in the midst of a headache. We see facial grimaces and watch him rub his head gently, as his movements and enthusiasms gradually slow to a crawl. Even if we try very hard to put ourselves in his shoes, even if we are true saints of empathy, our own being is not delivered over to the headache in the same way that his life is. Between my life as it executes itself and the life of another as seen from outside, there is an absolute gulf—a kind of ontological difference. But notice that this unbridgeable rift is not confined to our perceptions of *other* people: the same dualism occurs even in cases of introspection. An expert phenomenologist or Proustian diarist might be able to draw up a thousand-page catalog of the inner fluctuations of a headache. Even the minutest contours of its misery could be recorded with staggering literary brilliance, so that seemingly nothing remained to be said. As a limit-case, we might imagine the perceptions of God himself, who could presumably exhaust the describable qualities of any act of his awareness or ours. Even in this situation, there remains an ineffaceable gap between the image of a pain and its execution. To *observe* something, no matter how closely, is not to *be* it; to look at a thing is not the same thing as to stand in its place and undergo its fate, even if what we are observing is our own psychic lives.

This breakthrough of Ortega's belongs to the same year as his surprisingly early critique of Husserl: 1914, five years before Heidegger's own Muse first becomes visible. What we learn here is that consciousness is not primarily an observer, but an executant actor. Introspection has no closer relationship with the intimate reality of my life than my vision of a dolphin has with the dolphin itself. Introspection is not true inwardness, but only a special form of that espionage or visual eavesdropping with which we survey the being of *all* other objects. The reality of a thing is always utterly different from any of our relations to it. With luck, this point will already have convinced a large number of readers. But Ortega takes a second and more radical step, one that was too far ahead of its time in 1914 to leave any lasting mark even on Ortega himself—a step that not only paves the way for his theory of metaphor, but also silently pushes him beyond the familiar boundaries of post-Kantian philosophy. For it turns out that the

distance between execution and image applies not just to us and other animate beings, but holds good for objects in general. The pronoun "I," says
Ortega, belongs not just to living beings, "but rather all things—men,
things, situations—inasmuch as they are occurring, being, executing themselves."[12] With this step, Ortega is far beyond what is called speech-act theory: what he gives us is object-act theory, comprising the action of rocks,
grapefruit, snakes, and peppermint tablets no less than of humans. Few
fans of Heidegger will need much convincing that a *human* entity might
be irreducible to any of its external contours, that it might have an active
inner reality of its own, unapproachable by means of the usual descriptive
categories. Ortega's additional breakthrough, already a half-step further
than Heidegger ever went, consists in his noticing that there is also an executant inner reality stirring behind the facades of buckets, candles, super-
markets, clay-pits, bank robberies, helicopter accidents, and trees. He cites
the example of a red leather box lying before him, and notes that the redness and smoothness of the box are mere perceptions in his mind, while
the box *itself* is actually embedded in the fate of being red and smooth—
unlike Ortega himself. In one of the most radical sentences of twentieth-
century philosophy, he tells us that "just as there is an I-John Doe, there
is also an I-red, an I-water, and an I-star . . . Everything, from a point of
view within itself, is an 'I.'"[13] Elsewhere, Ortega speaks of true inwardness
as "anything in the act of executing itself," as "the true being of all things,
the only sufficient thing and the only thing whose contemplation would
completely satisfy us."[14]

Note that Ortega's "executancy" has nothing in common with what is
now called "performativity," despite their apparent meeting point in the
German word *Vollzug*. Performativity is a recent concept forged to fight all
notions of hidden essence, which it replaces with a kind of nominalist
essence fabricated on the outside by a series of public actions. Execution,
by contrast, is an essentialist concept through and through, even if not in
the traditional sense of an essence that could be made present in an adequate *logos*. Rather than an essential list of properties that the philosopher
could gradually make visible, the executancy of a thing is a dark and stormy
essence that exceeds any such list of properties. No catalog of qualities, no
matter how important and exhaustive, will ever *use up* the reality of
Ortega's red leather box, just as Husserl's or even God's surveillance of my
life does not step in and *replace* my life and live it for me. The weakness of
phenomenology, even in its existential form, is not just that it ranks visible
profiles higher than the horizons into which human Dasein is thrown.
Instead, the real weakness of phenomenology is its failure to capture the
objecthood of objects, the "I" of sailboats and moons, by granting them
an intimate interior of their own. To change objects from visible targets of
consciousness (phenomenology) into concealed potential background tar-

gets for consciousness (hermeneutics) may appear to some observers to be a great philosophical advance. But it does not yet liberate objects into the full autonomy they deserve.

Ortega holds that the inwardness of things is a depth that can absolutely never be fathomed, insofar as it is not interchangeable with any sum of its attributes (cf. Kripke's objection to Russell's theory of names[15]). The growth of knowledge is a process of digging away at this inwardness of things and attempting the ultimately hopeless task of bringing it to light. "This," says Ortega, "is the task of language, but language merely *alludes* to inwardness—it never shows it."[16] In more melancholic terms, "a narrative makes everything a ghost of itself, placing it a distance, pushing it beyond the horizon of the here and now."[17] The fate of language, as of perception and (we will see) of all relation, is forever to translate the dark and inward into the tangible and outward, a task at which it always comes up short given the infinite depth of things. And precisely this is the importance of aesthetics for Ortega. "Imagine," he announces, "the importance of a language or system of expressive signs whose function was not to tell us about things but to present them to us in the act of executing themselves. Art is just such a language; this is what art does. The esthetic object is inwardness as such—it is each thing as 'I.'"[18] Art is granted a sort of magic power, allowing us to confront the impossible depth of objects. Or rather, art is only granted the power of *seeming* to be able to do this, since even Van Gogh cannot *really* put the internal executant being of shoes onto a piece of canvas. For now we can restrict ourselves to asking how this process works, though we will eventually want to know why aesthetic productions seem able to present executant things while nonaesthetic experiences do not.

As already noted, Ortega confines his discussion of art to the theory of metaphor. The metaphor of choice in his essay comes from the poet López Picó of Valencia, who sings that the cypress tree "is like the ghost of a dead flame."[19] To simplify his analysis, Ortega strips away the "like" that turns the metaphor into a simile, and drops both the ghost and the deadness of the flame. For the purposes of his analysis, the kernel of the metaphor is this: "the cypress is a flame." He first notes that this attempted union of cypress and flame is based on a truly deep coincidence in their being, not a merely literal resemblance or contrast. "Metaphor," he insists, "is not . . . the mutual assimilation of real qualities."[20] In fact, for some important reason, metaphor seems to work only when it utilizes *inessential* qualities.

We can show this using examples of our own. It is clearly no metaphor to say that "a dollar is like 87.153 euro cents," or "a dollar is like a euro because both are hard currencies." But it is possible that we might begin to feel poetic sentiments about money and generate metaphors based on the Aristotelian ratio that dollars are to euros as America is to Europe. Haunting refrains can easily be invented on this basis. A Leftist poet could call the euro "a dollar that funds no wars." A right-wing bard might counter by berating the five-euro cent coin: "Europe, whose nickels Jefferson fled in shame." Presumably both political camps could agree on a neutral melody like this one: "a dollar is like a euro etched in green, / the green of distant Neptune and the cold and deathless sea."

We can say the same thing of metaphorical contrasts no less than comparisons. Obviously, no real poet would tell us "a shield is not like a cup because one is used in battles and the other in restaurants" (unless we were dealing with some sort of literary Dadaism, a special aesthetic scenario that need not be considered here). But the poet might easily follow Aristotle's example, and refer to a shield as "a cup that holds no wine."[21] In the *Poetics*, the connection drawn between cup and shield is their respective use as symbols of the gods Dionysus and Ares, which even for an ancient Greek would hardly be regarded as what is most typical of these two objects. For most of us, if this metaphor works at all, there will be some other sort of connection between them. But neither a shield's similarity to a cup, nor its uselessness for holding wine, are the sorts of qualities that jump to mind if we are asked to describe a shield.

The question before us now is why only the inessential qualities seem to provide an effective basis for metaphor. The answer, it turns out, has mesmerizing implications for the thinghood of things.

B. The Plasma of Things

Let's return to Ortega's own pared-down example, "the cypress is a flame," and follow his account of how one object merges with the other. As already noted, the metaphor tends to fail if it too closely approaches a genuine similarity; to say "a cypress is like a juniper" strikes too close to the truth to be effective. Any literal similarity between cypress and flame in the practical world will border on the trivial. Most likely, what we have in mind if this metaphor works for us is the similar physical shapes of the cypress and flame, and these shapes are far removed indeed from what strikes us as most essential about these objects. But on the basis of this pretext, this mere shell of a similarity between cypress and flame, the poet becomes an audacious liar who claims *absolute* identity between them (ignoring the special case of similes), as though the cypress as a whole were equivalent to the flame as a whole. The mind of the reader resists this identity, as it must. "The cypress is a conifer" fails as metaphor precisely because the names *can* be fused together with ease; "the cypress is a flame" succeeds only because they cannot.

What we have is an apparent likeness used as an excuse to bring into
play an *unlikeness,* as in Max Müller's point about metaphor in the Hindu
Vedas, which displays its *via negativa* in naked form: "he is firm, but he
is not a rock", or "the sea roars, but it is not a bull."[22] Whatever we normally associate with the name "cypress," whatever we customarily attach
to the word "flame," these associations are broken into pieces as soon as
we hear that the cypress is a flame. In Ortega's own magnificent words,
miles removed from the neurasthenic jargon of the postmoderns: "The
result . . . is the annihilation of what both objects are as practical images.
When they collide with one another their hard carapaces crack and the
internal matter, in a molten state, acquires the softness of plasm, ready to
receive a new form and structure."[23] A new object is created, neither quite
tree nor quite fire, but a vaporous hybrid of both: one that cannot even be
described in terms of definite tangible properties.

Ortega's description of this process makes sense only in light of his previously described ontology, in which the world is forever torn apart
between the inwardness of things and their effects upon us: his intriguing
dualism between the thing as image and as execution. If we speak of the
cypress or the flame, we can only *allude* to their innermost reality, the "I"
or self that each of them enacts. No cataloguing of the properties of these
entities, in no matter how many different moods and under no matter
what lighting conditions, can ever fully exhaust the cryptic essence
deployed in each of these things. My relationship with the tree cannot suck
it dry to the marrow, since the tree always eludes contact with us.
Language and all forms of perception seem doomed merely to point
loosely at the inner execution of things, at their subterranean being, without ever reaching full intimate union with this being. Ortega's claim for
metaphor, of course, is only that it presents the inner execution of the
things in *simulated* form. Poets cannot *really* crossbreed trees with flames:
perhaps only wizards could do this, and their race has vanished from the
earth.

The question, then, is how the poet makes such crossbreeding *seem* to
happen. In attempting to answer this question, Ortega develops an interesting and quite novel concept of what a "feeling" is. Against any psychol-
ogistic notion of feelings as internal mental states or physiological
excitements, he insists on the close connection that feelings have with
objects. "Every objective image," he says, "on entering or leaving our consciousness, produces a subjective reaction—just as a bird that lights on or
leaves a branch starts it trembling, or turning on and off an electric current
instantly produces a new current."[24]

This beautiful description entails a *second* fundamental split within reality, one that resembles the distinction between image and execution but
does not entirely coincide with it. If I say the phrase "snow leopard," for

example, there is obviously no presence of the real leopard in this phrase. Snow leopard *the thing* is a warm and dangerous creature stalking its prey in the Himalayas, whereas snow leopard *the phrase* is without bodily temperature, strikes no fear into any nonhuman animal, and is no more at home in Nepal than on the moon. The same is true, *mutatis mutandis*, of snow leopard *the visual image*.

This second rift in reality lies entirely on the level of thing-as-image, not that of thing-as-execution, just as we saw with the gap between intentional object and sensual quality for the carnal phenomenologists. On the one hand, there is the cypress as a set of distinct qualities: its shrublike texture, its twisted and stunted upward motion, and its dull, dark green hue. On the other hand, there is the cypress as a unified thing that I encounter, that fills up some part of my life as I adopt a definite lived stance toward it, however faint. Insofar as the cypress enters the sphere of my life, it is not just a sensory image, but also a single executant reality within my life, an actual experience that I undergo, a mysterious unity at which all my attitudes aim. Considered as an apparition that enters my life and sets up shop, the cypress-feeling is not the same as the real cypress that grows and dies on the plain. Nonetheless, even within the narrow limits of my life, in which all objects are reduced to caricatures, the cypress-feeling still exceeds all of the hundreds of millions of things that might be said about it. None of these would exhaust the total cypress-effect that plays itself out in my personal world. In each instant of my life alongside the cypress, I vaguely recognize it as a unit, as a kind of inscrutable monad of my world beneath its multitude of describable features.

The point is important, and bears repeating. The cypress is not only an image sparkling with diverse features, but also a murky underground unity *for me*, and not just in its inner executant self. And it is from this strange concealed integrity of individual images that metaphor draws its power—not from the genuine reality of each thing, which language is powerless to unveil. On one side we have the cypress-feeling, which as a single executant experience of my own can never be fully described, but perhaps only vaguely illustrated: maybe it is a shadowy intuition of brooding vegetative power combined with funerary gloom and the fear of lurking criminals. On the other side there is the flame-feeling, with its festive joy, its delight in destructive power, its jubilation of infernal color, and its hypnotic void of information. Naturally, the flame-feeling can only be split into parts in this way by analysis, since it generally begins as a united experience of the flame as a total reality, a kind of image without organs. What happens in usual language and perception is that our attention is seized by images alone, as the nature of things requires. I grasp things by their shape and color or by the musical sounds they generate, and also by meeting them with a unified "feeling" in Ortega's sense, not by touching their nethermost reality.

The same thing happens if we follow a Kripkean theory of reference, using proper names to point to some unknown X called "gold" or "Richard Nixon," names that remain distinct from any known properties of these objects. What we have with proper names as rigid designators are the feeling-units "gold" or "Nixon," not gold and Nixon *in themselves*, since these consist only in executing their own reality and can never be reduced to names or thoughts any more than to definite descriptions. A proper name is simply *not* the thing itself, even if it points more closely to that thing than does an adjective. More relevantly for us, notice that the proper name is also not yet a metaphor, even if it strikes some theorists as being closer to the essence of a thing than all of its numerous properties are. But the situation changes drastically if some poet writes: "gold has forged the keys to Nixon's tomb." Here, we have left both names and descriptions far behind. Gold and Nixon are no longer convenient nick-names for gigantic lists of known facts about certain entities, but neither are they just pointer fingers stretched towards inaccessible things-in-themselves. What probably occupies the reader's mind instead is some sort of tragic hybrid network that links the thirty-seventh president with scandals, greed, fate, death, and the sparkling seduction of gold.

And here is the marvelous point: according to Ortega, the metaphor does this not by painting an image of "Nixon-gold" from the outside, but by compelling us to live executantly a new object born in our midst in the very moment that it is named. More concretely, it forces us to live a new *feeling-thing*, and not a new thing itself, which can never be directly lived by any other thing. To return to the case of the cypress and the flame, in metaphor their images are destroyed, and even their independent existence as proper names is swept away. If someone tells me that a cypress is like a juniper, what happens is that my attention is absorbed by a set of remarkably similar qualities; I am adrift in a world of *attributes* of things. But if someone tells me that a cypress is a flame, then I have entered the magic world of a cypress-flame-feeling-thing. Since the two images are unable actually to melt together instantly by way of their truly minimal common qualities, the cryptic essences that my life senses in them remain before me in a kind of permanent collision. My executant feeling of the cypress and my executant feeling of the flame attempt to fuse with one another, but without final resolution: their hard carapaces crack as they fill each other with molten plasm. And as Ortega admits, "even when a metaphor is created we still do not know the reason for it. We simply sense an identity, we live executantly this being, the cypress-flame."[25] This new being may be constructed out of feelings, but given Ortega's object-oriented concept of feeling, it is actually a new *thing* that has entered the world, and not just a private mental state of mine. To create such an object is to de-create the external images that normally identify it, reshaping the plasma of their qualities into a hybrid structure. What we call a *style*, says Ortega, is nothing other than a specific mode of de-creating images and recreating them as feeling-things.

Before pausing to consider a few other authors, it should be noted that Ortega's concept of the executant object deployed in its private reality has nothing in common with any supposedly naive theory of "the proper"— that favorite piñata of the Derrideans. The candle-in-itself and the horse-in-itself do not claim any univocal, literal, proper meaning for Ortega, because they do not have a *meaning* at all. What they have is an intimate reality, a foot permanently jammed in the door of the world. To try to approach their "meaning" in any way is necessarily to do so from the outside, by means of a relation—that is, by means of some sort of image. In this respect, there is certainly an unmasterable polysemia to the meaning of things, one dependent on context, text, perspective, system. But this vaunted unmasterable polysemia is far less interesting than the unmasterable *kryptoousia* or hidden reality that actually makes up each entity: its irreducible execution amidst the cosmos, utterly distinct from the execution of anything else. In this latter sense, the object is indeed univocal: this candle is this candle; it is what is proper to itself. To say this is not to lapse into some sort of gullible, fateful, traditional, reactionary, power-hungry white man's imperialist *mythos* (as Derrida suggests in such grandstanding fashion[26]). It is only to recognize that the infinite dissemination of meaning does not entail an infinite dissemination of being. In other words, the fact that the "proper" of the candle can never be univocally spoken does not mean that there is no such thing as the proper of the candle.

We will now see that it is only Derrida's tacit antirealist bias, typical of phenomenology and its French inheritors, that allows him to equate the being of a thing and the meaning of its name. The infinite inward depth of candles, stars, and moons is far more interesting than the supposed infinite complexity of multiple meanings—an increasingly academic notion that may be useful for endlessly beating conservatives to a pulp, but is quite useless for unleashing the music in the heart of things.

C. Reality without Presence

No figure in the history of philosophy is simultaneously so observant and so irritating as Jacques Derrida. This is not meant entirely as a compliment. Some of Derrida's least appealing traits as a writer are borrowed directly from Heidegger, while others are present in his forerunner only in germ. Among those habits shared with Heidegger is a similar attitude with which both authors approach the history of philosophy. For one thing, neither of them can ever have a simple point of *disagreement* with a past philosopher—it is always a matter of some dark, fateful error that has conditioned all Western discussion of such-and-such ever since. Another example is the monotony with which both of them see little in past philosophers other than naive invocations of *presence* (generously granted to be inevitable), as if all bad cities were bad only for parking their police cars on the street, and never for different reasons. Finally, the followers of both Heidegger and Derrida share an uncommon resistance to stating the teachings of their masters in the form of an actual *thesis*: indeed, these followers imply quite openly that anyone who tries this is a ham-fisted blunderer who merely inscribes himself in the very discourse that has already been overcome— or whatever. One senses a deep-rooted fear of criticism in this strange wish to be utterly impregnable, to turn the enemy's weapons back against the enemy rather than meeting them openly with equal and dissimilar force.

Among those unfortunate traits that belong to Derrida to a greater degree than to Heidegger, at least two come to mind. One is the insufferable use of puns that seem designed to expose a none-too-accidental connection between the terms they unify, but which are often just doubly arbitrary. For instance, there is Derrida's mention of the *heliotrope* to refer both to the supposed "metaphor of metaphor" of Plato's sun,[27] and also to "a kind of oriental jasper,"[28] hinting a bit too preciously at some sort of deep-seated connection between the very gesture of philosophizing and Orientalist imperialism—a connection insinuated elsewhere in the essay but never really argued. Another frequent annoyance is that Derrida's essays, like his bottomless public lectures, are invariably far too long. In the case of "White Mythology," as in many other cases, we find a hard-hitting ten-page core surrounded by an additional fifty pages of highly mannered intellectual collage. For what it's worth, I think that this is no way to write, and cannot comprehend those strange souls who regard Derrida as a master literary stylist, or even as especially witty: reading Derrida after any of the carnal phenomenologists is like moving from a delicious meal to something midway between solving a rebus and auditing a tax return. Nonetheless, the central philosophical claims of "White Mythology" have genuine merit, and show Derrida at his clear-sighted best. Even more than Heidegger, Derrida resembles a skilled Coast Guard captain preventing the illicit return of Presence to any shore. In "White Mythology," this takes the form of a proposed ban on any notion of "literal" meaning.

When it comes to Aristotle's distinction between the literal and figurative meanings of words, Derrida notes an inner complexity to this doctrine, which "does not recur to a very simple, very clear, i.e. central opposition . . ."[29] In a primary sense, there is the chief or literal or ordinary meaning termed *kurion*, as when Aristotle says that "by the ordinary word I mean that in general use in a country."[30] This is the proper name in the strict sense, and obviously varies from place to place, which is why archaic or uniquely British terms often have a metaphorical effect in American English. But although metaphors are obviously not proper names in this sense, there is obviously another sense in which they can be more or less proper than others: this is not *kurion* but *idion*, which can include rare words as well as metaphors. Paradoxically, then, "one may speak properly or improperly of what is not proper to the thing, its accident, for example . . ."[31] The sphere of the proper both excludes metaphor *and* inhabits it as a kind of internal measuring stick to judge its proximity to the proper in the strict sense. Surely this is already ontotheology, since despite an apparent gap between proper names and descriptions, certain descriptions will be closer to the thinghood of the thing than others, more appropriate to it: "Here, the two values properness/improperness do not have the same locus of pertinence. Nevertheless, the ideal of every language, and in particular of metaphor, being to bring to knowledge the thing itself, the turn of speech will be better if it brings us closer to the thing's . . . proper truth."[32] In short, the proper lies *outside* the metaphoric realm, but is also that which gauges all progress and improvement *within* the metaphoric realm. And given that we do not live in a world where the things have a direct and immediate presence to us, this difference between *kurion* and *idion* is what allows language to exist at all: "The space of language, the field of its divisions, is opened precisely by the difference between . . . the proper, and accident."[33]

A similar difficulty occurs in Aristotle's remarks about the nature of metaphor and of poetic genius. For on the one hand, metaphor is constitutive for our species as a whole, since it is a talent for noting resemblances, and "imitation is natural to man from childhood, one of his advantages over the lower animals being this, that he is the most imitative creature in the world, and learns at first by imitation."[34] But although this skill belongs to all of us, some of us have it more than others, and even have this superiority from the time of birth: "But the greatest thing by far is to be a master of metaphor. It is the one thing that cannot be learnt from others; and it is also a sign of genius, since a good metaphor implies an intuitive perception of . . . similarity . . ."[35] Even though all metaphor remains adrift in the world of the improper, some metaphors are said to make a closer approach to the proper than others. And some humans, despite the fact that we are all highly specific individuals, come nearer to the very human essence through their innate genius for resemblances.

Derrida has an especial brilliance for detecting a similar tension in virtually everything he reads, reminiscent of Heidegger's scent for the historical dominance of presence-at-hand. For as long as philosophy is done in this world, Derrida deserves to have this insight linked with his name—an insight that does push philosophy a definite step forward beyond his predecessors along this front. Heidegger has numerous flirtations with the same insight, but generally relapses into the ontotheology he should have been able to overcome: making Angst a privileged mood that steps outside all moods, or theory a privileged relation to objects that outstrips all objects, or peasants more genuinely Dasein than city-dwellers, or Germans more thrown into the void than ruinous Americans and Bolsheviks. But in all fairness, it should be observed that Derrida is no less predictable than Heidegger in many of his views, which inevitably adhere to the mildly radical branch of the Center-Left: criticizing the actions of NATO or of Pennsylvania judges rather than the equally "metaphysical" deep ecologists and antiglobalization protesters. A right-wing version of deconstruction is quite conceivable, and would seem no more or less intellectually justified than the political attitudes of Derrida's more typical readership.

But for the most part, Derrida is admirably cautious about ranking humans and other entities according to their proximity to a realm of the proper, and has even been a peerless teacher of such caution. Any theory of the proper, especially any attempt to engrave it somewhere in visible presence, is quickly showered with poisonous darts in his works. And this puts us very close to the deadlock of post-Heideggerian philosophy, which has lost any valid mechanism for dealing with specific entities, and has abandoned any hope of the "proper" in favor of a shifting holistic world of interrelated significances that shun any thing-in-itself. Derrida describes our necessary reflection on the proper as "an immense task," which is certainly true, and also as one "which supposes the elaboration of an entire strategy of deconstruction and an entire protocol of reading,"[36] which is more questionable, for the same reason that Heidegger's massive program of a history of being is questionable. An "entire protocol of reading"— sending everyone to the library to consolidate Derrida's gains—may be effective in unmasking detailed abuses of the proper in many different places, now that his basic critique of the proper has long since been published. But such a "protocol" will do little to demonstrate the basic validity of Derrida's philosophical position, which is marked everywhere by a damaging prejudice. I refer to Derrida's tendency to shift from the impossibility of proper *meaning* to the impossibility of proper *being*. In fact, these are two completely separate issues.

What worries Derrida about Aristotle is his apparent fondness for univocal speech, for proper names as the genuine meaning of things. "No philosophy, as such, has ever renounced this Aristotelian ideal."[37] Derrida concedes that Aristotle allows for multiple meanings of a single word: "This is a fact. But this fact has right of entry into language only in the extent to which the polysemia is finite, the different significations are limited in number, and above all sufficiently *distinct*, each remaining one and identifiable. Language is what it is, language, only insofar as it can then master and analyze polysemia. With no remainder."[38] The philosopher is the one who has only one thing to say, in opposition to the Sophists and other long-winded chatterboxes. And in a stunning indictment of Aristotle's supposed harshness, we hear that "each time that polysemia is irreducible, when no unity of meaning is even promised to it, one is outside language [according to Aristotle]. And consequently, *outside humanity*."[39] But anyone reading these passages of Aristotle carefully will see that they have a different purpose from what Derrida imputes to them. What Aristotle actually says is that "it makes no difference if one says [a word] means more than one thing, [as long as it is] *only a limited number* . . . But if one were not to posit this, but said it meant infinitely many things, it is clear that there would be no definition; for not to mean one thing is to mean nothing, and when words have no meaning, conversation is abolished, even with oneself."[40] With this statement, Aristotle's purpose is not to enter language like some brutal rogue cop and force everyone to regulate their speech according to literal meanings. Note that for all practical purposes, the polysemia of language remains limitless for Aristotle, since new poets and new contexts will continue to shine fresh light endlessly on all horses, mountains, chariots, and olive wreaths. The point of the passage is not to regulate the production of *meaning*, but to secure the reality of *being*, by insisting on the identity of separate substances.

Aristotle's point is really quite simple. If everything had a truly infinite number of attributes, everything would necessarily be the same, "so that all things would be one, since they would be synonyms."[41] We can certainly allow that a thing might have different names or attributes at different times or in different respects; indeed, the ability to have different attributes at different times is one of the key features of substance according to Aristotle. But we can never allow a thing to *be* different things simultaneously—a simple, fundamental distinction so lost to present-day continental philosophy that it would probably strike many as just a word trick. Aristotle considers "the case that what we call 'human being,' other people call 'not human being'; but the thing raising an impasse is not this, whether it is possible for the same thing at the same time to be and not be a human being *in name*, but in respect to *the thing*."[42] With this, his target is not only the Sophists, but also Anaxagoras, with his holistic cosmos in which everything is mixed with everything else: "if contradictory things are all true of the same thing at the same time, it is obvious that all things will be one. For the same thing would be a battleship and a wall and a human being . . . And so the claim of Anaxagoras comes true, that all things are mixed together, so that nothing is truly any one thing."[43] The fact that Aristotle insists on the identity of individual substances beyond every possible multitude of descriptions does not entail that he wishes literal meaning to dominate all figurative language. Not at all: his obvious admiration for poets speaks loudly to the contrary.

Here we have the same cardinal error that haunts all of Derrida's work: his tendency to confuse ontotheology and simple realism. In other words, the fact that Heidegger is unjustified in holding that Germans more closely approximate the human essence than Spaniards does not entail that there is no human essence. The incapacity of the proper to be visibly incarnated in privileged specific objects does not entail that there is no proper. And more generally, the fact that there is no proper of meaning does not entail that there is no proper of being. For Derrida, any object-oriented philosophy could only be metaphysics in the bad sense; he and his followers, were they to read this book, could only view it as a retrograde step. On the contrary, I hold that they are the ones who occupy the retrograde position: for it is they who force us into a false either-or choice between a reactionary philosophy that judges all beings by their approximation to the proper, or a Sophistical or Anaxagorean cosmos in which everything is everything, in which I the author am simultaneously a battleship, a wall, and a human. But every interesting possibility in philosophy lies somewhere between these two options. To reverse Leibniz's old maxim, Derrida tends to be right in what he denies, but wrong in what he affirms.

This misreading of the genuine problem of the proper eventually becomes quite disturbing in Derrida's interpretation of Aristotle's *tone*, which he bizarrely regards as sinister. Anyone reading the relevant passages of the *Metaphysics* with an open mind will enjoy a half-dozen good laughs thanks to Aristotle's defense of substance against his opponents. His tone is no less jovial than cutting. When his opponents claim that everything is everything, Aristotle has his share of good clean fun, not only by referring to them as no different from plants unable to converse even with themselves, but also by asking why they walk to Megara rather than sitting still, or why they do not walk off of cliffs. Since this is Aristotle, and not some random vulgar realist barking testily at innovators, his points have a compelling edge backed by a highly detailed theory of substance. But from reading Derrida's account of the matter, one would get the sense that Aristotle is some sort of demonic tyrant ready to declare the Sophists and his other opponents as subhuman—as if the comparison of his opponents to plants were an incipient, foreboding political gesture, heralding imperialism, Auschwitz, and the Gulag. Once again, *realism* is blamed for something that is really, *at most*, the fault of ontotheology.

I do not jest. Late in his essay, Derrida introduces a set of sweeping statements about "the West" and its desire to "interiorize" and "recollect"—i.e., to pin down all polysemia by means of some fixed literal meaning, some proper presence. Derrida actually implies that this is the cause of imperialist violence by the West, as can be gathered from his citations of Hegel belittling the use of figurative speech in Oriental poetry.[44] It is even insinuated that male humans are more caught up in this process than females, as in Derrida's gratuitous, even nauseating remark that "some have more nature than others, more genius, more generosity, more *seed*."[45] Most carelessly of all, it is cemented into the very title of his essay, since "White Mythology" turns out to refer to the mythology of *white men*: "Metaphysics—the white mythology which reassembles and reflects the culture of the West: the white man takes his own mythology, Indo-European mythology, his own *logos*, that is, the *mythos* of his idiom, for the universal form of that he must still wish to call Reason."[46] My gripe here is not with Derrida's political convictions, but with the sloppy and crowd-pleasing way in which he links Aristotle's *Poetics* with a fairly shallow interpretation of universal history. Perhaps a detailed case could be made that the ontotheology of presence is responsible for a good deal of actual political oppression, by some people or nations having been defined as *more* people or nations than others. (Though it is hard to believe that this was never done outside the scope of Western philosophy.) Derrida has not actually made this case, any more than Heidegger ever made his case about the link between *Vorhandenheit*, technology, and the crisis of the West. Anyone who makes a habit of reading good, basic historical writing will already demand much better from both of them.

Ortega's theory of metaphor is already more sophisticated than this. His initial premise is that the reality of each object is a definite executant being *and* that this being can never fully come to presence in perception or in word. With this simple first step, Derrida's habitual confusion of realism and ontotheology is avoided, and guerrilla metaphysics descends from the coffee farms to fight the reactionaries of Left and Right alike.

D. The Wolf-System

Ortega's essay is not widely cited in the literature on metaphor. Despite its merits, it still functions as a kind of island oasis in its field. For this reason, it may be useful to link his findings briefly with those of a more familiar classic essay on the topic. The one I have in mind is Max Black's famous article "Metaphor,"[47] which displays several points of convergence with Ortega's theory. This convergence is all the more striking given that Black falls squarely within the recent Anglo-American tradition, whereas Ortega emerged from the neo-Kantian and phenomenological milieu of pre–Great War Germany. Black's article shows us analytic philosophy at its finest. Every school has its vices, and the worst sort of analytic thought is known to mix self-righteous claims to ruthless logic with a Bazooka Joe level of wit. But in Black's essay we find nothing but the analytic virtues: lucidity, precision, innovation, flashes of democratic collegial warmth, and the sort of healthy self-confidence that offers us a freedom from paralyzing traditions.

What Black most opposes is the common understanding of metaphor that views it as a surrogate for literal meanings. The name he gives to this viewpoint is the *substitution* theory of metaphor. Consider this simple case: "the chairman plowed through the discussion." The substitution theory holds that this statement is a more or less exact equivalent of more commonplace terms that might have been used: "Instead of saying, plainly or *directly*, that the chairman dealt summarily with objections, or ruthlessly suppressed irrelevance, or something of the sort, the speaker chose to use a word ('plowed') which, strictly speaking, means something else."[48] If we convert the sentence into "the chairman dealt summarily with objections," the substitution theory would hold that we have lost nothing at all, having merely deprived the sentence of a bit of decorative sparkle. Black forcefully opposes this conclusion. Obviously, Ortega must oppose it as well, since for him the ultimate terms in a metaphor are inscrutable executant realities, not literal meanings that can be exchanged for other such meanings like trading cards. Naturally, Derrida would also oppose such a substitution theory—but for the *opposite* reason. Ortega, like Black, actually grants the existence of literal meanings of words. For Ortega the problem is that these meanings are simply incapable of touching the secret depth of things, while for Black they are mere social commonplaces that metaphor will somehow manage to outstrip. For Derrida, however, there is no such thing as a literal meaning in the first place, since this would require some sort of univocal referent that exceeds our various articulations of it. In other words, Ortega and Black both accept a distinction between metaphor and normal language, while Derrida does not. What this entails is that both Ortega and Black need to zero in on some sort of realm that *exceeds* everyday language, though Ortega is more explicitly metaphysical in his way of doing so.

As a variant of the substitution theory, Black also considers the *comparison* theory of metaphor, modeled more closely on similes. Justly mocking an inane traditional example, Black asks us to consider the statement "Richard is a lion." The substitution theory might say that this is simply a different way of saying "Richard is brave." The comparison theory, not so different from its cousin, would parse the metaphor as saying "Richard is like a lion, insofar as they are both brave." According to both theories, there is no net energy loss when the lion is replaced by explicitly stated adjectives. Given this total cognitive equivalence between metaphor and literal meaning, it might be asked why anyone would use metaphor at all. For both the substitution and comparison theories, the answer is clear. As Black notes, both "agree in making metaphor a *decoration*,"[49] just as some believe that an author's style is nothing more than decoration added for cosmetic purposes to a fixed literal content. With typical relaxed irony, Black cites another reason offered by both theories for the existence of metaphor: namely, that metaphor provides "a shock of 'agreeable surprise' and so on. The principle behind these explanations seems to be: When in doubt about some peculiarity of language, attribute its existence to the pleasure it gives a reader. A principle that has the merit of working well in default of any evidence."[50]

But there is an even deeper assumption that both theories share, one that Black addresses only in passing. Namely, for both the substitution and comparison theories, metaphor is concerned with *properties* of things rather than with things as a whole. When Richard and the lion are combined, the traditional theories simply pick and choose the most easily convertible features from the two entities, dumping the rest along the roadside as irrelevant. Black senses this when he laments a conceptual relapse by I. A. Richards, when at one point[51] Richards seems to backtrack on his earlier theory by expressing agreement that metaphor only brings *certain* features of its terms into play. "He is on firmer ground," Black counters, "when he says [on page 125] that the reader is forced to 'connect' the two *ideas*. In this 'connection' resides the secret and mystery of metaphor."[52] Again, what Black and Ortega share is an insight that metaphor is concerned with unitary ideas or things, not with specific sets of qualities.

By contrast, Derrida is allied in certain respects with the substitution and comparison theories, since he does not allow for any existence of a unified thing apart from the knowable features of it. At most, he would simply add the postmodernist twist that all metaphors are equal, since there is no standard by which to determine which descriptions are more proper than others. But even with this gesture, he would remain trapped on the level of qualities and properties.

But Black disagrees that metaphor works by observing similar qualities in things and then pushing the things together on that basis. As he sees it, metaphor actually *generates* the similarity in question: "There is some temptation to think of similarities as 'objectively given'. . . [But] it would be more illuminating in some of these cases to say that the metaphor *creates* the similarity than to say that it formulates some similarity antecedently existing."[53] But this implies that we are concerned with more than just discernible qualities: what we have are *integral units* of some kind, whether one wants to call them things, objects, ideas, names, or words. What is important here is only that they are entities with singular personalities that exceed any of their graspable features; it is these units that are brought together in metaphor, and not just comparable qualities. This is what Black calls the *interaction* theory of metaphor, a term that could be applied to Ortega's position just as well.

Black proposes that we consider the striking statement "man is a wolf." Several things are happening here. On the one hand, what we have are two simple *unities*, human and wolf, whatever they may be: no one in the world can give an exhaustive description of the features of these entities. The words point us vaguely towards recognizable stock characters of the cosmos without specifying any of their traits in particular. On the other hand, human and wolf are not just units, but *determinate* units. Although none of us can sum up everything there is to know about these two very dangerous animals, we can all give a fairly rough description of them. We all generally regard the wolf as "fierce, hungry, engaged in constant struggle, a scavenger, and so on."[54] And most likely, none of us wrongly believes that wolves are vegetarians or easily domesticated.[55] What we are dealing with here is what Black delightfully terms "the system of associated commonplaces" or "set of current platitudes" associated with any term. Some of our beliefs about wolves might actually be false. Some of them surely might be culturally relative: Black notes that "[those who] take wolves to be reincarnations of dead humans will give the statement 'Man is a wolf' an interpretation different from the one I have been assuming."[56] Ultimately, the commonplaces must even vary slightly between each individual person, giving the metaphor an ever so subtly different effect for each of us. But the point is that there always *are* such vague commonplaces associated with any word.

Now, the traditional theories would say that metaphor works by mixing and matching these commonplaces between the two objects, "taking pleasure" in discovering that both humans and wolves have backbones and two eyes, inhabit portions of Alaska, and live in violent hierarchical packs. But Black's interaction theory simply denies that this is what is happening: what is being brought together are *things*, not properties. Although he lacks Ortega's ontological commitment to a secluded world of executant objects, Black agrees that a metaphor can never be reduced to a comparison of traits, but must be some sort of fusion of entire independent units.

In a phrase of staggering beauty and probing insight, Black observes that the meaning of the wolf is really "a *wolf-system* of related commonplaces."[57] In most cases there is not one wolf-quality in particular that catches our eye, since the metaphor leaves vague what exactly we are supposed to look at. Instead, there is a kind of electrical infrastructure of half-intuited wolf-marks and wolf-tokens. And in the metaphor, what happens is that the wolf-system is somehow translated into the system of humans. As Black describes this process: "A suitable hearer will be led by the wolf-system of implications to construct a corresponding system of implications about the principal subject [i.e., 'Man']."[58] Or even more memorably: "Any human traits that can without undue strain be talked about in 'wolf-language' will be rendered prominent, and any that cannot will be pushed into the background. The wolf-metaphor suppresses some details, emphasizes others—in short, *organizes* our view of man."[59] Black compares this process to looking at the night sky through a piece of smoked glass with only certain lines left transparent, or like being forced to describe a battle in terms borrowed from the game of chess. The chess metaphor does not only pick out chesslike features from the military scene before us. Instead, it actively *shapes* our perception of the battle, perhaps playing up the brilliant tactical positioning of the two armies while suppressing the shock and trauma of those wounded horribly in action—a gruesome feature of warfare for which chessboards provide little analogy. The same thing happens when we say "man is a wolf." For as long as this metaphor rings in our ears, we tend to forget all instances of human musical skill or mathematical ability, the invention of airplanes, and all other human things that have no name in wolf-speak.

There is nothing in all of this that would contradict what Ortega said about the cypress and the flame. These two objects, just like the human and the wolf, fuse together as *entire systems* rather than simply coming to handshake agreements about shared qualities. What Ortega says is that we take some minor shared quality (in this instance, physical shape) as a pretext for combining the most intimate realities of cypress-thing and flame-thing. Black never really addresses how such a pretext might function, but he clearly believes that metaphor takes us beyond any overlap of isolated qualities, and on toward a marriage or cybernetic merger of the two things as a whole. Even if we imagine a reader who is utterly obsessed with the single human/wolf similarity of ferocious competition (say, a Marxist economist), this reader will still experience the metaphor as resounding into vulpine chasms reaching far beyond the limited theme of market competition.

We should end this reading of Black's theory with an interesting possible objection that he himself anticipates, and which applies to Ortega as well. When the wolf-system is imported into the human-system, it seems as though some of the commonplace traits of both objects would *also* undergo metaphorical transformation. That is, there would be more than a single metaphor between human and wolf, since the meanings of ferocity, scavenging, hierarchy, and struggle would also become markedly different in the cases of humans and wolves. Black concedes that "the primary metaphor, it might be said, has been analyzed into a set of subordinate metaphors, so the account given is either circular or leads to an infinite regress."[60] In fact, he admits that he is not sure how to handle this objection. He begins by saying that changes in the attributes in question are not necessarily metaphorical, and that "many of them are best explained as extensions of meaning, because they do not involve apprehended connections between two systems of concepts."[61] But he then goes on to add that, even if the features of humans and wolves *do* turn out to be subordinate metaphors, they are so much fainter than the primary metaphor that they can safely be ignored, much like the overtones of any musical note: "to attach too much 'weight' to them is like trying to make the overtones sound as loud as the main notes—and just as pointless."[62] For practical purposes it may be enough to ignore the series of overtones in any metaphor. But when dealing with the ontology of the interaction theory, we should indeed wonder whether the metaphor spirals into an infinite regression— and whether this is even a problem. The question can safely be postponed.

I have already mentioned that Ortega defends a full theory of withdrawn executant things that has no correlate in Black. In this sense there might seem to be a big difference between their respective positions. But as concerns the theory of metaphor, the difference is actually irrelevant, since it turned out that the executancy of the things themselves plays no role in Ortega's model at all. Remember, it is not the executant cypress and executant flame that participate in our metaphors, since these are utterly unreachable by language. What really collides in the metaphor are my executant *feeling* of a cypress and executant *feeling* of a flame: in other words, the cypress and flame as intentional objects, not as real ones. In this sense, Ortega would speak of a wolf-feeling-thing that would be no different from Black's wolf-system of associated commonplaces. Both are underlying unities that exceed all delineable qualities even while loosely implying them, and both are also unities that need not necessarily exist in an outside world to be metaphorically effective. Ortega and Black could both be full-blown Berkeleyan Idealists without having to alter their theories in the least, since the underlying unity of the wolf-system is internal to my own experience. For Derrida, there is no such underlying unity at all, because this would imply some sort of "literal" wolfish substratum onto which all descriptions would be grafted. For Derrida, no literal language is possible, and for this reason everything tends to look equally metaphorical in his eyes. This is not the case for Ortega and Black. As they see it, we are trapped in a literal language from the start through our fixation on tangible properties, and can escape into living metaphor by bringing unified objects into play as shadowy wholes. For them, the distinction between the dead determinations of literal speech and the living force of metaphor that points to a systematic underground is very real indeed.

Black's interaction theory is criticized by Donald Davidson, who regards it as "fundamentally confused."[63] What Davidson rejects is the idea that metaphors can have any sort of special *meaning* at all that differs from the literal one, and for him Black is as guilty of this view as any of the more traditional theorists. When Black asserts that the metaphorical fusion of human and wolf cannot be paraphrased, Davidson is incredulous: "How can this be right? If a metaphor has a special cognitive content, why should it be so difficult or impossible to set it out? . . . Why does Black think a literal paraphrase 'inevitably says too much—and with the wrong emphasis'? Why inevitably? Can't we, if we are clever enough, come as close as we please?"[64] In other words, there can be no secret meaning lying behind the literal meaning of words. To believe otherwise is to be trapped in secret kiddie code games, and anyway, "to suppose [that a metaphor] can be effective only by conveying a coded message is like thinking a joke or dream makes some statement which a clever interpreter can restate in plain prose."[65] Put differently, Black and others supposedly defend "the thesis that associated with a metaphor is a definite cognitive content that its author wishes to convey *and that the interpreter must grasp* if he is to get the message."[66]

But this is precisely what Black denies, and it is shocking that Davidson says otherwise. A metaphor, and by analogy a joke or a dream, is precisely what the interaction theory believes *cannot* be grasped or restated in plain prose. Davidson fails to see that there can be any difference between a kind of language that deals with isolated attributes of things, and a kind that evokes those things as cryptic totalities, as wolf-systems. Indeed, he overlooks this point repeatedly: "There is, then, a tension in the usual view of metaphor. For on the one hand, the usual view wants to hold that a metaphor does something no plain prose can possibly do and, *on the other hand*, it wants to explain what a metaphor does by appealing to a cognitive content—just the sort of thing plain prose is designed to express."[67] Davidson's central prejudice is his notion that there is only one kind of cognitive content: that of plain, literal prose. In fact, there are exactly *two* kinds of cognitive content. There is the kind concerned with attributes, and the kind concerned with a thing as a total infrastructure that unifies those attributes. This is already quite visible in the ambivalence of the very phrase "wolf-system," since any system is both singular and plural simultaneously: a *system* of features, and a system *of features*.

Davidson even believes he has a devastating counterargument to the interaction theory when he suggests that, if metaphor really has a secret meaning that surpasses everyday prose, then this meaning should become visible once the metaphor dies. "Why doesn't 'He was burned up' as now used and meant mean *exactly* what the fresh metaphor once meant? Yet all that the dead metaphor means is that he was very angry—a notion not very difficult to make explicit."[68] To answer the question in Davidson's first statement, there is a very good reason why the current, dead use of "he was burned up" (and I have never used this phrase or heard it used) does not mean the same thing once meant by the fresh metaphor. Namely, the dead metaphor now deals only in the coin of specific attributes (heat, anger), whereas it once achieved a mysterious hybridization of human-system and fire-system. Through overuse it has now lost its touch, lost its capacity to dig underground into the cryptic life of things.

For Davidson, all meaning is necessarily literal meaning, an exact inversion of Derrida that hides their near-total agreement on essentials. All meaning can only be a kind of prison from which metaphor must find an escape if it is to function at all. Davidson thinks he has found an escape route in the *use* of words rather than their meaning: "If this is right, what we attempt in 'paraphrasing' a metaphor cannot be to give its meaning, *for that lies on the surface*; rather we attempt to evoke what the metaphor brings to our attention."[69] He misfires when he states that "it should make us suspect the [interaction] theory that it is so hard to decide, even in the case of the simplest metaphors, exactly what the content is supposed to be."[70] But that is precisely the point. For the interaction theory, the metaphor differs from literal prose not because it is like a secret code wrapped up inside a cigar that will eventually be read once the cigar has burned away. The reason we cannot decide the literal content of a metaphor is because it has a meaning that can never be paraphrased. For this reason, Davidson sees only one alternative: metaphor has nothing to do with contents of any kind, but rather "we are in fact focusing on *what the metaphor makes us notice.*"[71] This is actually far more vague than anything found in Black's lucid article, but Davidson does attempt to spell it out:

> When we try to say what a metaphor 'means,' we soon realize that there is no end to what we want to mention. If someone draws his finger along a coastline on a map, or mentions the beauty and deftness of a line in a Picasso etching, how many things are drawn to your attention? You might list a great many, but you could not finish since the idea of finishing would have no clear application . . . It's not only that we can't provide an exhaustive catalogue of what has been attended to when we are led to see something in a new light; the difficulty is more fundamental. What we see *is not, in general, propositional in character.*[72]

> The theorist who tries to explain a metaphor by appealing to a hidden message, like the critic who attempts to state the message, is then fundamentally confused. No such explanation or statement can be forthcoming because no such message exists.[73]

In the end, it almost seems as if Davidson has simply misunderstood the interaction theory, and has inadvertently come to agree with it despite his supposed critique. The interaction model does refer to the "cognitive content" of metaphor, but this is certainly not something *propositional* in character, not some secret code that a clever critic could decipher. Max Black stands puzzled before the reality of the wolf-system just as Ortega stands bemused before the union of cypress and flame—obviously, neither of them pretends to be the special initiate who knows the secret meaning of these metaphors, as if they guarded a forbidden cavern. Then again, it might seem that this misunderstanding is unimportant, and perhaps Davidson is offering a version of the interaction theory after all.

But in fact, there are crucial differences. Most important among them is that Davidson shifts the focus of metaphor from knowledge about *things* to knowledge about *ourselves*, much as continental interpreters of Heidegger like to do on every possible occasion. For someone who regards Black as "fundamentally confused," Davidson is surprisingly unclear in explaining what he means by saying that the key is what metaphor "makes us notice." Along with the notion that the contents of any metaphor are endless, which we can accept, it also seems to mean that the source of this endlessness is human being itself, which we cannot in any way accept. When it comes to meaning itself, Davidson assures himself that all meaning is literal, that all lies at the surface. Although he and Derrida have drastically different interpretations of the phrase "literal meaning," they agree on a much more fundamental point. Namely, both agree that there can be no hidden proper depth of things that the meaning of words is attempting to signal. Indeed, Davidson already takes on Derridean tones when he states on the first page of his essay, "there are no unsuccessful metaphors, just as there are no unfunny jokes."[74] This statement would make sense for anyone who thinks that all language plays out on the same plane, the plane of human access, and that metaphor can take place only by being folded back into the human subject. But there *is* such a thing as unsuccessful metaphor, because there *is* such a thing as language that merely shuffles qualities and properties around without being capable of bringing *objects* into play. Granted, it is hard to give *examples* of failed metaphor, because poetic genius is always capable of creating some context that allows virtually any metaphor to flourish, as with Rimbaud's familiar but endlessly startling link between vowels and colors. The point, however, is that some metaphors *do* fail—and the way they fail is by never pushing us toward the world of unified things, remaining frozen instead on the layer of inert qualities.

The position occupied by Davidson and Derrida, which views all meaning as a matter of surface qualities and articulations rather than of objects and essences, is bound to still seem avant garde to many readers. They are skeptics, master debunkers of any secret realm, and this is still very much the publicly accepted role of philosophers in our era. It is too seldom seen that this sort of debunking is now tending to become empty, and that most of the untapped energy now lies on the other side of the fence. In fact, Davidson and Derrida are really rather predictable defenders of the central philosophical orthodoxy of the past two centuries, which disdains all talk of autonomous objects released like wolves and salmon into the wild. It is Ortega and Black who actually point to something new, something truly immune to any of Derrida's and Davidson's criticisms: a secret content that is never presentable.

Rather than summing up what this teaches us about the carpentry of things, we should move on to the allied phenomenon of humor, waiting until the end of the next chapter to consider the lessons of metaphor and comedy jointly.

[9]

Humor

As already noted, Aristotle sees the imitative faculty of metaphor as one of the key features of human being. If we take tools to be metaphorical extensions of the human body, as many do, then the frequent reflections on the "tool-making animal" also come within the fold of metaphor. Along with these traditional theories about what defines humans uniquely, there is the topic of the risible or laughing animal, the great comedian of the universe that the human being always is. Somewhere in this vicinity there also lies the pivotal topic of dreams, with the condensation and displacement of the dreamwork displaying both metaphorical and comic elements. As Davidson put it, "metaphor is the dreamwork of language."[75] In this book, we will have to bypass the topic of dreams, despite its obviously promising connection with two of our central topics, simply because a reading of Freud in terms of object-oriented philosophy would require more than a few pages.

It is puzzling that continental philosophy has undertaken endless studies of tragedy, but has done virtually nothing with comedy. After all, the central importance of comedy in human life is hard to deny even from direct observation, quite apart from the tradition of the risible animal. We know from experience that even the dullest humans are often capable of lethal jests. This talent extends back to the earliest days of infancy, and even down into the higher mammals, if not further. Dolphins play tricks with balls and imitate one another's tail movements. Dogs play so many well-known jokes that any examples would be superfluous. Parrots mock our pretensions, while ravens pull clothespins from drying shirts and laugh as they fall to the ground. It is also widely known that we tend to value a sense of humor in our human companions above perhaps everything else, and a rare degree of wit usually provides even more charisma than sheer physical beauty.

But much like metaphor, humor is a universal feature of the human race that is also nonetheless dependent in its effects on a specific culture or

125

age group. There are certainly great classics of humor who travel well through time and space: Aristophanes, Don Quixote, Falstaff, and lower-rent figures such as Harlequin and Punch. Even many younger devotees of cinema still adore the Marx Brothers or Buster Keaton, though this is by no means universal. All the same, certain features of comedy do not translate well into other life-worlds. For North American and British children of Generation X, give or take a decade in each direction, the satirical newspaper *The Onion*[76] has recently emerged as the gold standard of contemporary comedy, rarely missing the mark except in unusually bad weeks. This periodical rarely fails as an icebreaker and conversation starter within vast strata of the Anglophone population. Yet its style of wit does nothing for those of my grandparents' generation; nor does it register especially well with my students in Egypt. Indeed, perhaps the greatest difficulty faced by those who are teaching students in a foreign culture for the first time comes from a sudden inability to produce effective jokes when required, even when there is no real language barrier.

There is definitely something contextual about humor, then, just as there was with metaphor. Max Black noted that cultures with different beliefs about wolves from our own will encounter the wolf-system somewhat differently from us. It is surely the same way with jokes. The fact that metaphor and jokes have a strongly contextual element might lead to the mistaken conclusion that all statements in themselves are inherently metaphorical and inherently humorous. This would be a false conclusion. The fact that any statement conceivably *can* be turned into a metaphor does not mean that any statement *is* a metaphor, even if a good number of postmodern critics make this sort of claim. If I were to say "wood is like a lizard," these people would claim that it really *is* a simile, because the hearer fascinatedly struggles to discover the meaning of this phrase no less than of "the sun is like a sower of seed." In fact, the wood/lizard simile is not a simile at all, but just an especially prosaic form of catachresis, or misuse of literal terminology. The attempted simile actually does fail for almost all of us. Based on the results of the previous section, the reason for the failure is clear: the identity it suggests is so patently unconvincing that we stay fixated on the level of their barely commensurable qualities, never making it to the deeper level of lizard-system and wood-system, which are much bigger than all lizard-qualities and wood-qualities. Given that Davidson and the postmodernists recognize no such deeper level, it is little wonder that they believe neither in failed metaphors nor failed jokes. The comparison of wood with a lizard probably *can* be made to work, if your name is André Breton or Marcel Duchamps, and you manage to generate an overall style in which this simile somehow manages to hit home. But this does not mean that all statements are equally metaphorical from the start.

The same holds for humor. If you are Dante, you can make readers laugh when demons stick pitchforks into damned souls floating in rivers of sewage. But this does not mean that such a scene in an actual Hell would be just as amusing as a Jay Leno monologue, as Davidson would appear to hold. If you have the literary genius of the Marquis de Sade, you can bring at least some readers to laugh at kidnappings and sex felonies, even if ninety-nine percent of them would be emotionally shaken when reading actual reports of such events in a newspaper. There is clearly a sense in which we have to be *prepared* to grasp a metaphor or joke, whether through the explicit labor of a particular author or comic, or through a broader sort of training that binds us to a particular nation and social class.

Here as with metaphor, humor is not the central theme of this book, and therefore will be followed only insofar as it links directly with our central topic, not considered in all its specific forms as wisecracks, puns, pranks, riddles, drolleries, *l'humour noir*, slapstick tableaux, and other comic variants. Luckily, we have at our disposal a concise and brilliant treatise that links comedy with the main themes of object-oriented philosophy: Henri Bergson's *De la rire*, available in English in a dated but usable translation.[77] This work is a classic. Whatever its shortcomings, it ought to have been taken as the foundation-stone for an ongoing philosophy of jokes, one that has never emerged during the full century that has elapsed since Bergson's monograph.

The alternative definitions of humor often used to dismiss Bergson strike me as obviously false, since they allow for numerous cases that are not funny at all. Among other attempted refutations, I have heard Bergson spurned by means of the counter-theory that humor actually results from a "sudden incongruity." But this notion can be falsified in a matter of seconds. If the Algerian rebels with their hatchets and guns were suddenly to show up at the front door of my parents' home in Iowa, this would certainly be a sudden incongruity, but by no means a funny one. Another, equally cavalier opponent of Bergson's theory once told me that comedy is simply "the absurd," a conception even easier to subvert. Melting highways, three-headed stray dogs, boiling oceans, rainstorms of molten lead, the moon floating about like an eagle—such phenomena would be absurd enough, but laughter would probably be the furthest thing from our minds when confronting them. But perhaps equally dubious is Freud's more serious theory of jokes, which fails Max Black's litmus test for bad explanation by explaining jokes as a source of *pleasure*. Freud holds that the pleasure of jokes arises from an economy in expenditure of mental energy, whether this energy had previously been allocated to inhibitions, investment of libidinal interest in objects, or feeling.[78] Here too, numerous counterexamples are possible in which I experience some sort of economy in the expenditure of energy without being amused at all. For instance, we may take courageous steps in our personal lives that short-circuit former inhibitions, or streamline our ways of understanding long-running conflicts, without anything funny happening as a result. Whether this rejection of "economic pleasure" as the source of the comic also affects the definition of dreams as "wish-fulfillments"[79] lies beyond the scope of anything that the present book can consider.

Bergson's model of humor, by contrast, is not vulnerable to counterexamples at all, since it strikes at the ontological root of comedy rather than merely treating a handful of its accompanying features. His theory is attractively simple: comedy results when we witness what is human reduced to a mechanism. At first glance this might seem at least as suspect as the rejected theories, but it actually turns out to be far more general in character. Namely, Bergson links humor to the innate *sincerity* of every object, its inability to free itself from a kind of fundamental ingenuousness. And since all human and inhuman objects have an innate naiveté in their being, all objects are potentially comical. But Ortega's point was that all objects are wrapped up in themselves at all times, without hope of escape. If this is the case, then we need to know why comedy does not occur equally at all moments, but only at certain times. An additional problem is that a thing's absorption in its own reality is characteristic not only of comedy, but of *tragedy* as well. The great tragic figures are wrapped up in the destiny that crushes them not so differently from the way in which Humpty Dumpty submits to the iron law of gravity, though he will not soon be sharing the stage with Antigone or Lear. As to this question, we should keep in mind Aristotle's view of the difference: "It is this difference that distinguishes tragedy and comedy also; the one would make its personages *worse*, and the other *better*, than the men of the present day."[80] It will turn out that there is more than a grain of truth in this criterion.

A. Reduced to Mechanisms

Perhaps no topic has generated more patently false philosophical theories than humor. In addition to the misfires already noted, Bergson adds others that are equally weak. He begins by dismissing the theory that humor is "patent absurdity,"[81] but we have already taken care of that one above. There is also the theory that "intellectual contrast"[82] leads to humor. This seems untenable due to numerous examples that might be imagined: to name just one, the offbeat contrast of using Aristotle's *De Interpretatione* to analyze Bugs Bunny cartoons would probably come off as forced, pedantic pseudo-humor rather than as anything truly funny. The "collision of two contradictions"[83] is an equally poor theory of humor, as seen when considering cases of international duplicity and unmasked love triangles, neither of which are often amusing. An even weaker theory comes from Alexander Bain, later one of Max Black's sacrificial lambs as well,[84] who traces humor to "the degradation of the dignified."[85] But this theory clearly fails to explain the humorlessness of atrocities against sages and nuns, unless they happen to be framed with the exquisite literary skill of a Sade. What all of these theories have in common is that they specify one particular *attribute* of certain kinds of humor, and wrongly postulate it as having universal explanatory force. In this respect, all of them resemble the theoretical bubbles blown by Euthyphro and Meno and burst by Socrates as quickly as they appear.

Bergson's most general statement about humor, one too often overlooked by his readers, is that it should be viewed as a type of *art*. This is stated only at the end of his essay, which is where we will begin. The theory of art offered by Bergson here bears an uncanny resemblance to that of Ortega. Whether his 1901 essay on laughter had some sort of background influence on the omnivorous reader Ortega, or whether their positions were developed in total independence, is impossible to determine. In any event, both authors agree that art differs from everyday life and speech by its attempt to reach what is inaccessible to all perception. This inaccessibility of the true world plagues us in the very structure of our senses: "If reality could come into direct contact with sense and consciousness, if we could enter into immediate communion with things and with ourselves, probably art would be useless, or rather we should all be artists, for then our soul would continually vibrate in perfect accord with nature."[86] Like Ortega surveying the absolute gap between executancy and relation, Bergson spies a fundamental chasm in the world: "Between nature and ourselves, [and even] between ourselves and our own consciousness, a veil is interposed . . ."[87] Perception will never be the exact equivalent of any of the things it perceives; it inhabits a private space of its own, surrounded by all the tantalizing entities it is unequipped to grasp. Which is to say that "we live in a zone midway between things and ourselves, externally to things, externally also to ourselves."[88] This suggestive sentence has now been in print for more than a century, but with little effect.

Striking one of the major themes of his own philosophy, and surpassing the Heideggerians in advance, Bergson observes that *praxis* no less than theory reduces things to mere surfaces of themselves: "what I see and hear of the outer world is purely and simply a selection made by my senses to serve as a light to my conduct; what I know of myself is what comes to the surface, what participates in my actions."[89] And again, "things have been classified with a view to the use I can derive from them. And it is this classification I perceive, far more clearly than the color and shape of things."[90]The problem with language, according to Bergson, is that it points only to generic qualities rather than specific things. The one exception he grants is proper nouns, much like both Husserl and Kripke. In most cases, "the *individuality* of things or of beings escapes us, unless it is materially to our advantage to perceive it."[91] The world of social and linguistic conventions forms an encrusted layer of usages that block our access to the things even more. And in a typically stirring image from this Nobel Laureate, Bergson declares, "the slow progress of mankind in the direction of an increasingly peaceful social life has gradually consolidated this layer, just as the life of our planet itself has been one long effort to cover over with a cool and solid crust the fiery mass of seething metals."[92] And yet, he adds so dramatically, "volcanic eruptions occur."[93] Art is the volcanic force of our planet, releasing magma from the hidden core of things.

Anticipating Ortega by more than a decade, Bergson tells us that the function of art is "to brush aside the utilitarian symbols, the conventional and socially accepted generalities, in short, everything that veils reality from us, in order to bring us face to face with reality itself."[94] But the gods never give all of their gifts at once, and no artist will unveil everything for us: "Even for such of us as nature has made artists, it is by accident, and on one side only, that it has lifted the veil. In one direction only has it forgotten to rivet the perception to the need."[95] The person who loves color and form for their own sakes winds through these dimensions, as if through endless subway tunnels, toward the heart of things. Others have the talent of seeing through the transient outer tokens of emotion that strike our consciousness, and approach the inner reality of mental states by playing with the resonances of words. What, then, are the materials of the comic art? The answer is not colors, shapes, sounds, or moods—but *sincerity*, that bedrock form of innocence with which all being is laced from the start.

Bergson does not actually use "sincerity" as a technical term; I import it from Levinas to describe a subject matter that is everywhere present in Bergson's essay on laughter without receiving a consistent name. What makes us laugh, Bergson holds, is a kind of rigidity or mechanism in the comic object. But not just any kind of rigidity: after all, we are not generally amused by the workings of gravity or the swaying of branches in the wind. Comedy arises not from all mechanism, but only when something becomes rigid or mechanical that *ought* to be flexible, adaptable, appropriately mutable. This is why Bergson insists that "the comic does not exist outside the pale of what is strictly *human* . . . You may laugh at an animal, but only because you have detected in it some human attitude or expression. You may laugh at a hat, but what you are making fun of . . . is not the piece of felt or straw, but the shape that humans have given it . . ."[96] It is not a question here of some sort of strained anthropomorphic theory of humor projected from human psychological qualities onto inanimate things. Bergson identifies comedy with the human only because comedy requires strife between rigidity and free adaptation, and the latter is simply much easier to see in human beings than elsewhere. If a running man trips on the sidewalk, we may be cruel enough to laugh, but Bergson notes that we probably would not laugh if watching a Hollywood stuntman performing this trick.[97] What we laugh at is the way in which human transcendence and free decision-making power are undercut by his being delivered to the force of things, unable to master them. It is a kind of rigidity or momentum that makes him fall: "the muscles continued to perform the same movement when the circumstances of the case called for something else."[98] That is to say, his body continued in the mechanical enactment of a procedure no longer flexibly adjusted to its surroundings.

We will not always laugh at such a falling man, of course, and perhaps not even most of the time. For as Bergson rightly observes, we can laugh at the reduction of freedom to a mechanism *only in the absence of feeling.*[99] This is easy enough to see. I have certainly known a few stone-hearted sadists with limitless capacity for enjoying the destruction of others. But most of us are sufficiently sympathetic to our fellow humans that the situation has to be harmless enough to grant us a sort of permission to laugh. For example, we probably laugh at the stumbling man only if he is not grotesquely injured in the process. It will also help if there is something unusually pompous in his attitude so as to give the situation an aspect of justice, or to make the contrast sufficiently delicious. If he is our mortal enemy or persecutor, we might laugh even if he breaks a bone or two in the accident. But only a sociopath would laugh if the tripping man were actually a child, a severely handicapped person, one's own grandfather, someone known to be terribly down on his luck, or a star athlete toasted throughout the nation. In other words, the mere contrast between freedom and mechanism is not enough: the contrast must be such that it places nothing genuinely at stake for us.[100] The comic object must be implicitly contemptible, beneath our station in the world in some respect. Or rather, this must at least be true for a passing instant—we have all laughed at the follies of close friends without holding them in any sort of deep or permanent disdain.

Here is the grain of truth in Aristotle's view that comedy presents those who are *worse* than we are. It is not that they are morally worse, less intelligent, or physically weaker than the rest of us, since we also laugh at the saints, geniuses, and boxers who we could never hope to equal. What really makes comic figures worse than we are is that, at least for a passing instant, they expend their energy in taking things seriously that we ourselves would never bother to trifle with. All of us are capable of seeing this in all others at certain points in time. Even our hero can choose a ridiculous shirt for a key public appearance; our most brilliant and beloved teachers have peculiarities of speech that provide fodder for comic imitations after class; those who are mighty enough to crush us like bugs are still felt to be beneath us when we chuckle at their pompous mannerisms and the sophistry that they wrongly believe will fool us. If we simply weigh the sum total of skills, defects, virtues, and vices of every human on the planet, it is likely that each of them is better than us in some ways and worse in others. And we know it. The sole way in which we *always* instinctively feel ourselves superior to all other entities in the cosmos is that we feel our own freedom in contrast with the mechanical predictability of the others. We fail to see the rigidity of our own characters, mannerisms, and tastes. It is always the other entities that seem like stock characters, not we ourselves. There are certainly those who like to ham it up or play a role in front of others, but they always see it as a game under their complete control, one that they can quit or modify at will. No one ever honestly says "I am *such* a character," despite the fact that we have all said it dozens of times about others. (We can also laugh at ourselves, but only by converting ourselves into objects just as the ego of phenomenology does.) The way in which we feel superior to all comic entities is simply that they seem like such *characters*, whereas what we sense within is primarily our own shapeless, noncommittal, adaptable freedom—which allows us to overlook our most robotic personal traits, though they are perfectly visible to the others who tease us for them behind our backs. The root of all human arrogance is not to be found in wealth, beauty, power, or popularity, but only in the lordly sense of being more *internally free* than other entities, even if they are kings and we are merely prisoners locked up in their towers.

But to repeat a qualification mentioned earlier, no event in itself is either inherently comic or inherently serious, since all of them can be skillfully framed to yield either result. This holds not just for the rare sadists who laugh at the fallen man as he slowly bleeds to death, but also for we ourselves. For the comic arts are able to make virtually *any* event appear both beneath us and lacking in any seriously harmful consequences. Many of the actions of the old Italian clowns or the Three Stooges would qualify as aggravated assault in all modern legal systems. We laugh nonetheless. In purely objective terms, it is not amusing at all when Harpo Marx pumps his bare feet up and down in the lemonade and burns the snack vendor's straw hat:[101] however unpleasant the vendor may be, he is probably living close to the poverty line, and will now go hungry for the rest of the week just to provide an evanescent gag for the spies Chicolini and Pinky. None of us would care to be on the receiving end of such a gag. And neither would we care to reside in large Japanese cities under assault by monsters, though even this is made amusing both by various framing devices as well as by a poor quality of cinematic execution. From the thefts and infidelities of *The Canterbury Tales* to the criminal incitement of Baudelaire's "Let's Beat Up the Poor," the comic universe is riddled with heinous acts that manage to bother no one as long as they are handled with sufficient skill, and as long as they avoid hitting too close to home. The often thin line separating the realms of comedy and horror can be seen in the now almost hackneyed role-reversals of clowns, portrayed by turns as carrying flowers and murder weapons.

We have already reached the heart of Bergson's theory. At all times, there is a dualism at work in human activity: "*tension* and *elasticity* are two forces, mutually complementary, which life brings into play."[102] Hinting at the entirety of his philosophical position, Bergson credits life with *spontaneity*, with a sort of pliant versatility when faced with new situations. "A continual change of aspect, the irreversibility of the order of phenomena, the perfect individuality of a perfectly self-contained series: such, then, are the outward characteristics . . . which distinguish the living from the merely mechanical."[103] The features of mechanism are precisely the opposite, marked as they are by "repetition, inversion, and reciprocal interference of series."[104] When a living organism becomes enveloped in helpless or unthinking routines, it takes on the air of "a jolted puppet."[105] This is why the absent-minded person becomes a universal stock figure of comedy, with Don Quixote the classic example, as all the formalistic routines of chivalry are redirected from actual enemies and princesses onto everyday objects that everyone views with contempt.[106] The reverse formula, though of more dubious taste, can also be made to work: comic figures who *underestimate* the dignity of things in their environment, using rare museum pieces as spittoons, or behaving before a United Nations tribunal as if at a down-home fish fry.

As a side-note, it is also not difficult to see the basic principle that separates good comedy from bad. Bergson says that "to imitate anyone is to bring out the automatism that he has allowed to creep into his person."[107] I would propose that good comedy identifies *deeper*, more *genuine*, more *unshakable* automatisms, whereas mediocre comedy deals only with superficial caricatures that belong to a person only accidentally. Richard Nixon provides an excellent example, since any random person on any American street can easily take a crack at holding up two fingers and mumbling "I am not a crook" while shaking the head with rapid horizontal vibrations. But in the three decades since Watergate, this routine has become so canned as to become almost unbearable, and it is fairly clear why. For however much Nixon has come to be identified with these typical mannerisms, he was until recently a living human being. For this reason, he could easily have tried to change his ways, perhaps embarrassed enough by all of these impersonations to alter his mannerisms to whatever degree possible for someone of his age. Notice that the fuel for bad Nixon mimics is always nothing but trivial external gestures—gestures that all of us have, but which any of us can change given sufficient negative feedback. A truly gifted mimic, however, will unearth those traits that Nixon could not *possibly* abandon without excruciating difficulty: the subtleties of his gait, the specific ways in which he slurs or articulates vowels, the personal rhetorical tricks that mark his conversation, the fears that haunt him uniquely, and the specific style of logical inference that belongs to him alone.

I once witnessed a lengthy party game in which the goal was to imagine the most impossible pair of conversational partners in the world. Strangely enough, the very first response to this question was one that has still never been topped: HAL the computer, and Popeye.[108] While not all readers will be as delighted as I was by this specific pairing, what is interesting is why later attempts to beat it inevitably failed. The failure of the other proposals stemmed from the fact that all of them contained at least one actual human—say, Mickey Mouse and Joseph Stalin. The failure of Stalin in this context is analogous to that of Nixon when performed by weak comic actors. Namely, however rigid Stalin may have been in his character, however cardboard-hewn he may seem to us today, he was once a living human. As such, he *would* have found some way to adapt to the strange scenario of a conversation with Mickey Mouse, and presumably could even have played along with it as a joke. But there is no such possibility whatsoever for Popeye and HAL: the lightheaded boastful sailor and the homicidal thinking-machine, forever frozen in their fixed and infinitely opposed world views, closed off to all adjustment.

It is also fascinating that I have never heard anyone list *himself or herself* as one of the two conversational partners in this game (though we rarely avoid talking about ourselves on any other occasion). For as already mentioned, it is unusually difficult for us to see *ourselves* as stock characters. All of us probably imagine that we are flexible and open-minded enough for a heart-to-heart talk even with Popeye or HAL. The comic character, says Bergson, "slackens in the attention that is due to life."[109] Such attention actually demands a certain degree of *insincerity*, of infidelity to one's previous thoughts or habits so as to let them be shaped by the shifting requirements of the instant. And although any of us might become laughable at any moment, we almost never reach the comic depths of Alceste, Pulcinella, or the Wife of Bath. For all of us there is still hope of change or adaptation, however remote. Try as we might, we will never feel as trapped in our own personae as the classic comic figures seem to be in theirs.

B. Sincerity, Comedy, and Charm

This would still leave open the question of the difference between comedy and tragedy, which are often separated by the thinnest of boundaries. All it takes to turn *Macbeth* into comedy is to dress the characters in Jimi

Hendrix outfits or have them inhale helium before delivering their lines. And likewise, all it takes to turn comedy into tragedy is to remove the special comic framework from Tom Sawyer's vandalism, and have it be ourselves or close friends whose property he damages. We have seen that for Bergson, comedy is intimately wrapped up with character, with the way in which the free resilience of life is haunted by some pregiven load of physical or moral destiny. But oddly enough, this is exactly what we say about tragedy as well, which speaks as clearly as comedy does of flaws and the punishment of hubris. We ourselves are wrapped up in our private destinies, trapped in our habits and mannerisms and fates, although normally we are deadened to this fact by our catching sight of a constant freedom within. The interesting thing is that both comic and tragic characters are united in seeming *less* free than we are, although the former are objects of ridicule and the latter earn our admiration as well as our pity. Everyday life is laced with sincerity through and through, in the sense that I really am doing right now whatever it is that I am doing—delivered over to that activity rather than to any of the possible others that might be imagined. Somehow, both comedy and tragedy make this *more* apparent than usual, just as metaphor makes more visible than usual the unified objects that are nonetheless always elements of our perception.

Sincerity is present *everywhere* in the world, not just in comedy. In fact, sincerity is already the proper meaning of phenomenology's definition of intentionality, that "all consciousness is consciousness of something." Intentionality is already a sincerity. Levinas might object to my saying so, but only because he wants to contrast the self-contained character of enjoyment with the intentional aiming at objects that points beyond what is directly here and now. My fascination with specific lighthouses and fishing-boats is actually no less sincere than my basking in the formless sea and sky: both of these dimensions of my reality *are what they are*, and both consist in being wrapped up right now in certain particular actions and no others. There is no such thing as a moment of life without sincerity, a term used here in a purely technical sense without cryptic moral insinuation. But the same holds good for Arabian horses, dandelions, and dead twigs, which are thoroughly absorbed at each moment in being precisely those characters that they are. As Ortega remarks: "Every attempt to dislodge ingenuousness from the universe is in vain. Because, in a word, there *is* nothing other than sublime ingenuousness, that is to say, reality."[110] When this passage is read in context, its target is obviously Husserl, accused by Ortega of granting priority to some sort of neutral, aloof, observing consciousness—a concept that Ortega famously detests. But although I am largely in agreement with his criticism, there is another sense in which Husserl is the philosopher of sincerity *par excellence*, since he defines consciousness by its act of paying attention to specific things at any moment. In short, the lack of ingenuousness in Husserl's position comes not from intentionality per se, but from the fact that the intentional object is regarded only as an ideal unity rather than a real force to reckon with in the cosmos.

This seems to be an opportune moment to pause and clarify some key points of terminology. As just noted, I will speak of sincerity or ingenuousness when speaking of a universal structure that is inescapable by any entity, one that is present at all moments in all parts of the universe. With this use of the term, smugglers, double agents, and poseurs are every bit as sincere as saints and infants, while tornadoes, landslides, snake pits, and moons are no less ingenuous than federal judges or the Michelin logo. All of these things are absorbed in being exactly what they are. This is true at all moments, as an ironclad ontological law.

But still, there are special variations on sincerity that *do not* occur at all moments. Comedy or humor is one of these, and Bergson has demonstrated that it works by somehow exposing something as a mechanism that ought not to be a mechanism. In fact, we are all partly mechanisms at each moment, delivered over to the power of various habits, routines, styles of speech, and facial features—which is why all of us are potential comic targets at any instant. The problem was that the same thing seems to hold for tragedy, the diametrical opposite of the comic. Here too, Antigone is wrapped up in herself, moved by sheer force of character to such an extent that she is actually less free than we are: just as Lucky and Jojo the clowns seem less free than we are, even when they transgress the behavioral restraints that we loyally observe. The difference, Aristotle already observed, is simply that the concerns of clowns seem so far *beneath* us as to awaken our contempt (slapsticks, round red noses, cream pies, pillow fights) whereas Antigone's worries play out in a league far *above* most of us (dead rebellious brothers, death-threats from the state). What comedy and tragedy have in common is that they not only *exist* in sincerity, as all objects do, but also somehow make it an explicit theme for the viewer. The comic puts this into play at a level somewhat beneath us, while the tragic does it at a level that commands our respect. Take away that respect, replace Desdemona on stage with a marionette or a cow wearing a blonde wig, and Othello will become an object of ridicule rather than of awe—unless the staging were put in the hands of some absurdist mastermind with the talent to pull it off.

However, it turns out that comedy and tragedy are greatly mismatched in scope: comedy is far broader. Any situation that brings a laughable form of sincerity into play will result in comedy. But the opposite is not true: *not* all respectable forms of sincerity lead to tragedy, since tragedy requires some sort of actual destruction of the sincere agent. But there are plenty of nontragic situations that bring the sincerity of agents visibly into play. The simplest of these are probably the actions of babies, small children, and young animals, which often cast a spell over us though not always making us laugh. Another example would be the style of a favorite author, whose workings immediately bewitch us as soon as we open the next unread volume. But this phenomenon expands to cover all sorts of situations: someone's memorable smile, or fascinating accent, or impressive way of commanding groups, or their signature move on a basketball court. In all of these cases, we seem to be not just focused blandly on the intentional objects of our experience, but also overcome by the *style* of something.

If in comedy we are attuned to an actor's absorption with an object and feel it as unworthy, in the cases of enchantment just described we are also aware of a kind of mechanism, but without feeling any contempt toward it. We are always partly mechanisms by the mere fact of dressing or speaking in our habitual ways. These typical styles that belong to each of us can also become fully visible without always becoming funny—they can be endearing or even tragic. To become attuned to the typical locomotion of monkeys or snakes, to bask in the presence of an infant's world with its countless delights in small things, is not always to laugh, and certainly not always to experience tragedy. In fact, the comical makes up only half of the sphere in which objects are made visible as mechanisms. For the other half, which includes tragedy as but one small part, I can think of no better technical term than *charm*. This word should be heard with overtones of witchcraft rather than those of social skills. What is at issue is not some sort of people-pleasing faculty in things, but a sort of magic charm or elixir that we sense in each thing, as when warriors devour tiger hearts or druids cautiously approach forbidden trees. The charm of objects is their innocent absorption in being just what they are, which in each case is something that we ourselves can never be. Packed full with deeply sincere agents, the world resembles the hideout of a sorceress, with its numerous medicines, poisons, vegetables, mushrooms, weapons, jewels, scents, tamed animals, gifts, toys, uniforms, and omens. In our most memorable moments, the world is certainly no less interesting than such a witch's hut would be. Comedy and metaphor are among the triggers that bring us into such a charmed universe, but there are plenty of others.

If the comical is what unearths sincerity and exposes it to scorn, then its opposite form can only be that which exposes sincerity to our fascinated attention. Instead of laying bare someone's hopeless style of dancing so that we might laugh at it, it brings this style before us contagiously, as a kind of magnetic force that realigns our nervous systems. There is often an ambivalence between comedy and this sort of charm, without their being the same thing. One moment I laugh at the antics of the dolphin, and the next I am captivated by the sorcery of its being. The same dark puppet show can move some of my friends to tears while being ridiculed by others, leading to conflict later on. When metaphor works, it is always charming: we cannot help noting the sheer sincerity of existence of the cypress-flame and wolf-human.

An interesting point here is that what charms us is precisely the person or thing that seems charmed *by something else*—that seems to have devoted its energy to taking certain things seriously in the world. This is somewhat easier to see in people than inanimate objects. What charms us in people is not so much a sweet voice, beauty, artistic tastes, or flattery, since all of these become repugnant when used for obvious favor-seeking or intent to defraud. We all make mistakes, of course, in measuring the level of good faith with which human charm is extended toward us. But what we at least *think* we see in the charming person is a certain total geography of objects, one that the charming agent acknowledges and inhabits to the exclusion of others. When entering such a person's world, whether they be a recording artist, a philosopher, a down-to-earth banker, a first-grade nephew, a zen monk, an ace video arcade repairman, a kindly taxi driver, a thug who hassles us on the sidewalk, or a diva on stage before us in Stuttgart, we tend to forget all other possible worlds: hence, the contagious effect of everything that charms. When bewitched by a saxophonist's style, we temporarily forget the equally adorable spheres of volcanic Greek islands, fresh juice, childhood reminiscence, and playful dogs at home. The charming character we encounter is immersed in something quite seriously, whether it be in their own melodious voice or personal grace, in the quasars or reptiles that obsess them and not the rest of us, or even in blackmail or offshore gambling. Whatever his or her interests may be, the charming character defines something as being very much *at issue* in the world.

This explains the familiar bit of wisdom that opposite sides in the same conflict often have a surprising degree in common, since the key to a style of character has less to do with the content of one's opinions than with the sheer fact of worrying about certain things and not others. It simply never occurs to me to think of private homes as intriguing targets to be invaded and robbed, though this undeniable possibility is a major factor in the lives of both security consultants and career criminals. Tamil rebels and Indian soldiers both expend their energy struggling for territory where I myself may never set foot. New Yorkers of all classes, ethnic groups, and lifestyles, including rats and seagulls, all have a certain stake in New York's existence and its rules and legends that I as an occasional visitor do not. We have seen that this sort of sincerity holds good for all objects at all times. But when it takes the form of charm or comedy, we see another agent in the very *act* of taking something seriously, and in a way that mesmerizes or delights us.

Charm limits and fixes our vision, as shown by the voluntary limitations of literary style—which, when skillful, is never "all over the place." Good style is fixed into place in a single world, and can extend the borders of that world only cautiously and at some peril. Kafka places us amidst senseless bureaucratic events and pointless lawyers, whippers, surveyors, and palaces. But his stories would be ruined if he *also* tried (like Tolstoy) to bring Napoleon into his universe, or if Josef K. had met up with characters in the style of Faulkner or Dickens, or if he had suddenly made a side trip to Edinburgh. Stylistic experiments do occur within the corpus of writers, but they are judged effective or ineffective based on the style of the universe that has already been created. Raymond Chandler occasionally sends his detective Marlowe outside of his usual Los Angeles haunts: up to a lake or down to San Diego or Tijuana on business, and with perfectly believable results. But any additional novel attempting to send Marlowe to the Galapagos for scientific research would have bordered on the ludicrous; the very suggestion already has the flavor of parody about it.

In the words of Alphonso Lingis, every style wants us to love it, and love it *exclusively*. These styles belong to places and objects no less than to people. The charm of Beirut or Prague consists in their saying "this is the way things are," and not by their trying to be everything to all people simultaneously. In Beirut you stroll the corniche endlessly or take a taxi up to the mountains; in Prague you climb to the castle or wander the side streets off Wenceslas Square in the dark. You do not *also* expect to place a central focus, while visiting these places, on gambling, solitary religious vision, rural relaxation, raisin farming, or Thai erotica. The charm of beautiful glass, platinum jewelry, or melons and cakes brings out certain features of the world while suppressing others. The jewelry can be viewed as a kind of Bergsonian "mechanism," not insofar as it is made of atoms and governed by chemical laws, but rather insofar as it behaves as though "platinumness" were what was at stake in the entire cosmos, as though it were *obsessed* with being platinum—which, of course, it is. As usual, it is *The Onion* that grasps this truth most brilliantly, with its numerous editorials written by computers, dehumidifiers, puppies, and bees.

Baudrillard observes that what seduces us about a thing is its weakness rather than its strength, and in this he is surely correct.[111] Strength always implies a certain resilient adaptability to shifts of fortune, rather than the comic flaw that edges us toward repeating routines regardless of context, a flaw of which humans and other objects are constantly guilty. And just as Baudrillard defines seduction as a way of bowing before the weakness of objects and obeying their law anyway, Levinas defines violence as a means of using weakness as a means of getting at strength. We cut into granite, exploiting its weakness, only to take advantage of its strengths. We pour psychological abuse onto an envied but highly sensitive rival, hoping in this way to gain power over his *strength*, since we would never bother to torment an absolute weakling. All of this makes violence an especially interesting form of hypocrisy. And although we should all hope to avoid these procedures in our treatment of other humans, we cannot avoid them in interacting with things. We use the strength of a ladder's rung to steady ourselves, only to pass beyond that rung and abandon it to its loneliness. We exploit the weakness of a grapefruit's skin in order to gain access to the strong suit of its juicy sweetness. It is easy to understand the charm of animals, who seem utterly occupied in doing cow-things or monkey-things, or in being trapped in the characteristic sounds they make. The same charm is present in foreign cultures, and for all the endless diatribes against "Orientalism," objects themselves are a perpetual Orient, harboring exotic spices, guilds, and cobras. The customs of our day-to-day world tend to become vapid trivialities for us, but can take on a mysterious charm for outsiders, whether we enter an actual foreign nation or merely a new subculture or social scene. And of course, every form of style or design brings out some features of the world while condemning others to oblivion. Nothing and no one can be everywhere at once. The attempt to be all things produces the dilettante, that perfect figure of free transcendence and liberation. And the need always to be above any sincerity produces the calculating operator, the careerist survivor, who sees no purpose in ever going down with any ship.

But in addition to being charmed by objects, we ourselves want to emulate them, and wish to charm the world. It is simply not the case that our fundamental wish is to be viewed as dignified thinking free subjects with a chance to speak at the microphone of the universal assembly. This opportunity is certainly preferable to being a war casualty or a slave, but it does not yet say enough about what it is that we want the microphone to do for our voices. The kind of recognition we would prefer is always far more specific, since we often feel ourselves to be so painfully mutable that *any* specific role will do—the friendly one, the one who cooks, the exotic traveler, the one who sings like Caruso, or just the one who likes to be spoken to in such-and-such a way and not another. The one book that all of us would approach with greatest interest, that no human in history would be able to resist opening, would be a book of anecdotes about *ourselves* as told by other people. The appeal of such a book would lie not in some sort of grotesque human vanity, but in our wish to be something *definite*, a desire at least as great as our urge to be free. There is a profound need to escape the apparently infinite flexible subjectivity within, which feels far more amorphous to us than to anyone else.

Contrary to the usual view, what we really want is to be *objects*—not as means to an end like paper or oil, but in the sense that we want to be like the Grand Canyon or a guitar hero or a piece of silver: distinct forces to be reckoned with. No one really wants to be a Cartesian subject, but everyone would love to be some version of Isis, Odysseus, Aquaman, Legolas, or Cordelia. While none of us wishes to be a slave, scapegoat, tool, or object of ridicule, we would rather be charmed and charming than be free, as our actions consistently show: we take out large mortgages to buy huts in forests or the seaside, or we trade our freedom to follow one unique person—and not always mistakenly. We may sacrifice years to thankless study in order to hunt some golden unicorn glimpsed one day in the library, even though it may never enter our grasp and no one else may even believe that we ever saw it. Freedom itself is never an absolute good, and is often a troubling void filled with addiction, hopelessness, confusion, or fantasies of triumph and revenge. By contrast, all great styles charm us even if they deliver us to bondage in repulsive places, whether these be libertine dungeons, Nibelung underworlds, fields of chemical warfare, or outright slaughterhouses.

Along with charm goes the closely allied experience of *courage*. Although it may sound paradoxical, courage is one of those moods in which we treat ourselves less as free subjects than as *objects*. To perform a courageous act is not to behave as a free transcendent self thrown out into nothingness: such a self is far too amorphous to stand for anything in particular. Rather, the unshakable core of courage inside you is simply the character in you that does not change, that stands for something, and that would rather be shattered by events than reconcile itself to any shameful compromise. I am courageous not as a thinking subject, but as the valiant leader or the tough-as-nails bastard that others always knew me to be.

C. Allure

Already, tragedy has turned out to be too narrow to make up the full opposite to comedy, and has been assigned to the wider category of charm. The same holds true of metaphor, which again covers too limited a slice of reality in comparison with humor. As seen with the cypress-flame of Ortega and even the wolf-system of Black, what happens in metaphor is that we somehow become attuned to the inner ingenuousness of things. The truly executant flame and wolf can never be perceived by any other object. But neither does metaphor leave us stranded at the level of perceptible qualities. Somehow, it manages to put the very sincerity of a thing at issue, by somehow *interfering with the usual relation between a thing and its qualities*—and this is precisely what charm means. Indeed, it seems likely that all forms of beauty and fascination have this sort of structure, including the beauty of people, birds, jewels, landscapes, cities, and the hypnotic power of ambient electronic music and roulette wheels. Such objects present a limitless field of inquiry, and I will leave it to some future book of aesthetics to begin to scratch their surface.

I have often noticed the dual sense of the word *cute*, which is used by adolescents mostly to refer to physical beauty, but in other cases points to the activity of creatures smaller or weaker than we are. Cute objects are either lovely, or else they are delightfully absorbed in some technique that we ourselves take for granted. That is to say, certain actions are performed by certain worldly agents with a regularity and ease devoid of any hesitation. Horses gallop, donkeys eat, humans write letters, and native speakers of a language use it fluently. The labors of such agents become "cute" when they are slightly underequipped for their task: a newborn horse trying to prance on its skinny, awkward legs; a sweet little donkey trying to eat a big pile of hay with its sweet little mouth and tongue; a child handing us a thank-you note with imperfect grammar; a foreigner misusing our language in slightly incorrect but delightfully vivid fashion. In each of these cases, the cute agent is one that makes use of implements of which it is not fully in command. All of these cases are able to make us chuckle with delight. They can veer into outright humor as soon as we lose sympathy for the actors involved: when a hated political candidate looks inept on horseback or on the dance floor; when a piece of hate mail arrives with questionable spelling; when a foreigner berates us with badly mangled curses from our own language; or when we find a dated book on etiquette whose bizarre advice on silverware and elevator manners we will easily ignore. But a similar cutting of the bond between an agent and its traits occurs in beauty, in which a thing or creature is gifted with qualities of such overwhelming force that we do not pass directly through the sensual material into the unified thing, but seem to see the beautiful entity lying beneath all its marvelous qualities, commanding them like puppets. But this topic, too, is worthy of a lengthy treatment of its own someday.

We have now distinguished charm and humor as two ways in which the sincerity of an agent can be placed at issue: in the first case this happens in a fascinating way, while in the second case it entails some form of mild or serious disdain. We need a general term to cover both the comic and charming ways of encountering the sincerity objects, and the best term I can think of is *allure*. Let's briefly review the terminology so as to avoid any confusion. The most general distinction is between *sincerity*, which always exists for all objects at all times, and *allure*, which occurs only in special experiences and seems to have something to do with separating the agent from its specific qualities. Within the realm of allure, there is a difference between *humor*, which feels superior to its object, and *charm*, which feels enchanted by it. Finally, we have given passing descriptions of many different sorts of charm, including *metaphor*, *beauty* in general, the *hypnotic* experience of repetitive drumbeats or machine movements, as well as the *cute* actions generally undertaken by small animals or children, or by strangers in new contexts who misfire slightly in copying the locals.

There are numerous different forms of humor as well, but they are sufficiently well known that no list is needed here. For the rest of this book, the
only one of these distinctions that will concern us is the broadest separation between *sincerity* and *allure*. The terms will reappear frequently in
what follows, so I repeat: sincerity occurs everywhere in the universe at all
times, since a thing always just is what it is; allure is a special and intermittent experience in which the intimate bond between a thing's unity and its
plurality of notes somehow partially disintegrates. This is an important
point that will require further development. But clearly it is just the sort of
thing we are looking for: the entire method of this book hinges on drawing up a geographic atlas of the bonds and joints between the four poles
of being, mapping their union and dissolution.

But two points need to be emphasized immediately. First, charm cannot place *only* the sincerity of its targets at issue, because then all jokes,
metaphors, paintings, and sparkling gems would have precisely the same
effect on us. It would be like the fate of Leibniz's monads without their
qualities, reduced to one and the same monad by the principle of the identity of indiscernibles. In other words, the specific content of a joke or
metaphor *does* obviously matter, even if all of them share a deeply important feature in common. Second, it should be clear that comedy and
charm, which we have called allure in general, makes no use at all of what
Heidegger calls the as-structure. For this reason, allure falls entirely outside the scope of any critique of ontotheology, since it makes no attempt
to bring the hidden kingdom of objects to direct visibility. There is indeed
such a kingdom: or rather, there are as many such kingdoms as there are
things. But allure makes no claim to get us closer to this shadowy realm,
since it plays out entirely in the realm of relations, not that of the things
themselves.

To laugh at the pratfalls of a charlatan does not bring us into direct
communion with this person's essence, nor even move us one step closer
to it. Not only do I never come into contact with subterranean charlatan-
being—I actually never even come into contact with the *intentional* object
"charlatan," the ideal principle of a series of appearances of the same person. Neither the real object nor the ideal version of it lodged in my experience can be summoned into presence, whether by jokes, metaphors, or
any other means. Objects always withdraw. What does occur instead is a
strange sort of interference between two moments of a thing's being, one
that does not occur at all times as sincerity does, but one that simply either
occurs or fails to occur. If it can be determined how this interference
occurs, we will have set an interesting precedent by distinguishing
enchanted experience from banal experience without recourse to any discredited categories of metaphysics in the olden style. This in itself would
be a significant breakthrough even if the current book were focused on

aesthetic issues alone. But it already has broader implications than this, since such a precedent would provide encouragement in dealing with the several *other* relations among the separate axes of being. Just as allure either occurs or fails to occur, so too does causation either *occur or fail to occur*, and certain qualities either *belong or fail to belong* to a given substance.

It would cheer the hearts of many to find some way to work back toward objects without implicating ourselves in the rubble of ontotheology. For along with the intrinsic value of such a program, it would also provide hope that we might someday be free of the endless spiral of increasing critique, irony, intertextuality, collage, deliberate fragments, scare quotes, questions of the question of the question, tracing(s) of the possibility of impossibility of impossibility of possibility, and other painfully reflexive contortions. The way to exit this dark and stagnant tunnel is not to turn around and resign ourselves to the regime of all the purported reactionaries. Instead, if merely navigated all the way to the end, the tunnel in which we stand issues directly into fertile valleys, volcanic landscapes, caravan routes, fields of pillars and windmills, and exotic ports. The next step in arriving at these places is to elucidate the quadruple structure of objects and relations.

PART THREE

Quadruple Philosophy

"The Show could always be combined with some story or comedy . . . Swimming. Extraordinary rope-dancer. Perilous leap. Show how a child can lift a heavy weight with a thread . . .We will bring the man from England who eats fire, etc., if he is still alive."

—G. W. Leibniz
"An Odd Thought Concerning a New Sort of Exhibition"

[10]

The Root of Vicarious Causation

This book has addressed two separate but deeply entangled themes. Part One, which described the sensual ether of the carnal phenomenologists, was concerned with the sheer immediate visibility of the world. It is true that the concept of tool-being points to a side of things that is always withdrawn from any human access; the same was already true of Husserl's intentional objects, though without the twist of realism that this book advocates. And nonetheless, we undergo concrete sensual experience anyway. We never simply aim beyond ourselves, swathed in indeterminate darkness as we point toward a shadowy underworld, but also bask in the taste of peaches and the gloomy facades of churches and armories. Each of us stands *somewhere*, as do each of the phenomena we encounter. And at the same time, even the hidden subterranean face of objects must stand somewhere and have some definite character, inaccessible though these objects may be—otherwise all of them would be identical, just as in Leibniz's initial worry about monads. All realities, whether they be sensual or endlessly withdrawn from the senses, are quite specific and positioned somewhere quite determinate. But this means that at bottom there must be a single type of reality, one form of self-contained being that belongs both to the phenomena encountered by the senses and to the tool-beings that recede from us.

For this form of reality, we have every right to use the term *immediacy*, since it refers to the side of things that is not influenced in any way by its relations with other things, but reposes in itself. While immediacy has been held in low philosophical esteem since the time of Hegel, there is no good reason to endorse this rejection of the term. A horse is what it is. We might try to sublate it, or draw it into an endless play of differences, or otherwise challenge its immediate selfhood, only if we view it exclusively as something belonging to the sphere of human awareness. But the horse *itself* is not a mere naive and one-sided determination that vanishes into some more sophisticated totality: the horse runs or sleeps, breaks free or is captured, prances in victory or utters cries of pain, grows sick and dies, and does all of this as *itself* rather than as a battleship, a wall, a human, or some trivial local modification amidst a systematic blur. In one sense the horse is part of a system with the sandy road on which it runs or the human observer who views it. But in another sense it is something perfectly self-contained, a stalwart diamond or steel ingot among objects. More than this: even if we consider the horse solely in its character as a horse-phenomenon, as an equine apparition in the consciousness of humans, it would still be a *horse*-phenomenon, not a volcano-phenomenon or lightning-phenomenon. In this respect, both the horse as concealed object and the horse as palpable specter are something partly *immediate, self-contained, and nonrelational.* The entire technique of the carnal phenomenologists is to survey the contours of this immediacy—at least insofar as it is accessible to the senses.

Part Two considered the situation of allure, in which a sensual object somehow breaks loose from its own qualities and meets them in a kind of duel. As we have seen, this can occur in numerous different ways. The comic dupe loses flexibility in adapting his features to the task at hand, and becomes dominated by his absurd mustache or monocle or his clumsiness in slipping on the ice. The beautiful object strikes us as an active power infused throughout its various beautiful properties while also surpassing them. Literary, musical, or personal style hints at a fertile surplus vaster than its sum of visible deeds, none of them ever capturing the style as a whole. Indeed, the concept of allure covers an almost limitless range of fascinating terrain—from adorable ponies and rainbows, to the sinister air of comets and epidemics, on up to the poisoning-scenarios of the more desolate brand of cabaret. We cannot consider here what sort of general aesthetic theory might emerge from this concept, even if it gives pleasure to wonder about this. The relevant point here is that allure displays a relation between poles of being that are supposed to be separate, but which in fact are engaged in constant interaction: in allure, there is a combat between the object and itself, between the monad and its own traits. For this reason, allure also seems like a good candidate for providing a key to the *other* forms of such interaction, serving as a kind of primitive atom-smasher for exposing the simplest workings of relationality to view. And since this book has already described the apparent impossibility of *direct* interactions between separate realities, there is a need to introduce some form of *vicarious* causation.

Already, we have distinguished three basic forms of vicarious relationships:

First, there are the relations that exist between the distinct objects of the world. These relations are a genuine riddle, given that objects or tool-beings are supposed to withdraw from one another, failing to grasp or exhaust each other despite their mutual interference through subtle connections and outright physical blows. These are the *causal* bonds between things, which will pose a problem for any philosophy in which objects or substances are never adequately translatable into any sort of relation. Occasionalism is the best historical example of such a philosophy, though its hasty invocation of God as the omnipresent occasional cause manages to avoid any detailed account of the mechanisms of such causality, and is responsible for the poor repute from which occasionalism suffers today. But beyond all pistol-shot theological claims, the great insight of occasionalism remains: the impossibility of one substance ever touching another if substance is defined as an object beyond all relations.

Second, there is the unremitting duel between an object itself as a real unity, as a single thing, and the same object as made up of numerous specific features. Along with the horse or flame or bicycle as a whole, there are various horse-traits, flame-attributes, and cycle-features. All of these notes or birthmarks of an object both influence the object and fail to influence it, just as they both affect and fail to affect each other. After all, some of the traits of a thing are clearly inessential and can be modified or removed at will without destroying the object. And even those that might be essential, to the thing do not in any individual case constitute its full reality as one thing, and therefore their exact relation to that thing poses a genuine philosophical problem. Yet there is another sense in which they must certainly belong to the thing, or we would not call them features of that thing in the first place. All of these considerations refer to the *physical* bond within any object: the cohesion between a rat and its speed and sneakiness, or between an ocean and its turmoil, saltiness, and darkness.

Third and last, there is a further partition in objects when they are considered not as independent subterranean realities, but as existing in relation to us, and perhaps even to other objects in general. This rift within appearance is the home turf of the carnal phenomenologists, with their shared insight into the discord between hidden intentional objects and their colorful facades. What is at stake here is the *sensual* bond in objects of perception. It is not yet clear whether sensuality is confined to the sentient perception of humans and other animals, or holds good for every interaction whatsoever.

Careful reflection on these three types of relations–the causal, the physical, the sensual—raises the gates on a midnight landscape that has been crossed only fleetingly, and never once mapped. The object in and of itself is merely doubled, split between its formal unity and its abundance of traits (the physical bond). But when it comes into relation with something else (the causal bond), or at least with sentient entities, this duplicity is itself doubled: the object seems to become *quadruple* (via the sensual bond). Yet the four poles of the perceived object suffer from a hereditary inability to touch one another, since each withholds its full being from the others. We are again confronted with the two central philosophical problems already raised in Part Two: (1) What is the medium through which different objects or poles of objects interact, and how does this interaction occur? (2) What is the reality of each of these objects or poles of objects in their own right?

A. Severed Qualities

The previous chapter observed that comedy, metaphor, and all forms of allure have an unusually enchanting effect not found in normal experience. This is merely a commonplace; the point of the discussion was to shed light on its metaphysical basis. What seems to happen in every form of allure is that a special sort of interference occurs in the usual relation between a concealed sensual object and its visible symptoms. What we have, in other words, is strife between an object and its own qualities, which seem to be severed from that object. So far, we have deliberately said very little about what "quality" means. Let this term continue to serve as a vague place-holder to be more closely determined later. If objects are what recede from us, qualities are simply defined as whatever *does not* recede, allowing us to bathe in them at every moment.

At first, the general difference between allure and its absence seems easy to describe: whereas normal experience deals solely with surface qualities, allure apparently brings objects directly into play by invoking them as dark agents at work beneath those qualities. It is true that the withdrawn intentional object is present throughout all perception; we are never purely immersed in formless sensory data, but pass straight to the elusive objects of our intentions. Yet in normal perception, these objects are bound up so directly with their carnal surfaces that we sense no distinction between the two realms—a car or pistachio seems to be equivalent to what we directly sense of it. True enough, if I approach a pickup truck with the aim of stealing it, I am well aware that there is more to the truck than meets the eye. I do not regard it merely as a flat metallic profile with a certain color scheme, since my plan is to break into the truck and drive it away, and this clearly cannot be done with a two-dimensional colored surface. Yet I am also not seeing flat metallic profiles and free-floating colors in the first place: the truck for me is already an object, not just a bundle of sensations. But in normal perception, the gap between truck-object and truck-quali-ties is hardly at issue for us as it is in allure.

To vary the example, I may realize that a house cannot be grasped fully unless it is circled at all possible angles, viewed from overhead by aircraft and from beneath by means of special windowed tunnels, its walls opened and each of its boards examined with magnifying glasses and finally electron microscopes. Even then, I might recognize that the house-object has not been completely exhausted by all of these far-flung techniques. But still, normal experience tends to regard the hiddenness of the house only as the current absence of other *perceptions* still unknown; it does not come to grips with the house as a courageous integral unit hovering somewhere beyond all features, but leaves it reduced to its traits. In other words, normal perception does not distinguish between objects and their sum total of qualities, despite realizing that many of those qualities are not currently available. The intentional object is of course already a unit even in normal perception, since otherwise we would encounter an indiscriminate blur rather than a landscape broken up into discrete personae. But the object *per se* is not yet at stake here, and neither are the qualities. There is not yet any split between the cypress as a unit and the cypress viewed through its many features. The same is even true of most theoretical comportment, which by offering improved descriptions of things in terms of more accurate qualities simply maintains the typical fusion of a thing with its features.

The situation is completely different when it comes to allure. Among all its wildly diverse forms, the *sine qua non* is that every form of allure makes a distinct separation between an agent and its qualities. In humor, the comic laughingstock loses all ability to adapt his properties to his surroundings, and is thereby clumsily split off from those properties. In metaphor, the cypress is invoked as an integral object distinct from any list of its traits. A cute baby human or animal attempts adult tasks with undersized bodily limbs or an awkward rhythm, thereby splitting apart the typical immediate fusion between a living creature and its own torso. Tragic or courageous figures break off from adaptable contact with their surroundings and fold back into special private destinies. The fascination of a beautiful sculpture exceeds any measurable list of elegant ratios and seems to arise from a hypnotic underlying daemon, as if the object made use of the properties as secondary instruments at its command. Any compelling style lurks beneath its track record of literary products like a concealed nuclear reactor, able to generate countless new effects at will, such that one can roughly imagine what a Shakespearean play on Churchill or Lincoln would look like, and given sufficient talent might even succeed in making a convincing parody of it. All of these cases show that allure contends with objects and notes *in separation* rather than through the usual fusion of the two.

Pushing the point further, the difference between stories well and poorly told is already the difference between allure and its absence. To tell a compelling tale is not to list all of the applicable facts of the case, which is simply the best way to bore everyone in sight. Instead, the winning technique is always to break up the story into a number of discrete central agents that the hearer can easily grasp, which undergo lucky or evil adventures in the events that follow. The speaker must prepare us for the climax of a story in the same way as for a gathering of unknown relatives or the start of a new basketball season—by surveying in advance the relevant actors who will participate in the story, their ultimate fates still in doubt. Otherwise, we get nothing but dull fluctuations in the known and unknown properties of things. The Chinese Civil War, hip-hop culture, the workings of the sugar trade, or a piece of office gossip can be made interesting to even the most bored auditors simply by bringing to life the central stock characters whose rivalries generate each of these worlds.

This invocation of objects is even the typical stratagem of seducers and manipulators. The seducer mumbles something under his breath, refusing to repeat it when she asks him, drawing her ever further into the clutches of his sham secret—or perhaps the secret is real. The academic manipulator listens to our plans, pretending to endorse them, but adds ominously that he is "not sure if the dean is going to like this," before coyly exiting the room to avoid scrutiny of his empty threat—or perhaps the threat is not empty. Surprisingly enough, this danger zone of never fully graspable lures and threats is even similar to the kind of knowledge sought by Socrates, who refuses to accept any of the explicit *qualities* of virtue or piety offered by Meno or Euthyphro, and demands instead a "definition"—a definition located paradoxically *beyond* all qualities!

In more recent times, this is also the best way to interpret Thomas Kuhn's notorious "paradigms" in the history of science. A paradigm is not an arbitrary principle constructed by a social community in a contingent time and place and imposed by the power of the mob, but rather the rule of a unified scientific *object* beyond all nail-filing arguments and contradictory evidence and public cataloguing of its traits. When the electron is introduced or phlogiston abandoned as sheer fantasy, the regime of objects has shifted, even when the jury remains out as to the details. "Normal science," like normal perception, tidies up our lists of known properties and fixes previous inconsistencies in our map of things, but does nothing to shift the underlying field of objects that are accepted as real. *Allure*, with its severing of objects and qualities, *is the paradigm shift of the senses*.

In any case, we should keep in mind this severing of objects from their qualities, whether in explicit cases of allure, in normal instances of perception, or even in the sheer existence of objects as something separate from their properties. The duel between things and traits is an important piece of the puzzle outlined in this book. Another such piece emerges when we globalize the rift between a thing and its features, no longer placing it under quarantine at the unique fissure where human meets world, but allowing it to spread throughout the cosmos to account for *all* interactions, including inanimate ones.

B. A Downward Spiral of Objects

If allure is the separation of an object from its qualities, then we should ask what these qualities are. And above all, we must remember that qualities come in two different kinds. On the one hand there is the ether of sensual traits without which no experience could occur at all, since the world would consist solely of unreachable objects receding from view in color-less, odorless fashion, leaving no impact on us at all. On the other hand there are the qualities of the objects themselves, quite irrespective of our contact with them, which we can follow Zubiri in calling *notes*, after the Scholastic *notae*. If we distinguish here between the public qualities and the private notes of an object, what both have in common is a specific char-acter distinct from the sheer *unity* of an object—whether that object be a real underground force in the world, or merely an intentional object elud-ing direct perception even while organizing it. We will focus now on qual-ities, leaving the question of notes for later. In this connection, it will regrettably be necessary to avoid any direct discussion of the problem of universals. As Porphyry puts it in the opening of the *Isagoge*: "I shall beg off saying anything about this problem. Such business is profound, and requires another, greater investigation."[1]

In this book I embrace a model of the world in which objects are always absent, concealed from human view but also from each other. An object or tool-being exceeds any possible access to it, and the intentional object of perception (which may not even be real) also evades contact with us. In this sense we do not live amidst objects at all. But neither do we live amidst pure sensory qualities, since there is no object-free layer of passive given-ness that would be shaped only by the human mind. The reason that no one has seen minute pixels of noncommittal sensory data is not because our eyes are too big for the job, but simply because no such perceptual dust-motes could possibly exist, as Husserl realizes. Paradoxically enough, the world inhabited by humans seems to be made up neither of objects *nor* of qualities. It follows that Levinas is wrong in one sense but right in another. For in one way, there is no passively received layer of raw sensory data free of all objects of the kind that Levinas proposes, since objects are at stake in even the most rudimentary sorts of perception. But in another way, he is right that there must be some sort of *immediacy* to perception: if everything simply pointed elsewhere in the manner of equipment, and were nothing in its own right, we would experience nothing at all. There is, then, a strange sort of ether in which immediacy occurs.

Whatever this mysterious sensual material might be, it is the glue of the world—the conducting medium that extends between objects and makes their interactions possible. Moreover, some version of this ontological cement must extend between all of the otherwise separate poles of reality, or they would belong to different universes. In other words, *the same sensual ether that spreads between things and their visible qualities will make possible the physical and causal relations as well.* It will be the source of all vicarious causation, and in this way will unify the numerous different layers of reality at a single stroke. As soon as we begin to wonder what this ether of the senses may be, we find only two basic possibilities. One option is that the qualities adrift in the world are made of an entirely different stuff from objects, which would leave us with a dualistic cosmos of objects and properties, perhaps along the traditional lines of form and matter. Another option is that the qualities are *themselves* objects—entities that somehow find a way to violate the apparent law that objects can never become present. This would give us a world filled with a single genre of reality known as objects, unaccompanied by any second, foreign principle.

In order to gain some foothold in this problem, let's consider the loosely proposed "battle of centaurs" from Husserl's *Logical Investigations.* We can imagine that Husserl has just finished a lecture and is now settling down at a riverfront cafe in the gloomy city of Halle. He recalls the reference in his lecture to a battle of centaurs, and lets an image of this battle take shape in his mind.

On one ridge he finds the Order of Chaos led by Arkhytas: tall centaurs draped in green cloths bearing the emblem of a snake; as they circle about and arrange themselves into ranks, martial music is heard from trumpets and pipes. The opposite ridge shows the Order of Stone, under their captain Creander: somber warriors clothed in dark blue with a jagged diamond-icon, forming perfect columns to the rhythm of snare drums. After some initial skirmishes on the wide plain separating the armies, the battle begins with a sharp volley of arrows. The Order of Chaos attempts the maneuver known as "right wheel," hoping to shatter the flank of the enemy with an enfilade of toxic darts. Sensing these plans, the Order of Stone launches a spearpoint charge to scatter the enemy's columns—when suddenly their forward units are decimated by an unexpected flurry of javelins. Their grieving comrades rush forward to save them, but advance too far into the center of the ranks of Chaos. From this point on, the result is foreordained: the Order of Stone is now caught in a double envelopment reminiscent of Hannibal's victory at Cannae, and the battle degenerates into a rout. While scattered fugitives escape the general slaughter, most of the elite centaurs of the Order of Stone are trapped. Thousands fall on the plain on this dreary, humid day, their corpses scavenged for treasure by the exultant forces of Chaos. Arkhytas celebrates atop the ridge as his wounded survivors are treated with herbal medicines. In a shocking result, he has pulverized the Order of Stone.

Professor Husserl's coffee now arrives, tearing his attention away from the battle in his mind and returning him to a diligent mood. Knowing that phenomenology applies to imaginary landscapes no less than to real ones, he ventures an analysis of the battle. Above all, he knows that he is not simply imagining a set of colored dots and then applying a subjective grid of interpretations onto them. Fictional or not, the imagined scene contains intentional *objects*—warriors, flags, canopies, weapons, dead bodies, musical instruments. What Husserl hears in his head is not imaginary sound waves, but imaginary *military music*, an organized aesthetic object rather than a series of discrete stimulations of the eardrum. And now, scanning this imaginary scene for Arkhytas, Husserl fixes upon the well-dressed and noble centaur performing a victory dance on the ridge, and concludes that this must be the general of the winning army. This act of phenomenological *recognition* is possible even though no centaur can be viewed in total adequate presence at any moment—since even a fabricated mental image only presents its object from some specific angle and in some more or less distorted lighting condition. Husserl notes further that the clothing of Arkhytas is of an unusually bright green, and that his trademark snake icon has a strange and ominous style. This might launch Husserl into a full deployment of his theory of categorial intuition, noting that the green of the centaur's cloth is a color, that the color is a sensation, and that the sensation is a reality, proceeding in this way by stages: "It is *essential* to [categorial] acts, in which all that is intellectual is constituted, that they should be achieved in *stages*."[2] For the chain of sensual categories is not a single pattern stamped into shapeless sensory matter once and for all at the start, but resembles an endless knotted rope in which each thing is tied into its nearest neighbor, each form successively locked into still further forms.

Every time we reach a new category in the analysis, it can overflow back onto the original perception and modify it, since it merely unearths something already present in the perception itself rather than something added magically by us.[3] For example, we can grasp Arkhytas explicitly as a wearer of green clothing rather than allowing this fact to linger quietly in the background, as we did when merely observing the celebration of this jubilant captain. Perhaps Husserl goes even further, and emphasizes that the centaur *is* wearing green and a snake image, or that he is wearing green *and* a snake image, invoking categorial intuition in a still deeper sense. Even these highly abstract concepts "is" and "and," although never directly *seen*, can still be called intuitions insofar as they are capable of intentional fulfillment. That is to say, if Husserl notices that Arkhytas simply *is* a centaur, "the *is* itself does not enter into the judgment . . . It is, however, *self-given*, or at least putatively given, in the *fulfillment* which at times invests the judgment, the *becoming aware* of the state of affairs supposed."[4] This is what allows Husserl to criticize Locke's notion that logical categories arise only through reflection on our own mental acts and therefore belong to the "inner" sphere of consciousness.[5] Against this,

Husserl contends that the "is" and the "and" belong not just to my mental reflections on the battle of centaurs, but *to the battle itself*, even though in this case the battle is a fiction. We could continue to analyze Husserl's daydream through a full technical discussion of all the layers of founding acts and acts of synthesis and the status of species in categorial representations. But the details of these processes are not important here, since this book is concerned with a different set of problems—in some ways a much simpler set.

Following Husserl, I survey the battlefield from a hilltop and view a host of live and dead centaurs. Clearly, what I see is not mere shapeless sense data; my field of vision is broken up into objects from the start. Nonetheless, the object known as a centaur is never actually present. It is the target of an objectifying act, yet becomes manifest only in a series of profiles or adumbrations. This leads us back to an important point. If we ask what these adumbrations of a centaur might be, we find that they are *still* not just raw sense data, but are composed of a number of familiar centaur-elements: human head with somber features, equestrian torso, miniature tail, a deliberate and purposeful gait. These parts are not mere abstractions, since the head and tail remain impenetrable to my perception no less than does the centaur as a whole: "we may call anything a 'part' that can be distinguished 'in' an object, or objectively phrased, that is 'present' in it."[6]

Moving in the opposite direction, it is equally true that an individual centaur can change from whole to part if I focus instead on the total object "*army* of centaurs." The fact that individual centaurs can reproduce and survive for many decades, while an army of them may last only for a single battle, is of no relevance for the moment. Both the army and the individual centaur are on equal footing, since they can either be singled out as individual elements of the situation or blend into a larger intentional object.

In this respect, Husserl has less in common with Aristotle or Leibniz than with his frequent adversary Locke: for both Husserl and Locke, "wholes" are only temporary local kingpins, not pampered monarchs that enjoy the status of primary substances at all times and in all situations. Husserl is quite clear that there are no preexistent wholes given to us by the grace of Mother Nature: "It is . . . possible to *dispense* with [the notion of the whole] *in all cases*: for it [we can substitute] the simple *coexistence* of the contents that were denominated parts . . ."[7] This way of putting it might seem to have a nominalist ring, as though unified intentional objects arose artificially from an arbitrary fusion of parts. And it still seems this way when Husserl adds that "by a whole we understand a range of contents which are all covered by a single foundation without the help of further contents. The contents of such a range we call its parts."[8] For after all, such a whole might be something unable to exist independently. In one of his occasional lurid examples, Husserl offers the case of a *horsehead*, which "could exist as it is, through an a priori necessity of essence, even if nothing were there outside of it, even if all around were altered at will . . ."[9] All of these remarks seem to reduce wholes to mere "things of reason" rather than actual realities in the world.

But nonetheless, Husserl strikes a Leibnizian note in denying that wholes are merely *arbitrary* products of thought. For "a mere aggregate or mere coexistence of any contents is not to be called a whole . . . 'Aggregate' is an expression for a categorial unity corresponding to the mere form of thought . . ."[10] Such an aggregate entails that "the objects themselves, being held together only in thought, do not succeed in founding a new content, whether taken as a group or together; no material form or association develops among them through this unity of intuition, they are possibly 'quite disconnected and intrinsically unrelated.'"[11] In short, to call something a whole may be *relative* to a situation, but it is never *arbitrary*—it is never merely nominal, but is grounded in the reality of the phenomena themselves. We can hardly claim that Arkhytas, a battlefield trench, a spyglass, and the River Styx form a single unit, unless some bizarre set of circumstances were to bring them into union. And more importantly, "no reference back to consciousness is . . . needed" to establish the proper relation between wholes and parts, and those theories that view it as a psychological question instead of an ontological one "are merely subjectively slanted expressions of a purely objective, ideal state of affairs."[12]

There is also a very specific order of dependence between objects when they are considered either as parts or as wholes, which we have already encountered as the progression through numerous stages of categorial intuition. As we seek the forms of individual centaurs galloping across the field, we might focus on various body parts and other indications of centaurhood. If we now look closely at the face of Arkhytas, we can distinguish lips, teeth, nose, eyes, and eyebrows. Looking more closely at one of his eyes, we can distinguish iris, pupil, and eyelashes. If we are close enough to see his eyes in detail, we might even be able to identify distinct flecks of color in the irises. But notice that "raw sense data" is nowhere to be seen—there are only *objects* here, no matter how tiny. If Paul Cézanne were with us, he might decompose the battle of centaurs still further into a series of isolated bulky hues and geometric contours underlying our perception of everyday objects (*Battle of Centaurs Before Mont St.-Victoire*, Louvre.)

But Husserl, much like Aristotle[13], insists that this progression through layers is not the result of an arbitrary decision. It is not as though we could either decide to see Arkhytas as made up of a head, torso, and legs, or *just as easily* regard him as made up of minute flecks of color. To argue that the centaur's true visible elements are chromatic smears is to show contempt for an entire range of autonomous intermediate parts such as iris, teeth, face, and legs, just as the claim that a centaur is made only of atoms or quarks would amount to arrogant dismissal of all the labors of zoology and biochemistry. These midlevel elements do not arise from an arbitrary personal decision about what scale of description to use: they are relatively independent objects, closing in on themselves while drawing their own constituent parts into their orbit. In short, the head of Arkhytas is simply *closer* to his total reality than are the flecks of color in his irises.[14] In this respect, Husserl's phenomenal world is not one in which concrete figures take shape once and for all against a formless background, but is instead a spiraling interplay of objects wrapped in objects wrapped in objects.

This brings us back to two pivotal philosophical problems. The first is that none of these objects are ever *accessible* to us. I never see Arkhytas, but only silhouettes and adumbrations of his unified reality. Among his most striking features are the possession of a human head and horse body and horse tail, all of them pointing toward an underlying Arkhytas-unity that never comes to adequate presence. But here is the problem: the head and body and tail are never present to view either, since all of them have the same degree of bulk and complexity and elusiveness as the total centaur— the same level of objecthood. Hence, none of them can ever manifest themselves through any series of external views, no matter how abundant. And even if we descend to the level of the streaks of color in the centaur's eye, we find that these streaks are not accidental fusions of pointillistic color dots, but embody a certain patterned form that endures even when manifested in different ways in differing moods or lighting conditions. We can move up or down to any layer of reality we wish, and in each case the problem remains the same: *where* is the unified object that supposedly holds its various adumbrations together? Husserl has already said that such an object is not an arbitrary product of our minds resulting from an arbitrary fusion of pregiven independent parts, for there are no such parts. For this reason, any theory of raw sense data is inevitably just as naive as the naivest form of naive realism: it merely posits passive sensory givenness as the one substance from which the rest of the world is built, instead of establishing horses, trees, and flowers as the privileged natural kinds.[15]

But Husserl privileges none of these levels. In the ontological democracy that he champions, each layer of perception has the same autonomy as every other. Indeed, this is the very point of his critique of naturalism, which wants to explain all levels of the world by means of one extra-important and extra-special level: that of whatever the natural sciences of the day regard as primary. By contrast, Husserl's own sensual universe is filled with limitless egalitarian strata of intentional objects, yet such objects are always hidden, elusive, inaccessible. In other words, *even though intentionality is always an objectifying act, it never really provides us with objects*. And in the same stroke we encounter the converse problem: *intentionality is supposed to point to objects by way of sensations, yet sensations as shapeless raw material do not exist*. In this way, it remains a mystery just what we encounter when we go about our lives.

It is worth dwelling on this situation just a bit longer, to etch its strangeness into the mind ever more deeply. What lies before us is not raw information, but objects—and yet objects never lie before us at all. What I encounter in perception is not a motorcycle clubhouse, but only certain visible profiles of the clubhouse that point me toward something that never becomes incarnate before my eyes, and that always exceeds whichever of its contours might happen to confront our senses. While these objects forever outrun us, we do have to stand somewhere, and that "somewhere" seems to be on a plane of sensory qualities. But herein lies the second, related paradox. The qualities that make up the clubhouse are not sheer qualities at all, but only further component objects that elude us every bit as much as the total object. I recognize the gang's clubhouse not in neutral streaks of white and green, but rather in its doors, windows, square bulk, slanted roof, chimneys, armed guards, heavy curtains, and sinister flags or logos. And none of these objects is any more fully embodied in the sensory realm than the others: all of them offer nothing but partial contours and shadows. Pushing things further, each of the component parts of the chimneys and windows and walls also turn out to be *objects*, not just prepackaged, shiny, disembodied qualities. The natural tendency of our minds is to assume that this process comes to an end somewhere, in some terminal point of pure givenness that can later be molded into a structure of increasingly objectified layers. But Husserl's analysis demonstrates the contrary: *perception is object oriented, not data oriented*. Against all expectations, sensuality is a realm dominated by objects.

To bring additional focus to the discussion, we can introduce the technical term *elements* to refer to whatever is actually encountered in perception. If *object* refers to the elusive centaur-unit, and *sensation* refers to some hypothetical piece of raw data later shaped into objects, then let *element* signify that which is neither formless and raw (as in Levinas's quite different use of the term), nor that which is subterranean and elusive. The sensual ether in which we bathe is made up of nothing other than *elements*: those vague yet distinct bits, chips, beads, flakes, fragments, shards, or glass blocks of being that neither recede into the dignified aloofness of objects nor flood us with incomprehensible rawness. There are two basic questions about these elements that we will need to answer: (1) How are elements the same as or different from subterranean objects and their notes, and from sensual objects and their qualities? (2) Whatever the answer to the first question may be, how can elements be encountered at all if they are also objects? As we answer these questions, the initial material lying before us is a strange upward and downward spiral of objects. Wherever we look, we find no sensual qualities, only objects—yet the *net effect* is that we still feel as though we are fully immersed in tangible qualities. One drop of water seems transparent, yet a great quantity of these drops appears blue or green; air is transparent when it is near us, but takes on deep colors when viewed over a large distance, or in certain memorable places such as Santorini, Kashmir, or Taos. Something analogous must happen with the object-oriented world in which we are immersed.

In any event, we have now lost any right to refer to the spheres of objects and of qualities as fixed zones that communicate across a permanently established border, since the fissure between objects and qualities reappears in every least crevice of the world. Perhaps even more importantly, this means that there is no way to bring qualities or notes into play without actually deploying full-blown *objects*. This resembles the problem faced by Max Black when he worried over an infinite regress of subordinate metaphors within any individual metaphor. When human and wolf were placed together ("man is a wolf"), there was the apparent problem that even the qualities in this metaphor—say, ferocity and wildness—cannot enter the situation without undergoing some sort of change in their own right. If we try to spell out what ferocity and wildness mean, the additional qualities we bring under their rubric will seem to undergo displacement in the metaphor as well. Hence, there seems to be nothing fixed or stable in the metaphor anymore, no controlled variables: even the qualities are mobile. Black answered this criticism by stating that even if this process leads to infinite overtones as with musical notes, we can safely ignore such additional vibrations and focus on the primary ones—a reasonable answer for the purposes of literary analysis, but unsatisfactory for settling the issue in metaphysical terms. But we now sense that if Black's problem of subordinate metaphors poses a paradox, then this is not due to any blemish in his theory, but only to the fact that an object *really is* the result of an endless ring of overtones beneath and above it. To bring the wolf into play is also to deploy its entire golden horde of elements. Yet the central problem remains: how can perception stand anywhere at all, given that qualities have now become objects, which should mean that they withdraw from all contact?

C. Elements

The state of the argument is now as follows. Sensual experience is concerned with objects even though objects never become present to it. Insofar as objects themselves elude us, the place where we stand is a fragrant ether or solar wind of tangible qualities that *do not* withdraw from contact—otherwise, we would be located nowhere and encounter nothing. And yet this ether of traits cannot be composed of formless sensory data, since no such thing exists: we encounter a centaur not through neutral color-smears, but through the centaur's proximate component objects. There is an endless regress of objects wrapped in objects. To the extent that these objects are encounterable by us rather than silently withdrawn, they are the *elements* that make up the sensual field, and perhaps even the inanimate world as well. Yet to the extent that elements are objects, they cannot touch their neighbors directly, since none of them can fully exhaust the reality of the others. Hence, the interaction between elements in the sensual sphere has the character of *vicarious causation*, and the sensual world is packed full with elements pressed up against each other, like vacuums or bubbles of reality somehow engaged in mutual influence without direct contact.

It also turned out that cases of *allure* display the vicarious relation between objects and their notes in especially clear fashion, although perception enacts this relation as well insofar as it already links withdrawn objects with their palpable elements. Finally, there seemed to be a quadruple structure of the world: an object itself is in conflict with its own notes, and the same object on the sensual plane is in conflict with its qualities, apparently giving us the same dualism in both the basement and the ground floor of the world. If this model of the cosmos seems too wild to be plausible, simply remember that the perceptual sphere is formed of objects rather than raw pixels of data, and recall in turn that these objects are deeper than any contact that can be made with them, so that any direct relations among this crowd of objects are impossible. This is already enough to suggest the model of the sensual world offered above—sensual elements that coexist, but in monastic isolation, chaste as the stars. But if possible, this model needs to be made even more compelling.

We have seen that the sensual bond between objects and their qualities comes in two versions: the normal case of perceptual experience, and the special case of allure in all its forms. What role do both of these versions play in the carpentry of things, and how does one transform into the other? We can begin with the second form, allure, in which objects become explicitly detached from their qualities. In Ortega's theory of metaphor as in Bergson's account of humor, it seems as though what becomes visible is the inner execution of the things themselves. Rather than remaining stupefied by the surface qualities of the cypress or the man slipping on the ice, we are supposed to come into some sort of simulated direct contact with these objects themselves. Ortega and Bergson are fully willing to admit that this access to depth is always a simulation, since any human access to objects will fall short of their reality in some way. In fact, what is described in both theories is the *intentional* object that structures perception, not the silent withdrawn reality of trees and injured humans in and of themselves. But there was a deeper problem here that both authors failed to note: namely, it *cannot* be true that the sheer executancy of the things is what becomes visible, even if in simulated form. For the executant reality of a thing would be a sheer formal unity, and in respect of unity all things are the same—a problem noted repeatedly by Leibniz, and already by Aristotle in certain passages of the *Metaphysics*. If what became visible in metaphor or jokes were simply the unified action of things, all metaphors and jokes would be the same, since all would unveil the same unity that all things share qua individual things. Against this, it is clear that the specific qualities or notes of individual objects play a key role in how allure functions: the beauty of the Grand Canyon is not that of a racehorse, just as a church seems quite different when metaphorically compared either to a beacon or a slaughterhouse.

In fact, the situation is the reverse of what Ortega describes. Instead of metaphor giving us a simulated experience of the executant cypress or flame, thereby turning the withdrawn into the visible, what it really does is make the visible seem withdrawn: that is to say, *metaphor converts the qualities of objects into objects in their own right.* In Black's example "man is a wolf," what happens is not the emergence to view of the unified executancy of humans and wolves, which Ortega admits is impossible anyway. What really happens is that all of the shadowy notes that tend to be bundled inconspicuously into our unified experience of wolves suddenly take on a human air. In the shadow of the wolf, we encounter a human rapacity, hierarchy, and desolation of a kind never before encountered. Many varied notes of the wolf are released as free *elements* into the world, unleashed on the road like a band of goblins. Instead of bringing underground execution to light, the metaphor actually grants subterranean status to a whole set of new objects, though paradoxically it does this by bringing them to our attention all the more. This addresses Black's worry about the infinite regress of subordinate metaphors: for in fact, it is no problem at all that the features of wolves, when described in terms of humans, should change their meaning in comparison with their customary usage. That is actually the very *point* of the situation, since it is these qualities or notes that come into play in the metaphor, though necessarily in some relation with the thing as a unitary whole. It also explains why metaphors are not reversible—why "man is a wolf" has a different effect from "a wolf is a man." If metaphor brought entire objects into view, then metaphors would have to work symmetrically, since both human and wolf would be brought to our attention as concealed unities. But in fact, with "man is a wolf" it is only the wolf-qualities that come into view, though with human overtones, rather than the human qualities taking on a lupine air. The qualities shift from one substance to another, like moons stripped from Jupiter by a more dominant planet.

This has the added virtue of clarifying Ortega's remark that inessential resemblances trigger metaphors more easily than essential ones do. To say that "my pen is like a pencil" strikes far too closely to what we regard as the inner reality of these utensils, so that we pass straight to the total unity of the pen without jarring loose any of its elements. By contrast, "my pen is an avenging viper" is an obvious catachresis that cannot take us directly to the pen as we know it, but unleashes its ink as a kind of venom, its ramrod-straight figure as a degenerate serpentine form, and its sideways motion as a slithering movement toward polemical ambush. The point is not that metaphor and literal statements both fail to grasp any hidden literal meaning and therefore are equally metaphorical. What marks the difference between metaphor and literal language is that metaphor actually generates new objects rather than passing straight toward those already stockpiled in our midst. It liberates qualities or notes from their banal servitude to withdrawn objects and sets them loose as objects in their own right. And it is precisely these new elements that somehow seem present to us in their execution—hence the grain of truth in Ortega's account.

The same is true, *mutatis mutandis,* for other cases of allure. What makes us laugh at the man slipping on the ice is not the mere experience of his agency converted into a mechanism. After all, this unified integral action is shared by all objects, and therefore cannot explain the difference between different jokes. What actually makes us laugh is the sudden prestige gained by entities that normally serve as transparent passages toward the things: ice becomes a cosmic power able to dominate human freedom; flailing arms become a new stock character in the world; the pratfall on the sidewalk brings the backside of the comic dupe into play as a portion of the universe to be reckoned with, whereas before (one would hope) it was barely noticed at all. And for humor as for metaphor, the jokes work better if they deal with inessential traits rather than essential ones. To witness a stabbing on the street is usually not funny, since the vulnerability of the human body to sharp instruments strikes too close to the truth of our mortal limits. Typical insensitive jokes about dead infants, physical deformities, or endangered races become almost brutally intolerable, especially when uttered amidst those most directly affected. They are obscene proddings at genuine vulnerabilities at the core of specific humans, and for this reason do little to split these entities from their traits, which is precisely what allure demands. For the same reason, teasing is tolerated when it merely picks us apart for trivial defects, but when it approaches the sober truth of our most painful shortcomings, it easily provokes cold glares and even brawls.

Analogous points can be made about beauty. What is at stake when the beautiful agent becomes separated from its qualities is not so much the agent itself, but rather its qualities, now turned into cryptic substances in their own right. Beauty is very different in the case of feminine or masculine features, a landscape, a show dog, or a piece of rare crystal, since the qualities set loose as objects are vastly different in each case. Here as elsewhere, one suspects that the inessential traits are more effective than the seemingly crucial ones. For in an obvious sense, the frequent attempts to derive human beauty from healthiness immediately run aground on the consumptive belles of gothic fiction, not to mention the common observation that human flaws often hypnotize us more than virtues. We are not left breathless by the triathlon victories or impeccable cholesterol levels of the beloved, but perhaps by the strange way they pronounce certain vowels, or the specific curvature of a cheekbone that bears no relation to health at all. A dog becomes charming by the way it tilts its head when hearing commands, not through immaculate dogness; a crystal goblet is beautiful not for its drinking utility but for its superfluous diffraction of light. In all of these cases of allure, the less essential traits of the object break free more easily into independent life, just as a planet's outermost moons are those most easily liberated.[16]

In all of these examples, we discover vicarious causation. It is found in the action of metaphor, since "the cypress is a flame" works only because the statement is *not* strictly true, and links these objects only by way of intermediaries rather than directly and in their total depth. The same is even more obvious in the *result* of allure than in its causes, since the entire labor of allure is to separate an object from its traits. But vicarious causes also lurk at the heart of perception in general: my interaction with trees and candles is not with these objects in their entirety, but only with a certain limited range of their qualities, as we have repeatedly seen. Still further, the same is true even of my pre-perceptual *use* of objects or simple *reliance* upon them, since these unconscious activities still encounter only a small part of the objects they deal with. And finally, this is not a special human curse, since we have seen that even the collision of inanimate objects is haunted by opacity and withdrawal just as much as the pathos of human reality is. Given that no direct links are possible between objects of any sort, we might wish to turn to the *qualities* of objects as the glue of the universe, as the tingling skin through which entities are able to communicate. Instead of arbitrarily invoking God as a global occasional cause, we might say that all relations in the cosmos form a vicarious link between objects by means of these qualities as intermediaries. Instead of God intervening in every interaction in the world, qualities as a whole now take on this formerly divine mission, and serve as the sole conduit between one entity and another.

There is, of course, a serious problem with this suggestion. Since qualities turn out to be impenetrable *elements*, or objects in their own right, it seems just as impossible for qualities to interact as for the underlying objects to do so, since the difference between qualities and objects has begun to seem merely relative. But if every quality of things turns out to be an object or element in its own right, we have a situation where nothing in the universe interacts directly with anything else at all. *Every* relation would be a vicarious relation. But this would mean that perception, allure, causal impact, and even the relation of a thing to its own essence all entail nothing but indirect contact. Instead of interaction, the cosmos would be a kind of fascinated side-by-side coexistence between objects and their neighbors. And this rather bizarre model of things stands in need of further description.

Although we have been discussing the sensual bond between an intentional object and its traits, the most distinctive features of this bond hold for the other two links as well. For we have seen that the sensual bond is a vicarious relation between an intentional object and its qualities. These qualities are not raw data, since the centaur we encounter is made of centaur-parts rather than infinitesimal color-smears. But they are also not objects, since objects are inaccessible while qualities are so carnally present that we bathe in them constantly. "Elements" is the term we have chosen for these quality-objects, which we have termed "elements" in the plural, as opposed to the Levinasian "element" which openly resists any articulation into parts. These elements have actually emerged as the key theme of the present book, since without them there is no way to begin to account for reality at all. The centaur-elements are not fully commensurate with the centaur, since it exceeds its elements precisely by unifying them. The elements are not the same as the parts, since all of these parts (head, torso, gait, style of speech) are objects in their own right not fully deployed in the centaur-unity, since they can be sounded or probed for interesting features that are irrelevant to the centaur as a whole. The elements are not sheer formless qualities, which we have already seen cannot exist.

Now, all of this holds good for the causal bond no less than the sensual kind. For it should be clear by now that causal interplay between two entities does not fully deploy the reality of either of them, which means that they can be linked only in a vicarious way. It has also already been seen that all relations must be viewed as objects, since if a relation is real then it has a reality inexhaustible by any interpretation of it or any collision with it, no matter how fleeting these events may be. And the causal agents belong to the object they generate in the same way that the parts of a sensual thing belong to it. In causation as in sensation, the objects fail to capture one another's full depth, which means that something is created that exceeds the parts of a causal relation. But a middle ground of elements must also be generated by causal interaction: after all, what is most crucial about elements is not that humans stand amidst them, but simply that they form a bridge between objects that otherwise could never interact. This bridge cannot be lacking even in cases of inanimate causal efficacy, since an element is not primarily a human experience, but a face turned by one object toward another. In causation as in sensation, elements are the crucial problem.

The remaining question is whether all of this is also true of the *physical* bond—the duel between an object and its own notes. For it is clearly true of the relation between an object and its *parts*, since this is merely a special case of the causal bond: a telephone does not utterly exhaust the total being of its diodes and plastic panels, but only siphons a certain portion of reality away from them. But this does not necessarily imply an independence of a thing's innermost notes or traits from the total thing, since the exact relation between parts and notes remains unclear. But in any case, whether the notes are the same as the parts or not, they seem to have all of the features that one could possibly demand of an *object*. First, they seem to be independent of the thing, since they are not identical with it, even if in many cases they cannot exist apart from it. Second, they also seem to be independent of each other, since if they interact at all it is still not a total, exhaustive interaction, and each of these notes retains an independent power to inflict blows on some objects and not others. It has been a puzzle since the time of Aristotle whether a thing is identical with its own essence,[17] and the solution will come only when a way is found to say both yes and no simultaneously. We can look by analogy to the sensual sphere, where the elements of the centaur belong in one respect to the centaur, but in another respect to the objects that compose the total centaur. The same must be true of the physical bond, since what is essential about the elements is their ability to serve as the interface between two completely separate objects, and not the fact that humans happen to be conscious of them. *Elements are the glue of the world, the vicarious cause that holds reality together, the trade secret of the carpentry of things.*

The several types of bonds in the world now begin to converge in a single point. The fourfold structure of quadruple philosophy remains in place, no less mysterious than before, though perhaps a bit less complicated. By now it should be clear that the causal relation is some sort of vicarious link between objects not in direct contact. Moreover, the causal relation serves to describe the interactions between all kinds of objects, whether human, subhuman, or inanimate. The collision of two rocks forms a new entity that remains inscrutable despite all efforts to probe it. For this reason, it is an object, and has the same relation to its parts that a clock has to its gears or a tree to its physical components. At the same time, the difference between physical and sensual/intentional objects has broken down. Although differences may still emerge between a tangerine's relation with its notes in independent reality or in sensual contact with us, that difference cannot emerge *here*. Both the physical and the sensual object are made of features, but both exceed these features and never quite master them. But the relation that an object has with its notes or qualities can never be the same as the relation it has with its parts—for by definition, an object does not deploy its parts in their total reality, since it cannot make use of their full objecthood.

In general, it can be said that the drama of the world comes from the tension between the causal bond on the one hand and the sensual bond on the other (the role of the physical bond will emerge later). The former involves the relation of an object with its parts, or an object and other objects, while the latter concerns a duel between an object and its notes or elements. The fate of object-oriented philosophy lies mostly in the latter domain, since it is here that all possibility of relations, contacts, or events is coiled up like a dangerous copper spring. Direct linkages of any kind seem in one way to be banished from the world, leaving only vicarious contacts in our midst. But elements seem to offer *some* unknown way to circumvent the impossibility of relationships, since relations and events obviously do occur. In one sense we still have a quadruple philosophy in which an object's relation with its own elements is repeated on the sensual level when that object makes contact with another thing, as when the duel between a palm tree and its traits is repeated as the combat between the intentional object "palm tree" and its sensually accessible features. But in some cases it might even be easier to think of object-oriented philosophy in terms of the number *three* instead of four. For what we always have in the world are two objects in relation by means of an interface made up of elements, which serve as a vicarious third term in the relationship. Whatever the numerology may be, what interests us is the vicarious relation of a thing with that which lies outside it. And the root of such vicarious causation is the coexistence of elements in the world.

To some extent, the highly technical nature of the preceding discussion will inevitably be repeated in what follows. But we should also try to make use of as many interesting examples as possible, since the human mind follows technical analyses only with the greatest difficulty.

[11]

Vicarious Causation

Elements are now the hero of our story, the central figure of guerrilla metaphysics. Without elements there would be no perception, given that neither objects nor raw qualities can ever be directly encountered. For objects by defintion cannot enter perception, while formless perceptual qualities simply do not exist. To say that perception is object oriented, enmeshed in a world of objects that forever elude us, is to say that perception bathes amidst elements. Object-oriented philosophy is necessarily a philosophy of elements. But elements are not solely the stuff of which *sense perception* is made. Spilling beyond unconscious praxis no less than they exceed the senses, elements are the basis of *all* relations, not just sentient ones. For not only is sentient perception object-oriented, bonded to fugitive objects in the night—but also interaction in general is saddled with this fate, and elements are the vehicle through which this destiny is enacted. Vicarious causation is not a special burden of human consciousness, but the very music of the world.

Perception is not object oriented due to some neurological quirk of human and animal consciousness, but through the inherent nature of relationship between one thing and another. Consider the circulation of the blood or the working of the lungs. In neither case is there anything like perception, yet in both cases our bodily organs reduce objects to caricatures. The body treats blood cells as mere circulable units, ignoring many blood-related features that are of great interest to mosquitoes or viruses; in the same way, our lungs reduce air to breathability, unconcerned with its majestic color at sunset. The same thing happens in purely inanimate cases: when rocks collide with windows or molten lava incinerates coniferous trees, these objects recede from each other just as much as from our human bodies and souls, given that no direct interface between objects is possible. From this it is clear that *no relationality at all* can allow one object to encounter another in person, since it is the nature of objects to withhold their full secrets from each other. What makes relations object

169

oriented is not the existence of representation in a sentient mind, since this is already quite an advanced phenomenon. Instead, even the most stupefied log or dewdrop is already adrift in a world of barriers that both entice and limit its action. And even these entities face the same paradox that haunts human perception: they are scratched or blocked not by mere qualities, but by *objects*, even though these objects forever recede from them. What we have called elements are not collateral features of human reality, but the sole means by which the universe allows *any* relations to occur. In this sense, Merleau-Ponty's stunning insights into perception are still far too humanized, like most of the philosophies that have emerged in the long shadow of Kant.

A few examples may help to show that objects encounter *other objects* rather than pure formless qualities. First, it should be clear that objects encounter their neighbors as unified *forms*, not just as tiny pixels of ultimate uncuttable matter. A rock breaks an entire window, not scattered points of isolated glass. What it confronts, what it breaks, is the thing as a whole. Conversely, the window is broken by the total piece of stone and not by independent dots of petrous matter. If scattered into clouds of stony vapor, the rock obviously could never have the wider-scale effect that we do in fact witness. The story of the world is a tale of interacting forms or objects of all possible sizes at all possible levels, not of pampered scintillae of underlying material. And neither could it be said that the rock and fire are merely confronting the *qualities* of other objects: fire does not burn "white," "flammable," or "cottonhood," just as rock does not smash "fragile" or "vitreous." Instead, fire burns cotton and rock shatters window. And yet these objects do not fully touch one another, since both harbor additional secrets inaccessible to the other, as when the faint aroma of the cotton and the foreboding sparkle of the fire remain deaf to one another's songs. In short, inanimate causation is trapped in the same puzzling middle ground as human perception itself—a no man's land belonging neither to qualities nor to objects, but which is only *oriented* towards objects, even while inhabiting a mysterious plane of tangible elements. All vicarious causation unfolds in this elemental sphere, whose inner workings remain a riddle.

Once we note that the sensual reality of elements extends well beyond the human sphere, we thereby revive and expand phenomenology and push its theater of carnality into previously abandoned realms. The world described by philosophy is no longer the mere eruption of foundationless qualities into human view, nor a tiresome collision of solid points of matter, but rather a drunken alchemy in which dolphins, strawberries, and protons transform each other ceaselessly into gold. Objects are no longer merely unverifiable hypotheses that perhaps lie somewhere out there beyond our perception and perhaps do not. Instead, though hiding from all comers, they extend their forces into the world like the petals of a rose or the tentacles of an octopus. The world is dense with sensual or elemental relations between things: a form of realism far more enticing than the tedious kind repeatedly denounced or evaded by human-centered philosophy.

We need to determine what elements are, since their workings are the skeleton key to the theme of vicarious causation, which along with the inner reality of objects or tool-beings is one of the two major themes of object-oriented philosophy. A preliminary result has already emerged: namely, that elements are the notes of intentional objects. But let's replace this Husserlian term with one better suited to the theme of this book, and call them *sensual* objects, never forgetting that sensuality in this meaning of the term exists even under the crudest conditions of inanimate reality. In this respect, we can say that *elements are the notes of sensual objects.* Consider the background of this statement. We already know that elements are not the *parts* of a sensual object, because each of those parts, such as the limbs of a centaur, has its own independent life not fully deployed by the centaur as a whole. Normally, objects and their intimate inner notes are untouchable for all other objects, given that they lie beyond all hope of contact. The sensual elements of sensual objects pose an exception to this rule. In the encounter with elements, we seem to find ourselves already within the volcanic core of the intentional object itself. The importance of this cannot be overestimated: for the first time, we find ourselves face to face with the *interior* of an object, with its internal magma or inner plasm.

The next question is where these elemental notes of a sensual thing come from. The rough preliminary answer is that they are somehow siphoned away from the *parts* of the intentional object, without however exhausting those parts. The bristly or solid look of the centaur as a whole clearly stems from the components of which the centaur is made: its coarse hairs and muscular limbs. In other words, the sensual object "centaur" becomes visible through certain features that it hijacks or enslaves from the head and legs and tail, without being able to put these pieces entirely into play. What we actually *experience* in the world, the very ether in which we bathe, is nothing other than sensual objects as comprised of their notes. We also need to know how this differs, if at all, from the way in which a genuine subterranean object relates to its own notes prior to being perceived. But at least on the sensual level of qualities, we find that we are living not in a univocal site, but a volatile point of intersection. There is the sensual pine cone that stamps its notes with its own personality even while remaining separable from them, and then there is the analogous process underway in the pine cone itself, buried somewhere deep beneath our vision. The object recedes from our grasp and the grasp of all else, while ceaselessly extending its notes toward other entities like a handshake or a fleeting kiss.

The reader may have noticed that this already sounds a great deal like what takes place in the allure of metaphor. In perception as in allure, the collision of inscrutable objects somehow generates an ether of tangible qualities in which both inanimate things and we ourselves reside. Allure is actually the clearest case we have seen so far in which qualities become visible. But perhaps metaphors, jokes, and beauty in general merely echo a process already underway in the most primitive inanimate sphere, and maybe they seduce us precisely with this archaic residue of causality—just as some hold that the mystery of the sea lies in its appeal to our distant ancestry. For this reason, it seems best to start with a closer consideration of allure and then work backwards toward a consideration of relationality in general.

Lurking in the background here is the abiding theme of the double axis of the world. The greatest philosophy of the twentieth century–that of Martin Heidegger—is dominated by a recurring opposition between absence and presence, as seen in the famous strife between tool and broken tool. At rare intervals, Heidegger augments this monotonous axis of reality with a second split that lies between the *specific* nature of a thing and the fact that it is *something at all*. Both of these dualisms resonate with themes found in the most classical currents of philosophy. We can leave this historical resonance for another time, since what is important here is what form this duality might take in *future* philosophy. But as a first step, it is necessary to commit an act of sacrilege against the Heideggerian temple and its fifty thousand security agents—some of them grim and haggard, others as chic as catwalk models. The sacrilege is that the opposition between tool and broken tool can actually be restated as *the duel between a thing and its parts.*

This rift is far more interesting than might be imagined, and has nothing to do with any sort of materialism. When a house is assembled from pillars, beams, baseboards, chimneys, and carpets, it siphons from these objects only the limited number of features that it needs. The house never fully grasps or even deploys the total reality of its stairwells and electrical cords, which withdraw from the house into the shadows of their private reality. In other words, a thing relates to its own parts in the same way that it relates to other things, and indeed in the same way that we ourselves relate to things: namely, by distorting them, caricaturing them, bringing them into play only partially. Since every genuine relation already forms an object, the terms of a relation can be viewed for this purpose as its parts.

Meanwhile, if this first Heideggerian axis is equivalent to the strife of things and their parts, the second axis can be rewritten as *the duel between a thing and its notes.* Now, the first axis is a clear case of vicarious causation, since the parts of a thing really cannot touch either each other or the thing as a whole. As for the second axis, we do not yet know whether a thing is in direct contact with its own internal features. In any case, we now need to discuss the nature and function of vicarious causation. We will do this by considering the action of each axis of the world, and how each of them relates to what we have called *elements*.

A. The Object and Its Parts

Let's pause briefly to review the cardinal tenets of this book once again. In Part One I focused on the carnal ether of phenomenology in which neither objects nor qualities are ever directly present, though both are firmly implied. But the phenomenologist secures this terrain only at the cost of making it a zone forbidden to natural objects, restricting it to a philosophy of human access. Defend Husserl from charges of idealism all you wish— he still has nothing to say about the interaction between mindless physical particles, since excluding such interaction from discussion is the founding gesture of his school. Levinas holds that the prehuman cosmos is a single anonymous rumble, a kind of *apeiron* of existence, so that the kaleidoscope of specific colorful and sonorous entities emerges only in a *human* experience that banishes the life of inanimate objects from sight. Merleau-Ponty brings humans and nature into reciprocal relation through the flesh of the world, but here too the mutual duel functions only as long as humans are on the scene. Moreover, his descriptive wizardry is burdened by a flawed conception of objects as nothing more than perspectives on other objects, never as anything in their own right. For Merleau-Ponty, as for Husserl and Levinas, the sensual vapors of the world envelop humans alone, and are not to be compared with the supposedly robotic natural causation that is thrown to the scientists like table scraps. Alphonso Lingis, unnerving explorer of our planet, is alone among the phenomenologists in sensing the many autonomous *levels* of the world. For Lingis, a sort of carnal plasma bathes the entire universe and all of its interactions, and the human being is only a traveler or sojourner at each of these levels, not the lionized guest of honor. But with this step, phenomenology mutates into something quite different: each zone and particle of the universe becomes a self-contained sensual reality, summoning us ever deeper while also reposing in its own immediacy. The key question in the wake of this theory of levels is as follows: how does one level grant access to the next?

In turn, in Part Two of this book I defined the concept of allure as a mechanism by which objects are split apart from their traits even as these traits remain inseparable from their objects. Above all else, it seemed to be aesthetic experience that splits the atoms of the world and puts their particles on display. While in Part One I tried to identify the island-like immediacy of the world at each of its trillions of levels, in Part Two I introduced a mechanism by which these levels might come into contact. It is now my task in Part Three to interweave these two themes, known to the classical tradition as objects (a.k.a. substances) and relations. Although a bit of flash and sparkle helps preserve philosophy from the gloom of schoolmasters and fan club enforcers, it should never be forgotten that we are following a most ancient path.

We need to identify the medium through which objects interact, and to this end several facts have already been established. First, the relation of objects must always be indirect or *vicarious*, since no object can enter fully into any interaction. This notion of the permanent incommunicability of substances is the enduring insight of all the various Arab and French occasionalists, whatever the other weaknesses of their positions may be. Second, the relation between separate objects is no different from the relation between a thing and its *parts*, since every genuine relation will have the status of a new object. But beyond this, we can also say that the relation of objects already has something like the structure of allure. For consider what happens when two objects enter into relation. They do not confront each other directly, but only brush up against one another's notes, like shadow governments communicating through encryptions or messenger-birds. And yet this encounter is not one that occurs between sheer pristine qualities—such pure qualities do not exist, given that each quality belongs somehow to the thing even as it breaks free from it. When we say that one object encounters another, what this *means* is that it makes contact with strife between the unitary reality and specific notes of its neighbor.

For this reason, if we now say that the universe has an aesthetic or metaphorical structure, this has nothing to do with the shopworn theme of a conscious human artist projecting values onto an arbitrary perspectival universe. Instead, it is an actual metaphysical statement about the way that raindrops or sandstorms interact among themselves even when no humans are on the scene. The point is not the old postmodern chestnut of "life as literature," but rather causation itself as music, sculpture, and street theater. When we speak of beauty, charm, humor, metaphor, or seduction, these are no longer perspectivist and humanized terms employed to flog naive realism, but are instead the basis for a haunting new realism more compellingly naive than any that has come before.

We can work backwards, beginning with the special case of aesthetic experience, moving on to perception as a whole, and finally entering the realm of causation in general. The examples of allure offered so far have all been specifically confined to human perception. The beauty of a lunar eclipse or the charm of a tormented mime plays out only amidst the sensual bond between an intentional object and the notes that grant access to it. Though our aim is to push beyond sensuality toward the causal bond between separate objects, it is not a bad starting point to reflect once more on the human experience of allure.

We have already encountered the metaphoric collisions of cypress with flame and human with wolf. Several different things happen in the course of this collision—when we say, for instance, "the cypress is a flame." In normal perception or language, the object at issue is fused together with sensual qualities and seems to be a composite made up of them, not a separate agent that dominates them. The banal cypress or insipid flame have numerous traits or qualities, which we will describe here as sensual notes. These should not be regarded as purely visual, sonorous, or tactile. For in the first place, even the simplest sensations go far beyond any pure data, since our sensuous experience is one of feeling cold glass or scenting vanilla rather than merely collecting puncta of sheer sense impressions. And beyond this, our perceptions of things are not confined to the five senses anyway: for example, the sensual notes of a cypress and flame differ somewhat for each of us, mixing our general knowledge of vegetative and flammable powers with our own personal obsessions and varying degrees of knowledge of Indo-European myth. To call the cypress a flame is to transport the entire complex of flaming notes onto the body of the mere cypress, some of them surviving the journey better than others. Put differently, the sensual notes of the flame are broken free from the flame-object and grafted onto the cypress. It has already been mentioned that this happens more easily when the identification of the objects is not *too* close.

"Goethe is Germany's Shakespeare" has a more bland and purely informative effect than "Goethe is Germany's Hercules." In the former case the resemblance is respectable enough that the *entirety* of the objects Goethe and Shakespeare are weighed against one another. In the latter, there is simply some peripheral yet still relevant degree of resemblance between Goethe and the Greek hero, on the basis of which absolute identity is nakedly asserted. By this means, the additional Hercules-notes are seized by a Goethe suddenly grown more violent, or more preoccupied with a series of discrete labors. The possible bizarre phrase "Hercules was the Goethe of the Greeks" would have a converse effect, softening the mythic warrior into a temperate renaissance man and wise aesthete by smuggling Goethe-notes into the Herculean orbit. We should also take note of those borderline metaphorical effects that occur in intellectual remarks that are not quite as peripheral as true metaphor requires, but which are also not immediately obvious. For instance, Harold Bloom writes of Dr. Samuel Johnson that "Johnson is to England what Emerson is to America, Goethe to Germany, and Montaigne to France: the national sage."[18] While too literally convincing to achieve a purely metaphorical effect, Bloom's remark is also just fresh enough to avoid the misleading banality of the old Goethe/Shakespeare parallel.

This suggests something about the status of theoretical comportment, which is not strictly metaphorical, but which must have something in it of the refreshing displacement of notes that occurs when a resemblance is at least mildly unexpected. In any case, we have now reviewed the major requirement of metaphor: that it shatters the usual immediate bond between an object and its notes, and uses one or more of these notes as a secret pipeline through which all the mysterious resonances of flame flow directly into the body of the cypress. This has at least three consequences:

1. *The cypress recedes into the distance, while still dominating its notes.* A normal cypress and normal flame lie before us, and seem to be accessible enough. Not so the flaming cypress of metaphor, which withdraws into a dark underground, leaving behind only its notes on the surface of the earth. The cypress now seems to be a brooding subterranean power, one that governs the notes we confront while never presenting itself directly. In this sense, it approximates the conditions of a *real* object, one that exceeds any sensual contact with us. The flaming cypress descends into a kind of relationless underground realm, striking a foothold outside any of the conditions of access to it. In this sense, it evades the entire critical arsenal of much contemporary philosophy and its signature trick: the denunciation of all hidden substrata, and the related demand that an object be judged only by the qualities it presents to view or the measurable effects it has on other things.

For many intellectuals today, this maneuver seems like the essence of all critical thought, an ingenious rupture with the naive dogmas of the past. But it is really just a well-meaning form of sophistry that never faces up to philosophy's abiding problem since Socrates—the fact that an object must be defined, but that no specific definition or set of qualities is ever quite enough. The metaphoric drama of the cypress causes it to split from the notes it dominates and to depart from direct access as if into the depths of the ocean or the center of the earth. But this underground object is not some "bare particular" or empty stratum of singularity uncommitted to any particular notes. After all, the withdrawn reality of the cypress is not that of a volcano, icicle, or star. The alluring cypress remains the warlord of its notes—but it is no longer identical with them, and flickers toward us independently from beyond. This simply does not happen in normal perception.

Notice that although some metaphors work better than others, we are essentially dealing here with a *binary* question of yes or no: allure either occurs or fails to occur. Either I am seduced by the poet into watching the cypress split from its qualities, or I am too bored and unmoved to see it. Note as well that this binary structure of allure gives it a disturbing similarity to physical causation, which despite its various degrees of efficacy must ultimately either work or fail to work. We can imagine a giant bonfire in Montreal melting wax figurines quickly and steel girders more slowly. But this bonfire has no effect whatsoever on the careers of Pavarotti and Julia Kristeva, and does not cause the planet Saturn to boil away into smoke. In other words, causation simply occurs or fails to occur, just like allure; it is not true that all things conspire. But if both causation and allure occur by quantum leaps rather than gradations, and if both are utterly unable to approach their objects even in asymptotic fashion, then they have nothing in common with Heidegger's troubled "as-structure," according to which the philosopher approaches the withdrawn being of things more closely than do drunkards or crocodiles. Allure does not take us any closer to the cypress, but merely translates it into flame-language. Yet this does not succeed in all cases, and the widely mocked distinction between living metaphor on the one hand, and dead metaphor or literal statement on the other, remains indispensable.

2. *The notes of the cypress are converted into sensual objects.* Begin by recalling that the qualities of an object are its sensual *notes*, not its parts, since the parts have an independent reality from which the object siphons away only a small portion of reality that is relevant to it. There is much more to the roots and branches of the cypress than whatever the tree manages to deploy; that which it manages to kidnap from the parts are what we call its notes. As a general rule, one object seems to convert another object into notes. In metaphor, however, it turns out that notes themselves are somehow converted into objects.

We can stay for now with Ortega's cypress and flame, whose relationship remains asymmetrical. To say that the cypress is a flame pushes the cypress into a withdrawn depth without doing this to any flame (unless the metaphor is reversed). Meanwhile, it is the notes of the flame that are transformed into sensual objects. The typical notes of a cypress remain packaged with the cypress as a whole, and somehow shift with it into the dark underground to which it withdraws. But the usual notes of a flame do not normally fit well with a tree. The cypress is perhaps initially bonded with the flame only through its ascending triangular shape, but the metaphor also loads the cypress with other flammable traits: painful heat, diabolical energy, insatiable motion, destructive power, hypnotic simplicity. These notes of the flame, impossible to fuse neatly into the cypress as we know it, come to be "at issue" for us, while the shared triangular shape of both tends to vanish as a mere given. It is the more surprising notes that seize our attention and come to the forefront of sensual reality. But the flame does not break down once more into its original component parts, as though the metaphor were returning us from the total thing to the ultimate physical segments of which it was formed. Instead, the notes that the cypress or flame had siphoned away from their parts are now converted into freestanding objects in their own right.

An independent object is created out of something that previously existed only through the marriage of two other objects. And this is of decisive importance. The flaming qualities in the metaphor are not mere universals, not just "hot" or "dangerous" in the same sense as all suns, geysers, napalm weapons, and electric stoves. Rather, they are notes *of the cypress.* We find ourselves face to face with cypress-heat and cypress-danger, and these are not exchangeable with any other force in the world. In other words, the notes are turned into objects in metaphor, but do not attain full independence from the haunting subterranean cypress, because they make no sense apart from it in the first place. To say that the cypress-heat becomes an object is to say what we say of all objects—namely, that it is an independent force to be reckoned with, but not one ever to be exhausted or directly approached. And recall once again that we are speaking of a *binary* operation. Although some metaphors work better than others, there is a bedrock sense in which either the notes of a thing are freed into independent objecthood for any one of us, or they are not—just as causation either occurs or fails to occur, even if some collisions are disastrous and others trivial.

3. *New tangible elements are released into the world.* What is created by the metaphor is a series of new objects, of flammable cypress-notes. These are the new elements of experience; the landscape of sincerity has changed. Whereas earlier our attention was absorbed by other objects, it is now absorbed by cypress-heat and cypress-flickering. Throughout this book we have been seeking the nature of sensual elements, in the knowledge that we could not call them either objects or qualities, since the former always vanish and the latter do not exist. We now determine, somewhat paradoxically, that *the elements of the world are nothing other than sensual objects.* I go about my life encountering not disembodied qualities, not a formless windy and starry elemental realm, but rather donkeys, crickets, pinto beans, and the cypress-heat of the poet. Near the outset of this book I spoke of two distinct senses of intentionality. There was the familiar "adhesive" sense of intentionality that binds the poles of subject and object, but also a "selective" sense in which it defines which objects absorb our attention as opposed to others. Metaphor calls our attention to certain objects at the expense of others, whose charms we now abandon. All perception does this, but only allure focuses our attention on solitary notes by converting them into objects.

I say allure more generally, rather than metaphor, because in this respect all allure is the same. In each of its forms, it operates by distancing an object from us and splitting it from its notes. The specific way that metaphor does this is by allowing the notes of one object to be gravitationally captured by another, thereby bathing those notes in the music of the new object that ensnares them. But we have cited numerous other ways in which this can happen. In the clown whose existence is dominated by a ridiculous spotted shirt, we no longer identify the clown with these ludicrous notes, but see him as a hapless agent held in bondage by contemptible round spots, entities taken seriously as cosmic forces by no one other than four-year-olds. In the crystal vase that sparkles as if from a distant void, the vase is no longer identical with its notes, but dominates them even while releasing them into view. The cute baby animal is a naive living force too awkward to use its ears or legs with easy fluidity, and thereby becomes separated from them. All of this is merely review, since we covered many such examples in Part Two.

To catalog each of the variants of allure, to show their structural relations and inner mutations, would be the work of a full theory of aesthetics that this book does not attempt. All I have tried to suggest here is that a single metaphysical principle explains the shattering power of beauty, laughter, tragedy, and all that is adorable. And once again we are speaking of a binary phenomenon: some cases of allure may be more potent than others, but there is an absolute gap between its occurrence and nonoccurrence. The metaphysical role of allure is to present us with the intersection point of objects and their notes, the point at which reality hesitates between existence and essence or substance and quality. Allure is that furnace or steel mill of the world where notes are converted into objects. The engine of change within the world is the shifty ambivalence of notes, which both belong to objects and are capable of breaking free as objects in their own right. Allure invites us toward another level of reality (the unified object) and also gives us the means to get there (the notes that belong to both our current level and the distant one). It puts its objects at a subterranean distance, converts the notes of those objects into objects in their own right, and rearranges the landscape of what we take seriously. This having been said, we now need to consider the more usual bond between a thing and its notes, the fetters of banality by which normal sensual experience is chained.

In fact, "banality" is a terrible overstatement, since the world is poor for anyone unable to recapture at will the wonders of perception. I have already cited in Part One numerous examples from the carnal phenomenologists in which the spell of the senses was warmly evoked. We are forever enshrouded by mists of color and sound, by the geometry of skyscrapers and Cambodian temples, or by the punishing blows of shoulder pain. While not yet full-blown cases of allure, even these experiences preserve a rudimentary form of charisma or witchcraft by which we are held in thrall. One of the pleasures of writing this book has been that each moment of fatigue was easily countered by a quick stroll through the city, and by the resulting encounter with the full menagerie of objects that belongs to guerrilla metaphysics at its theme. Once we give up the notion that specific objects are merely "ontic," that philosophy should deal only with the conditions of possibility of objects or of human access to them, everything changes. From that moment on, every aspect of our experience, from the simplest motion of dogs and waiters to our dealings with ruined glass, wire, and cardboard in a garbage dump, begins to bear witness to a genuine metaphysical event. While these normal cases of perception must differ from allure, one feature they share is that both contend with distinct objects. We never occupy a formless sensory medium, but only a landscape of determinate *things*, even if these things seduce us with a full arsenal of what seem like kaleidoscopic surface-effects.

To this extent we have already expressed partial disagreement with Levinas, who speaks of an indeterminate carnal element from which individual things are condensed as if from the vapors of a steam bath. His admirable motive in doing so is to rescue the immediate finality of carnal experience from Heidegger's tool-analysis, in which every entity is swallowed up in subservient relations to some total set of ulterior purposes. This valid criticism of *Being and Time* is one of the cornerstones of the present book, and Levinas deserves full credit for the insight. But what must be rejected in the Levinasian position is the split between a prior, shapeless, carnal medium on the one hand, and specific objects such as telephones and monkeys on the other. Still worse is his conviction that only human consciousness is equipped to carve up the world into specific entities by way of hypostasis. Quite the contrary: the world itself is an ongoing movement of hypostasis, with every object emerging into a local sensual medium of its own. Our present task is to contrast how this happens in normal perception and in allure.

We have seen that allure accomplishes three things. First, it pushes the sensual object to a distance, as if transforming it into something like a real object rather than just an intentional one. The cypress, diamond, or clown becomes a kind of *eminence grise* lying behind the notes that it extends to view, dominating them even while vanishing into the underworld. Second, these notes become sensual objects in their own right, rather than disappearing into the thing to which they belong as happens under the usual conditions of perception. Third and last, allure also rearranges our comportment so that we now occupy ourselves directly with notes that were previously enslaved to some other object of our attention. It is important to see how normal perception plays out in each of these three moments. It should also be stated that we are not actually speaking of a relation between perception and its objects, since that would be a question of the *causal* bond between me and the real mailboxes or army ants that I perceive. Rather, we are still speaking only of the relation of the elements within the *sensual* field to one another, a relation that allows all of the sensory layers of Husserl's centaurs to coexist even while retaining autonomous reality.

We can begin the discussion with two rough hypotheses about perception, both of them subject to further modification. The first hypothesis is that *whereas allure changes notes into objects, perception follows a contrary movement by converting objects into notes.* The latter statement rests on our earlier conclusion that any sensual object, such as a centaur, is made from a stack of other such objects, each of them siphoning features from its most proximate neighbors. The second hypothesis runs as follows: *an object is identical with its notes.* This has potential implications going well beyond the human sphere, since it is meant to apply even to the structure of objects themselves in the physical bond. In this way, it suggests an answer to the ancient question of whether a thing is identical with its own essence. The answer would be yes, since the notes of a thing would not be universal qualities that would need to be glued together in a substratum, but are linked to the thing from the start. Yet the answer would also be no, given that the notes are manifold and can be broken off from their object, as in allure. But we should cover each of the two hypotheses in more detail.

Both allure and normal perception unfold in the sensory realm, in the zone of what is accessible to us rather than amidst the secret life of things apart from our awareness. On this basis, perception obviously shares the third feature of allure—sincerity. For even simple perception already causes us to expend our energy focusing on certain realities rather than others. Whether we laugh at pranks, admire theater backdrops, or simply trace the flight of birds, we are not also concerned at such moments with geology, Japanese cuisine, or the shoelaces that have now come untied. More than this: as we watch a bright red cardinal in a snowy tree, we are not directly concerned with the cardinal's wings and beak, but solely with the bird as a whole. This was already the point of our reflection on the many layers of the centaur, each of them dependent on its most proximate components. And this returns us to the second major feature of allure, one that normal perception does not seem to share. Whereas allure converts the notes of a thing into fleshly sensual objects in their own right, perception merely seems to capitalize on the various parts of the cardinal or centaur, reducing them solely to those notes that are significant for the object of our attention. Here there is an inversion of the second calling card of allure— rather than notes being liberated, objects are exploited. The countless objects of the perceptual field are rendered subservient rather than set free as independent forces, even if the notes do exist independently to some extent and are thereby set free. We complete the triple portrait by recalling that the *first* key trait of allure is entirely lacking in normal perception. For unless we cross the line and become especially charmed by the cardinal sitting on its branch (as happens often enough to me) this bird is not a shadowy presence that lies behind its notes while eluding direct access. Instead, the cardinal seems to lie *within* its notes, animating them from the inside, not acting as their concealed puppeteer from some crawl space or hidden cubicle of the world. Let this serve as a preliminary sketch of the differences between perception and allure.

In asking the question of whether perception shares the three main features of allure, we are really asking about three forms of *noise* that surround an object at any moment. We can begin with the subtlest noise of all: that of an object's own qualities. When allure splits a cardinal or snowflake from its own traits, the cardinal-object or snowflake-entity becomes a dark nucleus of being that deflects its own features as if they were side issues, treating them as dispensable, as mere emeralds or gold chains of the thing itself. Although this does not seem to happen in normal perception, some muffled variant of it must nonetheless occur, since the separability of notes from the thing would be entirely impossible if the initial fusion were too absolute. Though our attention may be focused on the cardinal as a whole, we also occupy ourselves as a rite of passage with its specific features: its beak and wings and eyes, its memorable falling and rising telegraphic song. These bird-features are not direct objects of attention, but also do not vanish entirely, preserving instead a sort of marginal identity in the experience as a whole. Here we have nothing less than a duel between the thing and its notes (or *substance vs. quality*).

Second, there are the changing manifestations of the thing even when its notes remain the same, as when alterations through changing sunlight or bodily movement present objects by way of different sensory details in each instant. To circle a radio tower, a bean field, a forest, a lake, or a crime scene is not to encounter a different object with each minor sensory alteration that occurs. The sensory notes of the tower remain the same for us as long as we consider it the same object. All the shifting fortunes of the various colors, shapes, and perceptual angles never convince us that we are continually seeing different towers; we look past the tumult of these minuscule changes and see exactly what we saw before. The multiplication of all these profiles, informative though they may be, are struck down as irrelevant by the object in question. We have already cited the theory of Lingis that the object itself commands us to approach it by means of certain specific modes that bring it into optimal resolution: we find the right volume for music on a stereo, the right time of day for a swim in the river, the right distance from which to observe a monument. This entails the obvious fact that many conditions of observation exist for the same object, and that objects phase in and out of various levels of resolution, shrouded in a fog of accidents that remains present even when we do find an especially compelling mode of perceiving the thing. And here we have a second kind of opposition: on the one hand there is the thing as composed of all its notes, and on the other the various fluctuations that play on their surface (or *substance vs. accident*). Allure and normal perception enact this duel to an equal degree. The tower can be viewed from many angles under many lighting conditions, the poet's audience can imagine the cypress as ten or fifty meters distant, and for most purposes the clown can have, indifferently, orange hair or blue.

Finally, there is the ambient chaos that surrounds an object without affecting it. A jazz ensemble seen through a plate-glass window is vaguely surrounded by street traffic and snowball fights that are somehow present for us, but which do not affect the sensory apparition of the band itself. To replace the various peripheral components of the environment, whether with more scholarly or more violent elements, would certainly cast the musicians in a different light. But we would still consider them the very same band whether the mood were holiday or wartime, and whether we suddenly recognized them as our mortal enemies or our fraternity brothers. The sincerity that we invest in an object, the energy with which we take it seriously, deflects all complicating peripheral actors from the inner sanctum of the object. Even when these collateral actors serve to change our opinions about the jazz ensemble, as when sudden news of world catastrophe grants the musicians an ominous status as oracles of coming darkness, the band remains what it is for us. It endures through all the perceptual ordeals that unfold in its orbit. We can call this the duel between an individual thing and all else that inhabits the field of experience (or *substance vs. relation*).

In this way, object-oriented philosophy resembles the classical forms of metaphysics in its concern with three important themes: how a thing relates to its own inherent qualities, to the inessential traits that skate along its surface, and to other separate things in the environment. All three of these problems can be clarified only if we take a closer look at how perception converts separate component objects into a single new object, thereby granting the new one its own constituent features (notes), gracing it with irrelevant and fleeting sensual facades (accidents), and both fostering and blockading its links with other distinct objects in the vicinity (relations). One feature shared by all three forms of noise is that all are object oriented. The notes of a thing, its accidents, and the vague background entities that surround it, are all structured as objects in their own right, given that no mere raw qualities are possible. Any noise exceeding the object of our attention is structured to as great a degree as the object itself. It is not a white noise of screeching chaotic qualities demanding to be shaped by the human mind, but rather a *black noise* of muffled objects hovering at the fringes of our attention. This metaphor can be parsed in several different ways. In one sense, there is the now familiar theme of an object as a black box entering into relations as a constant actor whose internal components are currently irrelevant. Here, black noise refers to the object-like status of the clouds of qualities surrounding such an object.

In a second sense, the object can be viewed as a kind of black hole whose interior has receded infinitely from view, but which also leaks a certain amount of radiant energy, as Hawking's discoveries have shown. And this is precisely what objects are for guerrilla metaphysics: inscrutable holes of withdrawn energy that somehow still emit fragrance or radio signals by way of the notes that ought to have collapsed entirely into their dark and unified cores, but have not done so. Here once again, black noise refers to the objected-oriented character of the radiation from objects, which surrounds us as a constant sensual ether. And finally, despite the lamentable rampage of punning wordplay through newspaper headlines and postmodern philosophy alike, we should also read the term *black noise* as a fortuitous tribute to its namesake, Max Black. For by recognizing the problem that every metaphor seems to have infinite overtones, Black brushed against the object-like structure of qualities, as seen in perception no less than allure. And not only does black noise exist in both allure and normal perception, it is also the very reality of notes, accidents, and relations—of all that is ejected at various times from the inner sanctum of objects. To show this in the case of perception requires some discussion of the sensual layers of the world.

We saw earlier that any sensual object, a centaur for example, comes to presence by subordinating a number of component objects. We do not encounter a set of colored data-points that are then immediately woven into a total object. Instead, there is a layering effect in which the centaur is not assembled equally from eyeballs, hairs, color-flecks, and atoms, but only from its most proximate parts, whatever those might be for any given viewer. Each of these centaur-pieces is capable of becoming the object of attention in its own right, and so on, downward and upward through the entire galaxy of objects—from the tiniest individual hairs of every centaur's pelt, on up to advancing hordes of these monstrous creatures. Any object of our attention rudely exploits its component objects for its own purposes, as material for establishing it own general reality. Still higher overlords can exploit each of these objects in turn. The parts of a sensual object are forcefully locked together into it, though this process does not exhaust those parts and only siphons away a limited number of their notes. According to our first hypothesis, this process amounts to an inverse form of allure: if allure converts notes into objects, then perception transforms objects into notes. The secret inner life of horseheads and windowpanes is reduced to caricatures, as these objects are coupled into vaster machinery that drains them of their juices.

We can now consider the three sorts of black noise that result from this process. Noise is defined as the peripheral material that accompanies objects on their promenade through the cosmos, with the adjective *black* indicating that this noise is at all times object oriented, not formed of loose universal qualities. We should speak first of the notes of the sensual object itself. In accordance with our second hypothesis, there is no difference at all between a thing and its notes. The green of a flag or a mosque is not some sort of abstraction grafted onto a lumpy underlying material, but is already the green *of* these objects. It is a note set aflame with the reality of the object to which it belongs. But even though the notes are one, unified in the total object, they are not *only* one. There is a leakage of individual notes from the essence of the thing, without which the object would have no sensory reality at all, since it would be a sheer unity without handles for perception to grab onto. Like radiation seeping from the core of a black hole, notes escape to some degree the "event horizon" of an object and offer tantalizing hints as to what lies at its core. If a cardinal is the object of our attention, its wings and beak do not vaporize entirely into the hegemony of mighty cardinalhood, but are simply subordinated to the object and take form as cardinal-beak or cardinal-wing. Their reality remains devoted to the cardinal as a whole, but is broken up into all the various surfaces and planes with which we make contact in our sensory life. And this is entirely a binary phenomenon, since a sensual object either has certain notes or it does not. Either the disappearance of the cardinal's wings would undermine its reality or not, quite independent of the difficulty of determining where the lines should be drawn—a question belonging to the theory of knowledge rather than to that of the structure of objects themselves.

Next, we can speak of the ambient objects that exist alongside the cardinal even while forming no part of it. The cardinal does not exist in a chaotic blur, a white noise of mere shapeless qualities, but rather in a black noise made up of the humming of ulterior objects. Here again we have a completely binary phenomenon: either an instance of black noise seems to belong to the cardinal, or it does not; it is always either interior or exterior to the thing. Granted, at different times and for different people one object may alternately appear as either a twig or a part of the cardinal's body. But in the moment when it seems to be one of these, then it does actually *seem* to be one of these, whether rightly or wrongly. Cases of uncertainty simply indicate that we are not yet sure whether to ascribe something to one entity or another—which only goes to show that this entity is in fact already distinguished from a zone external to it.

Finally, and perhaps most interestingly, the cardinal is also adorned with accidental features that belong to it, but without qualifying for membership among the ranks of its essential notes. For instance, it may bathe in bright illumination when the sun emerges from the clouds, and at other times be shrouded in dusky shadow. The cardinal can be dusted briefly with snow when it stirs up a cloud of flakes, and can also be viewed from virtually any angle or distance. Unlike the previous cases, the kingdom of accidents is not binary at all, since all manner of variation is possible here without disrupting the regime of objects in the least. If the cardinal has been placed in my private indoor zoo, I can modulate the lighting up and down in cycles while endlessly circling the bird and varying my distance from it, and none of this convinces me that I am seeing a different bird in each instant. *Perception is primarily the kingdom of accidents*, and offers the necessary leeway for an object to undergo numerous transformations in quality while still remaining the same thing and retaining the same essential notes. Interestingly enough, this is also the only one of the three cases of black noise where qualities both seem to belong to an object *and* are capable of a range of variations. After all, notes belong to their object even when split apart from it, but they do not vary—since notes *are* the thing, and to modulate them would destroy the thing. And at the other extreme, the relations of an object vary constantly, yet they are completely external to the object itself. Accidents are an exception, belonging simultaneously both to the inner and outer sphere of a thing. Here, an important insight begins to take shape, for this very ambiguity is also the central theme of vicarious causation—that one thing touches another, but only indirectly, just as an accident belongs to a thing but only indirectly. And in fact, the form of black noise known as "accidents" will turn out to be precisely where vicarious causation unfolds.

Before passing to some remarks on causation per se, let's make a final review of the differences and similarities between allure and normal perception. Foremost among the differences are these: (a) perception identifies an object with its notes, whereas allure splits objects and notes from one another, and (b) allure unleashes objects into an inscrutable depth, whereas perception preserves them on the surface of experience. But there are also definite similarities. After all, both perception and allure unify objects by means of shared features, while also having to contend with the aftermath of these objects' *unshared* features, which are ejected into explicit view like qualitative residue. This is obvious in allure, when the similarity in triangular shape of cypress and flame links them as invisible glue, and we focus instead on all that resists easy transition between one object and the other. But the same thing already happens in normal perception. For we have seen that all of the parts of a visible centaur are united by some shared underlying reality, and yet the full sensory radiation of this beast flows from the unused portions of its parts, which become what are called accidents. That is to say, the entire carnal or sensual realm seems to arise from a quasi-metaphoric tension between an object and its parts. And not just the most proximate ones: with the centaur's parts stacked on parts stacked on ever smaller parts, the situation resembles a chord being struck on a piano, with countless layers of increasingly faint overtones of black noise found in any perception. The sensual realm resembles a pile or slag heap of accidents, and not of raw sensations, since all accidents are object oriented.

But we have already spoken of another, more striking similarity between perception and allure. Namely, the very accessibility of the notes of a sensual thing indicate that those notes are not *entirely* sucked into the reality of their object, so that some sort of separation of object and notes must already occur in even the most banal perception. For when I approach a tower and see it by means of slightly different qualities at each moment, I ignore these variations as unimportant, as if they were the mere jewelry of the princess rather than the Royal Highness herself. In general, perception is the zone of the accidents of a thing as distinct from the thing itself. The sensual realm, in other words, unfolds in a space that always lies somewhere *between* objects in their duels with one another. As we have seen, it is possible to view the cardinal under all sorts of different conditions, with greater or lesser degrees of distance and clarity—sometimes perhaps with too much nearness or clarity, since having one's face pressed directly against the bird would hardly provide a useful vantage point. But this is still not a question of the as-structure, since none of the views of the bird come any closer to it than any others: each of them simply unleashes certain features rather than others, translates them in different words than the others, even if some translations must prove superior in ways that are still unclear. Perception is one special sort of reality in the cosmos, since it defines the immediacy of the world—and not just for human perception. Allure is yet another special sort of reality, one that awakens numerous overtones of an object now grown deeply hidden.

The next sort of reality that needs to be discussed is the causal relation between separate objects, the topic to which the foregoing discussions have been leading. So far, we have already seen two forms of vicarious causation at work. First, there is the stacking up in layers of all the objects of perception, none of them fully exhausted by the further objects into which they are interlocked. Here, the various objects are present simultaneously in the perceptual field, most of them in the form of black noise rather than as directly perceived. It is clear that they are linked vicariously through their notes, rather than directly, since none of them are used up by their labor as components of other things. Second, there is the case of allure, in which the object is both in direct contact with its notes and not in direct contact with them. But we now come to the still more vivid case of vicarious relation that occurs between actual separate objects. Two kinds of such relation can be distinguished. The first kind merely creates a new relation in the world, and *ipso facto* a new object—since every genuine relation has an intimate reality irreducible to what is perceived of it, and thereby qualifies as an object. The second kind actually destroys one or more of its components by shattering its notes and ending the very existence of the object to which they belong.

We will focus here on the first kind of vicarious relation, since the second would require a discussion of the concept of time. Here too, we have seen that one object never affects another directly, since the fire and the cotton both fail to exhaust one another's reality. Clearly, one thing encounters another only through the intermediary of a certain number of its notes, not by touching the thing as a whole. In this sense, brute causation is no different from human perception. Indeed, all human and animal vision, all vegetable probing, and all inanimate impact must simply come under the head of "relations," without drawing distinctions between these for now. But it needs to be described how the causal relation functions, especially in contrast with the other phenomena we have discussed.

We have already observed that causation is purely binary—like the yes or no of allure, but unlike normal perception with its kaleidoscopic leeway of numerous closely related accidental profiles of things. That is to say, causation simply either occurs or fails to occur; an object either relates to an object in some way or fails to do so. Even in those philosophies that assert everything is connected, it is still held that there are certain connections between things rather than others. Such influence is never regarded as limitless. Namely, even if the shifting of sand on the Mediterranean floor is regarded by extreme holists as somehow affecting the Seattle opera season, no one claims that the entirety of the opera's repertoire is penetrated through and through by the motion of the sand-grains. The impact is a highly determinate one, limited to a distinct range of minuscule effects: it does not cause cast members to lose their jobs, or convert their dressing rooms into platinum or bushels of grain. This obvious realization is already enough to set important limits to holism and to demonstrate the binary nature of causation, since it shows that objects are to some extent barricaded behind firewalls, influenced by some events while remaining serenely aloof from others. To repeat, causation is binary—like allure, but unlike the accidents of perception. And indeed, causation must have something like the structure of allure, since there is no other possible option now that both direct contact between objects and contact with mere free-floating qualities have been ruled out for various reasons.

To call the causal bond between objects binary is also to call it instantaneous. For if two objects are capable of coming into relation, and are not prevented from doing so by any sort of barrier, then they will do so. And as we have seen, any genuine relation is already a new object, since it has all the familiar properties of an object: unity, withdrawal from all relations, a surplus of reality beyond any of its discernible features. The apparent time lag needed for some relations to play out is actually either a progression of the relation between different parts, such as when a fire eats slowly through a house, or else it involves a gradual alteration of many of a thing's notes in sequence, as when a corrupt master slowly erodes the moral fabric of an apprentice, one virtue at a time. Thus, there is a sense in which the causal bond is no relation at all, since it instantly subsumes its terms into a single broader entity, giving birth to a unified total reality made up of numerous distinct notes siphoned from its various parts. We have been speaking all along as though the sensual bond between an intentional object and its sensual notes was analogous to the physical bond between the real thing and its real subterranean notes. After all, both of these seem to mark the relation between one individual thing and its own properties, whereas by contrast the causal bond seemed to unfold outside of any one object. But this is inaccurate. In fact, *the physical bond is identical with the causal bond, and is not analogous to the sensual bond at all.*

Notice that both the causal and physical bonds are unified realities made up of a plurality of notes drawn off of other objects. Both are binary relations without any range of possible degrees of variation. And both fend off any extraneous accidents or relations, staying focused on the essence of the situation. But it is not merely a question of two separate bonds sharing numerous features in common, since there is no difference whatsoever between the causal and physical relations: they are two names for exactly the same thing. In this way, the three apparent bonds in reality are reduced to two. The world is now made up of a single pair of forces: perception and causation. This may seem at first glance to be equivalent to the weather-beaten modern distinction between mind and matter. But it is nothing of the kind, since perception and causation in our sense refer to ubiquitous forces in the cosmos, not to specific limited regions of the world as opposed to others. Perception is no more restricted to animal brains than causation is to stupid meteors and limestone blocks. Instead, perception and causation are everywhere intermixed.

But an even more intriguing variation arises on this theme. If two objects can interact at all, they must both already be suspended in the same ether, linked by the vicarious cause of a larger object that they themselves both use as a base or alibi for their relationship. Simply put, causation requires a prior shared medium, since otherwise it would be impossible. This medium cannot simply be their own relationship, because this would result in tautology—we would be saying that entities can relate because they relate. Instead, objects must both belong to the same medium, have some sort of fascinated side-by-side relationship, before they enter into total vicarious relation and fuse directly into one another. All objects relate only on the inside of another object; all perception occurs on the inside of an object. Hence, *causation and perception are equivalent to objects and the interior of objects.* To say that the entire universe is made up of causation and perception is to say that it is made up solely of objects and their molten interiors, excluding vacuums of any sort, but also excluding any relations or accidents that might float in empty space outside the interior of some object. To perceive is not to represent, but rather to live within the interior plasma of an object. And this is where we now turn—to the relation between an object and its own internal reality.

B. The Object and Its Notes

The central notion of this book is that philosophy must turn its attention toward *objects*. The bedrock and inspiration for this approach is found in Heidegger's famous tool-analysis, the greatest moment of the past century's greatest philosopher. In this analysis, human consciousness turns out to be a thin layer of awareness atop a massive assemblage of things unconsciously taken for granted: the failure of hammers, truck engines, or bodily organs suddenly alerts us to their presence in an explicit way for the first time. The supposed moral of the story is that all human theory emerges from a dark background of untheoretical praxis. But this usual reading of the tool-analysis is superficial. The point is not just that theory fails to live up to the full wealth of unconscious action. Beyond this, both theory *and* practice fail to grasp fully the objects with which they are involved; action, no less than thought, is constantly surprised or undercut by the force of the world. In other words, the central rift is not between conscious and unconscious human activity, but between objects and our relations with them, whether these relations be explicit and lucid or tacit and vague. But this contrast between objects and relations is not confined to the human realm. Mammals, beetles, amphibians, and serpents all fail to exhaust the total reality of the trees and rivers that surround them, and the same holds true even of inanimate beings, which brush up against only a small part of the realities they touch. All loose initial prejudice concerning the supposed gradation between different types of living and inanimate entities must not be smuggled into the realm of basic ontological distinctions.

Our subject matter is not human access to objects, but objects themselves. Objects are no longer a popular theme among philosophers, who pride themselves on a suspicious attitude toward all mysterious substrata and unverifiable things-in-themselves lying beyond all hope of contact. In most quarters, philosophy tends to become theory of knowledge, even theory of language in the narrow sense. Those rare philosophers who continue to venture beyond the human sphere (Whitehead foremost among them) tend to favor concrete events over withdrawn unified objects, and to cast doubt on any notion of an object as something not fully expressed in the current state of the world. One remains wary of anything that might be deep and hidden, or which might lie outside the world in any way at all. At most, one grants the existence of "powers" or "potentials" not currently expressed. But this is merely a way of wrongly conceding that actuality can never mean anything other than specific expression in the world here and now, and of passing the buck by defining any surplus of reality beyond expression solely in terms of what future effects one object might have on others. The inherent reality of things is never addressed.

But any radical theory of events that excludes objects altogether is faced with two serious problems. First, it will have difficulty explaining how multiple simultaneous perspectives are possible on the same object: if a hammer or tree is taken to be nothing other than its manifestations or outer effects in the world, then there will be nothing but a series of "family resemblances" between distinct and specific events referring to the "same" thing in name alone. Instead of a single redwood tree there will be only a sum total of different perspectives for nearby lumberjacks, owls, carpenter ants, mushrooms, and pollen, as We the Enlightened Ones smirk at the naiveté of those who believe in any deeper substrate underlying these various profiles. In many circles this sort of maneuver is still regarded as the gold standard of critical philosophic thought, and is enforced as an initiation rite no less cruel than any drunken midnight swim. Yet it is based on a highly opinionated metaphysical theory, and a rather arbitrary one, since it is zealously committed to an ontology in which specific manifestations are assumed to be more real than their unifying underground source. This supposedly liberated standpoint holds that simple objectless qualities are more directly given to perception than the unifying objects themselves. It treats highly determinate, particular qualities as the one genuine item in the cosmos, and asserts that any notion of an underlying union for these qualities is merely some sort of credulous superstition that any true philosopher would instantly debunk. But Heidegger's tool-analysis already subverts this ontology, granting objects the dignity of being able to surprise us with a reality beyond all their shifting facades. Indeed, such dignity is already granted by perception itself, since Husserl shows that we see a total chair-object from the outset and do not just leap wildly from objective discrete qualities to some gullible fetish of an underlying chair-nucleus. In short, it is false to think that we encounter particular visible manifestations of a thing before we encounter the thing as a whole. This is arguably the central insight of phenomenology, though Leibniz already makes the case in his one-way debate with Locke.

Second, any philosophy that completely eliminates independent objects from the world in favor of events or networks will find it difficult to explain change. For if an object were nothing more than its sum total of current expressions in the world, then it would hold nothing in reserve from which new surprises could emerge. But given that such surprises occur constantly, and indeed make up the very fabric of the universe, we need to ask about the reservoir from which objects radiate their startling novelties. Heidegger's insight into the hammer that withholds its secrets from human view (and even from unconscious human action) already gives us an ontology in which objects withdraw from the universe of relations. It is from this tacit Heideggerian model of the world that guerrilla metaphysics takes its cue. But only by dehumanizing Heidegger's tool-analysis can we remove it from the chilling shadow of Kantian critical philosophy. We do this by endlessly multiplying the levels of the world, ceasing to regard the rift between objects and human perception as the sole chasm in the universe. The gap between substance and relation is not just a special neurological gift of people or even animals, but puts all types and sizes of objects at war with one another from the start.

While some say they find it "useless" to speak of withdrawn objects at all, our definition of objects certainly does not result only in negative conclusions. Negatively speaking, an object is a reality that infinitely recedes from any of its particular profiles or specific relations with other objects. But the point is to speak of objects in positive terms, not just as withdrawn X's or irreducible ciphers. The object is not just an empty substratum onto which external properties are grafted via outer relations, for then all objects would be alike, as Leibniz saw with the monads. For this reason an object is not just dead shapeless matter, but rather a specific entity with a specific form that has set up shop in the world in some particular way. The first positive statement we can make is that since objects are different from one another, they must have interior notes or qualities. And even more importantly, we have seen that the interior of an object is a specific level of the world, a determinate sensual space. As a result, there are two ways of looking at the world. One is to say that it is made of nothing but objects, and the other is to say that it is made of nothing but the interiors of objects. In this sense, objects are never merely withdrawn, since we are never anywhere but inside of them.

The major concerns of this book are now as follows. The first is the status of *elements*. Since experience never encounters either full intentional objects or free-floating universal qualities, it remains a question just what sensual experience manages to run across. "Elements" is simply the term we have coined to focus on this issue. The second concern can be denoted either as the *levels* of the world or as *vicarious causation* in general. That is to say, we need to know the paths along which one level of reality passes over into the next, and how all are interconnected, always through indirect or vicarious means. Third and last, we need to know about that highly special form of connection and disconnection between realities known as *allure*, and what wider sorts of gradation it makes possible. While elements and black noise should be present at all times in equal quantity, allure seems to occur in some cases and not in others, or at least more intensely in some cases than in others. For this reason, it may provide the vehicle for passing from global ontological statements to descriptions of specific and apparently heightened forms of reality such as sentient perception, art-works, theoretical propositions, and ultimately philosophy itself.

All reality unfolds in the interior of an object—or rather, in the interiors of countless objects, stretching above and below each other indefinitely. If the whole of reality is conceived as made up of objects and relations, of the immediate reality of each thing and contact between multiple things, the interior of objects is the homeland for both of these. For on the one hand, we have already seen that objects can enter into relation, can affect each other, only if they belong beforehand to some shared common medium. This means that relations unfold only on the inside of an object, since every medium is nothing less than such an inside. After all, the space in which objects meet must already be a unified space if things are able to meet within it. We have seen that a relation enjoys an integral reality irreducible to any of its effects on other entities, and also that it serves as the autonomous support and referent for all of these effects, which never manage to drink it dry. And on the other hand, while an object exists negatively in withdrawing from other entities, it must still exist positively somewhere. This "somewhere" is an interior reality that is not only unified under the aegis of the object, but is that object, since the interior of the object is nothing other its essential notes, suspended in some still unknown plasma.

The inside of an object is a fiery cauldron in which other objects show their faces and sometimes manage to affect each other more deeply than before. But such effects are not instantaneous, and do not melt the total interior of an object into a piece of homogeneous slag. This indicates that there must be barriers of some kind between the different segments of the interior. Although everything in the volcanic core of an object is unified simply by the fact of belonging to that object, this is merely unification from above; on the inside, it is articulated into countless facets, notes, qualities, accidents, and other halos, echoes, and shadows. Since all relations are objects, and all objects are formed in turn of a swarming internal empire of relations, the basic model of the world that results is both simple and endlessly pluralistic: namely, *nothing exists but the interiors of objects, since objects are nothing but their interiors.* A windmill, screwdriver, blueberry, or star is not the sum total of its effects or even its possible effects, but only the totality of internal notes without which it would collapse. For this insight we can thank the ingenious but neglected Xavier Zubiri (1898–1983). Yet Zubiri remains content with a fixed duality of the world in which a single layer of real essences is opposed by a single derivative layer of relational effects generated entirely by humans, with no sense at all of the countless levels of the world. In this manner, Zubiri falls prey to the hereditary exaggeration of all forms of realism: his magnificent system leaves reality and relation frozen in unyielding dualism, not interwoven endlessly as the world actually demands. Furthermore, he grants humans alone (or at best animals) the power to distort or translate realities from one level to another.

To repeat, objects are nothing but their interiors. And in these interiors only one sort of reality can be found: elements. If we say once more that nothing exists in the world except objects and the interiors of objects, this can be rephrased to say that nothing exists but elements. What, then, is an element? Elements are not real objects, because they lie directly before us rather than receding into infinite distance as real objects do. They are also not sensual or intentional objects like the obelisks and pyramids now in my field of vision, since elements are concrete and detailed incarnations never fully identical with the objects they display. Most objects can be rotated to reveal ever-changing faces and can bathe by turns under the different luminosities of lantern, sun, and moon. And all objects can endure to some extent through time, radiating distinct energies from one moment to the next even while riding out the storm of relations in which objects are forever immersed. Whitehead wrongly views this as impossible, since for him entities are always utterly specific and hence do not undergo "adventures in space and time," as he puts it. In other words, Whitehead fails to distinguish between objects and elements.

To summarize, elements are far too particular, far too specifically carnal, to share in the mysterious lack of presence that belongs to real objects. But all the same, elements are also not just an army of discrete qualities violently bundled together by the laws of human psychology. If elements are carnal in the way that qualities are supposed to be, they are also unified like objects are supposed to be. *An element is a sensual object incarnated in highly specific form.* If the sensual object is the monkey that seems identical to us through all variations in our perceptions of it, the element is always the monkey at twilight or dawn, viewed from a specific angle or in a determinate mood, and currently eating, climbing, fighting, or screeching mournfully across a Peruvian lake. An element is a sensual object coated with accidents, like a car glistening with ice after an overnight storm. Elements have no alibi for their actions at any moment, and seek none: they stand before us, utterly and fully deployed in specific form, sincerely being just what they are. If objects hedge their bets within any specific perception, elements bet the farm on being exactly and specifically whatever they are, right now.

Earlier in this chapter I stated that elements are the notes of sensual objects. This is certainly true in one sense, insofar as the notes of a sensual object are always immediately present to us, unlike those of a real object that recede into the background along with it. It was also important to establish that elements are not the *parts* of a sensual object, since the parts are much richer in reality than whatever is siphoned from them by the objects that make use of them. But even so, elements are much more than notes, since an element also includes features that we would have to call purely variable or accidental. An element is always one specific, ruthlessly sincere incarnation of a sensual object. An element is not just the monkey in its pure perceptual monkeyhood, enduring over time, but rather the monkey down to every last trivial detail of its actions and physical posture. What we encounter in the world are neither real objects (they cannot be encountered) nor raw qualities (they do not exist) nor sensual objects (which are always less committed to specifics than our experiences actually are). We encounter only elements.

The most obvious feature of elements is that they coexist side by side rather than fusing immediately together. Numerous elements are present in consciousness simultaneously. The same is true of the sensual objects that lie within perception but are not identical with any specific profile they might generate. We simultaneously perceive factories, boxcars, steam, birds, and airplanes. All of these objects, which have taken on concrete elemental form, are certainly united in the sense that they all belong to my unified experience at this moment. But in another sense they are not fused together at all, since they maintain autonomous and mutually discernible force alongside one another. And yet they also belong together every bit as much as the distinct bulges in a carpet. The same is not true of real objects, which maintain a guarded suburban privacy, locked away in gated communities to which no access is possible. The real factory and the real steam simply are what they are, and for this reason they withdraw from all relational contact or even contiguity with other objects. Not so with the factory and steam as distinct sensual objects of experience, which belong to the same perceptual space from the start. We have said repeatedly that every relation immediately forms a new object, since every relation has a full inner life not exhaustible by any outer perception of it. But this might be cause for confusion, since the word "relation" is generally used to describe the relation between two things that *do not* fuse together into a new object. The numerous keys and toothpicks lying before me can obviously be said to relate to each other in a certain sense, but we have been employing the term "relation" for a closer kind of fusion between parts that give birth to a new thing.

Instead of saying that the various side-by-side elements of perception are related, we will say instead that they are *contiguous* or *adjacent*. While every real relation immediately forms a new object, this is not true of contiguity or adjacency, which we now employ as technical terms. The almonds, juices, and dried apricots on the table at sunset appear as contiguous within my perception, and do not immediately fuse into some separate new object—or at least not for perception. The elements on the interior of an object are contiguous rather than related in the strict sense.

And of course both things can happen simultaneously: the wings, tail, and engines of an airplane are separate and adjacent for perception, but on a different level these objects enter into true relation and create a new internal reality that, peripherally speaking, is also capable of numerous unprecedented effects. But this does not stop contiguity and relation from belonging to two entirely different orders of being. Contiguity deals with the interior of any given object, or the strife between an object and its notes. By contrast, relation forms a kind of wormhole linking separate objects so as to create a new one, and in this sense is equivalent to the duel between a thing and its parts.

Now, it might be wondered whether there is any such thing as sensual objects at all. It might be thought that sensory space is made up solely of elements that hint or point toward *real* objects as their unifying underground source, with no need to posit an additional layer of sensual objects. But this suggestion does not fit the world as we know it. In my dealings with the world, I look straight to objects, even if their particular elemental incarnation is different in each case. I look past the specific diffractions of light in each moment to see the same drinking glass constantly, and I hear only a door slamming no matter how specifically it slams. The sensual objects are there, carving perception into chunks, even if they always seem to be locked into a specific and accidental form, and even if some of them do not correspond to anything in reality: after all, even hallucinations are packed full with sensual objects, and every perception probably has something hallucinatory about it anyway. One sensual object is always contiguous with the others. And this leads us to a pair of interesting observations. First, it will be recalled that side-by-side coexistence also appeared in the case of allure. The cypress and flame of metaphor did not entirely fuse, but also resisted one another as somehow partially indigestible. This strongly suggests some sort of parallel structure between metaphor and perception. Second, there is the apparent fact that all forms of black noise imply contiguity, since immediate fusion would entail that everything belonged to the same homogeneous object in the first place in such a way that black noise would not exist. Hence, we can say that black noise and contiguity are one and the same. A sensual object is adjacent to the accidents that play along its surface, and also adjacent to the other sensual objects against which it nestles.

Throughout this book, we have spoken with Husserl of the ever-unfulfilled character of the perception of intentional objects. It seems that a tower, crypt, or silo is never entirely present in person, and only yields various limited adumbrations to any human perception of them. But the time has come to renounce this false doctrine, which arises only to the extent that Husserl conflates the features of real objects with those of intentional ones. In the first place, recall that Husserl acknowledges no real objects in the strict sense. In his zeal to wall off philosophy from the natural sciences, he brackets any real comet out of existence as an independent cosmic force to be reckoned with: instead, the comet becomes a unifying principle of a series of comet-profiles transmitted to us by telescopes, binoculars, eyeballs, and mathematical models. Pure fulfillment of our perception of the comet never occurs, since something will always be sheltered in reserve (to speak in terms that Husserl himself would never use). Only partial fulfillment will be possible, tending toward a limit of pure bodily presence of the comet to human view. But herein lies the problem: Husserl attributes a kind of withdrawal to intentional objects that only belongs to real ones. For it is the real *comet* that does its work in the cosmos and unifies its own internal notes while resisting any attempt to probe its mysteries entirely. This is not true at all of the intentional or sensual comet. *The comet as sensual object does not withdraw in the least.* It is there before me as soon as I acknowledge its existence.

If the real comet represents an unfulfillable desire for perception, the sensual comet is already completely fulfilled from the outset, as pure sincerity and immediate presence. This point can easily be clarified. When I encounter a comet, monkey, or volcano, I recognize them as such because they seem to have the essential features of these objects, whatever these may be for me. It might be asked who judges whether a given object passes the test to be considered as a volcano rather than as a normal mountain. The answer: it is each of us who decides. Remember that we are not talking about real objects here, but only about the personae that fill up perception. Human perceptual mistakes occur constantly. But nonetheless, if I think I see a monkey, then I think I see a monkey. This means that I believe myself to be in the direct presence of the essential monkey-notes, and in this respect my monkey-perception is always entirely fulfilled from the start. While it is true that the monkey can be circled or probed in various ways to yield new information, this does not affect the sensual object per se. As long as I am convinced that this is the same thing before me despite all the swirling elements that embody it at various times, the changes that occur in my perception of it do not affect the reign of the monkey.

An additional complication is posed here by the theory of Kripke. Namely, while the object before me will always be "this," it might easily turn out not to be a monkey at all, but rather a cat, a squirrel, or a toy monkey. Fair enough. The decisive question for us is whether the "this" is actually something present within perception and separable from its notes, or whether it only points obliquely to a subterranean real object that is by definition free from sensual notes (though not real notes) in a way that the sensual object is not. Kripke's "rigid designator" is meant to serve as a proper name pointing to something that remains identical even when all known features of the thing are altered, so that the moon remains the moon even if we turn out at some future point to have been catastrophically wrong about all its properties. The question is whether it turns out to be the same thing even if it is not a moon at all—in other words, even if the properties that caused us to regard it as a moon in the first place turn out to be false. I would agree with Kripke that on some level the answer is yes. However, the question for us is whether the inviolate "this" beneath all apparent properties is something lying within perception, or is instead a real object lying somewhere beneath it. To be specific, if I suddenly change my mind and conclude that I am circling a mere toy rather than an actual monkey, has the sensual object changed into a different one? I hold that it does change into a different sensual object, though not a different real one.

This theme deserves a longer treatment than it can receive here; it never posed a difficulty for Kripke, since he did not cut the sensual realm in half in the way that we are obliged to do. The basic point is that we can no longer simply distinguish between a sensual world of properties and a deeper hidden core of the essential "this." There is also a deep core of essence within sensuality itself, though not exactly a hidden one. Not everything in the kingdom of the senses is on the same footing: this zone has two layers. Namely, there is a difference for sensual experience between a sensual object itself and its mere passing features, since we recognize the red flash from a saxophone as a transient incident triggered by a police car speeding by, whereas the same musical instrument when sawed in half by vandals would seem to have lost something essential. And I hold that this essential something belongs to the sensual realm, and that it is something immediately fulfilled and present rather than deep and hidden. I hold that the deep and hidden belongs only to the sphere of real objects, not intentional ones.

To return to the previous example, the difference between my perceptions of a monkey and of a toy monkey far outstrips any difference between the respective perceptions of the same monkey at five meters and ten meters, since in the latter pair we see right through the minor fluctuations and reach the same object. More generally, we have already established the central notion that *an object is identical with its notes*, and this is true for sensual objects no less than for real ones. To recognize no longer the presence of a monkey before us, to decide in our minds that it is only a toy or simulacrum monkey, or even a kitten, is to alter the essential notes of what is before me to such a degree that it would no longer be recognized as the same object. And to repeat, if it is now asked who serves as the judge of what is essential and inessential, the answer is that we ourselves already serve as such judges at every moment. The stakes here do not concern real objects, but only our own sincerity in dealing with the world. When it comes to sensual objects, the ultimate arbiter of the difference between unaltering substratum and shifting surface qualities is simply the one who perceives and recognizes them. This is not relativism, since we are not granting humans the almighty power to determine what is real and what is accidental in the universe, but merely recognizing that humans do constantly make such decisions within their own experience, no matter whether these decisions live up to the demands of reality or decay into falsity and wishful thinking. The "this" may be separable from all sorts of specific and falsifiable features, but it is never separable from a specific essence, and is therefore no "bare particular."

Even for Kripke, the rigid designator points ultimately to the essential Richard Nixon, and not to some empty lump of indeterminate presence lying back behind Nixon. Or expressed in the terminology of this book, the rigid designator is pointing to a subterranean President Nixon with real notes, though by definition it is impossible in the case of real objects to determine exactly what these notes are. And while it might also be difficult to verbalize exactly what belongs to the essence of a coniferous tree or dog as *sensual* objects, it is not difficult to gain immediate access to these essences at least in cloudy form, since they are present from the outset in all perception. To acknowledge the presence of a coniferous tree (whether it's really there or not) is to acknowledge the presence of something that remains such a tree for us no matter what angle we view it from and no matter what background music may be playing or what lights may be flashing. Here it is not a question of dark crystals of hidden inaccessible reality, but only of the act of human sincerity, which takes some incidents to be accidental and trivial and others as having a devastating impact on the essence of a thing.

If for example we are relieved to discover that the terrifying hanged corpse in the public square is merely an effigy *en papier maché*, we cannot immediately agree or disagree with Kripke that the thing is still the same thing despite the massive falsification of its essence due to our discovery. The sensual object has clearly altered to its core, since something snaps in us and we no longer acknowledge the same thing. Yet the underlying hidden entity from which this apparition somehow exudes can indeed survive the alteration in the sensual object. All of this can be summed up by saying that there is actually no black noise between a sensual object and its notes. A sensual object *is* its notes, plain and simple, and cannot do without them. The same is also true for *real* objects and their notes. This is simply axiomatic for object-oriented philosophy, for without this principle, we would have nothing but featureless chunks of presence indistinguishable from other such chunks.

We have now seen the precise difference between real objects and sensual or intentional ones. The real object is never present and always lies elsewhere, in some inaccessible crawl space of reality. By contrast, the intentional object is all too present: not only do we get the comet and volcano from the start, we also get all the various accidental shimmerings of carnal radiation along their facades. Sensual objects are always completely present, they simply are not present in naked form, but instead are clothed in notes stolen from other, contiguous sensual objects. If the surplus of real objects consists in their bottomless untapped oil reserves beneath all perception, the surplus of sensual objects has an opposite character—it entails *too much* presence, too much sensuality, too much oil and perfume always already pouring into the streets. It is not that the sensual object always exceeds what is present of it (the case of real objects), but rather that it always *falls short* of the full richness through which it becomes present to us. Real objects are more than we think they are; intentional objects are less. The implications of this are extremely important, and they are missed by Husserl's theory of intentionality no less than by the Heidegger/Derrida critique of this theory. For all of these standpoints agree that the objects of the senses are unfulfilled, and disagree only as to whether fulfillment is possible, and as to whether a greater or lesser approach toward fulfillment should be utilized as a measuring stick for judging the degree of ontotheological incarnation of any particular thing. But the entire debate is poorly framed, since no *process* of fulfillment is possible at all—fulfillment already lies there before us directly. Real objects can never be brought to presence even partially, while sensual objects are always completely present from the start. To repeat: sensual or intentional objects are completely fulfilled at all times. It is only real objects that forever slip away into the craters and shadows of the world. While real fulfillment is impossible, sensual fulfillment is automatic. It follows that there is no such thing as Husserl's "empty intention." Simply to mention a church or graveyard, even without calling up any specific mental image of it, already brings this thing before us as a force to be reckoned with in our current experience. No startling mismatch can occur between such merely verbal phantoms and their subterranean reality, since this reality can never be fully translated into the sensual realm in the first place—there is never anything *but* mismatch.

To review the central conclusion of all this, the "too much" or superfluity of presence in an intentional object makes it the exact opposite of real objects, for which no presence is ever possible at all. But we need to ask the source of all the excess superfluous features of sensual dogs, blimps, tar pits, and watermelons that constantly vary along the surfaces of these objects without causing us to lose faith that we are still experiencing the same objects as before. The source of this surface variation can only be other sensual objects, since there is no further option. The watermelon as we know it gains its excess features either from its parts, or from other adjacent objects in the vicinity. When all the parts of a centaur unite to form this monstrous entity, the leftover features of the parts cluster around the core of essential notes like jewelry, or glow from its surface like neon. Steamships, flags, and nuclear plants convert the crucial features of their sensual parts into notes, while the superfluous features remain humming in the air as a kind of sensory residue. Now, certain similarities may be noticed between this case and the case of metaphor as described earlier. There too, objects were united only along one front, while their excess residues thrust themselves before our eyes, as when the union of cypress and flame employed their shared physical shape as a kind of invisible structural skeleton for their relation, while their other, more potent and more contradictory features pressed themselves directly upon us.

But there are also major differences between the two cases, not to mention outright reversals. First of all, metaphor was seen to work by unifying inessential features, whereas the present case works by uniting essential ones while emitting the inessential ones as excess sensual radiation. Second, metaphor was shown to work by converting the notes of things into independent objects, whereas the present case of perception does the reverse by converting objects (parts) into notes. Third and most importantly, while metaphor was shown to put objects at a distance, the present case does nothing of the kind, since the notes of sensual objects are already entirely fulfilled from the start in my simple act of taking the thing for what it seems to be. In searching for a general term for this inversion of metaphor, I can think of no better designation than *metonymy*—for in perception, as in the familiar rhetorical trope of this name, objects appear in the guise of their parts. The passage from the slimmed-down sensual object to the full richness of a superabundant element requires a kind of metonymy for any sensual object. For an object to appear in specific incarnated form means to appear amidst all its residues. (Levinas: "a thing exists in the midst of its wastes.") While metonymy has been a celebrated term for decades in postmodernist circles, their use of it lacks the strong dose of realism that the present case demands, and hence their take on the problem is of minimal value to us. Let metonymy simply serve as another name for what we have called contiguity, adjacency, or black noise, a phenomenon that will be examined shortly.

While an object is the same as its interior, the *experience* of the inside of an object is not the same as that interior. For to enter the inside of an entity is not just to encounter notes, but also to enter a total atmosphere made up of accidents and contiguities as well. Human life displays one prominent example of this process, but not the only one. My interaction with express trains or roses forms an object, an immediate unity between me and the object perceived that lies beyond the mastery of both of us. But what I perceive cannot be that unity plain and simple, since this is merely the glue that holds us together even while the specific details of the relation oscillate through numerous different permutations. Moreover, the immediate unity between me and a flower is experienced differently by the two of us, and this means that the interior of our relation must be something other than the way that each of us experiences it. To repeat: an object is indeed its interior, but only this interior itself, and not the interior as manifested to any of the components of that object. The various gears, pulleys, diodes, and wires plugged together in a machine are united into a new object, and the way in which each of these parts comes to terms with the machine as a whole, participating in it and resisting it, is not the same thing as the machine itself. But this means that every relation, every object, is already born into a state of disintegration—for it immediately sets up an internal space in which the union of its parts is no longer entirely unified, in contrast with its sleek unity from the outside. In this interior space, I encounter the flower and it encounters me as well, and the components of the relation press up against one another and encounter each other sensually without being entirely unified. We could call this an "excess" of the relation, except that it lies not outside of the relationship, but nestled deep within.

Although I have said previously that every entity is a descent into its own particles, it would be more strictly accurate to say that every entity's particles descend *into it*. My relation with the rose suspends both the flower and me as discernible adversaries on its interior even while unifying us. It is important to note that I descend into my *relation* with the rose, and not into the rose itself—something which only the parts of the rose can do. To descend into the relation means that both objects have become truly linked, and we sink into the infernal depths of our bond, within which the relation between us varies wildly in its manifestations. The full formulation of the concept of intentionality is expressed, of course, in the phrase "intentional *inexistence*." This is supposed to mean that intentionality has its objects inside it in the manner of a container, a feature by which Brentano tried to distinguish mental acts from mere inanimate causal relations. But what the phrase really turns out to mean is that intentionality lies *inside of other objects*—namely, inside of the relations that I have with the objects of my perception. To repeat: intentional inexistence means to exist on the inside of an object, not to have the object inside of oneself. And whereas the usual model of containment seems to exclude anything other than animal sentience from the title "intentional," the new model we propose is open to any entity whatsoever. Every object is intentional, because every object enters the inside of its own relations, its own overriding master-objects. And what it encounters inside of those objects is what we have called *black noise*.

It should be noted that black noise plays two different roles in any relation. On the one hand, we have seen that two objects can come into contact only because they are suspended inside of yet another object. This means that they are somehow related vicariously by means of the black noise that they emanate into that stormy space above, and which can be shaped into sensual objects signaling the underlying real ones but never identical with them. In other words, real objects have to become sensual objects inside of a higher object in order to make contact in the first place. Or put still differently, the rose and I must first be contiguous or adjacent inside another entity before we can ever form a link. Something must happen in the larger entity containing us both in order to change us from merely adjacent to actually related, to let us finally enter a genuine relation with a stormy interior of its own. On the other hand, objects also point down toward the interior of their own relations, each with a different window on the black noise within, even though all are somehow experiencing the same interior. The rose and I both point down into the same infernal inwardness of the rose-and-I-relation, but both perceive it differently, which means that the interior itself is made up not of accidents (which are irrelevant) or real objects (which are unattainable) or of elements (which are different for both of us) but of something else that truly defines the interior. Stated more poetically, the parts or components of a relation cluster around the rim of the object and face down into its depths, as if circling a whirlpool filled with colorful flame. An object does not descend into itself, but merely is itself; it can certainly relate to itself, as when humans or ducks look into a mirror, but then this image is always something different from its own very act of being. I descend not into myself, but into my relations with moths and gaslights and zookeepers—relations in which these objects show flickerings of their true colors just as I display my own facets to them, whether these objects be sentient or inanimate. No one and nothing ever sees an object from the outside; objects are seen only from within, making any notion of "transcendence" even more absurd than before, so that "descendence" would actually be a more accurate term.

All of this will be so unfamiliar as to border on science fiction, and I will try to approach it in more palpable fashion in the coming pages. But it may be useful to rephrase what we have already seen in more prosaic language before continuing. To relate to something is to join with it as a single object, but also to be pressed toward the interior of that object. This interior is ultimately defined by the essential notes that the thing needs in order to be what it is, though it is still unclear just what form these notes assume. For instance, the entity made up by the rose and me is somehow unified from above, yet is broken into separate components below in a way that contains and displays all the essential notes of the relation. Yet these notes do not appear to us directly and in naked form, but only amidst a swarm of flickering accidental features and mutual relations between all of the portions of the interior: that is to say, only as elements. The notes of the relation are none other than the sensual objects that lie at its core. Yet from Husserl and our modification of his position a few paragraphs ago, it is already clear that these sensual objects are never directly accessible in naked form. Instead, what we make contact with are the forms of black noise—namely, the accidents and contiguities that are distinct from the sensual objects in question, but which themselves have an object-like character, since raw qualities simply do not exist. How this works has not yet been spelled out. And although it is best to avoid sterile technical terminology whenever possible, there are times when a convenient word can serve as a kind of paper clip for organizing a group of related ideas. In this spirit, we could refer to the foregoing paragraphs as the outline of an "endo-ontology," a metaphysics of the interior of objects. While this term is too irredeemably ugly and too reminiscent of dental surgery to deserve extended use, it may prove useful every now and then. The obvious first maneuver for such an ontology is to look at how black noise functions, at how the different forms of it belong together and play off of one another so as to link each level of the world to the next. I have already given a rough outline of how this process works, but it should be clarified more fully if possible.

The phrase "black noise" obviously consists of two parts, each of them referring to one of the essential features of this phenomenon. We can begin with the noise before shifting to the blackness. The meaning of noise is something audible that accompanies a central message while somehow remaining extraneous. It hums in the background but is generally phased out as attention is focused elsewhere. When perceiving a pineapple or ruby, we look past the surface fluctuations on each of these objects and go straight to the thing, thereby piercing the black noise or fog of accidents. Additionally, we isolate each of these things not just from its own inessential properties, but also from its neighboring objects, distinguishing the accidental specific gleam of a ruby from the weddings or solar eclipses occurring nearby. This refers to the black noise of that which is adjacent or contiguous, meaning that a sensual object is always surrounded by numerous other such objects from which it is always strictly demarcated, even if erroneously so. We also considered whether a thing might be separable from its own notes or essence, and concluded that this cannot be the case. A thing is identical with its essential self, and to alter the notes is to alter the object, whether we speak of real objects or only sensual ones. This indicates that there is no black noise between a thing and its notes. We see from all of this that black noise is always a matter of contiguity. If we speak of parts united in a real relation, then they simply unify, and no black noise is present in the united thing insofar as it us united. And since the interior of an object is the only place where contiguity is ever possible, black noise is a phenomenon pertaining exclusively to the interior of an object—to the smoldering volcanic core of things.

Second, there is the blackness of the noise. This simply means that the inessential surface-effects on a dog or comet, not to mention the adjacent nearby objects, are not mere disembodied qualities attached to some neutral substratum of *je ne sais quoi*, but are objects in their own right. Somehow, objects are affixed to other adjacent objects without fusing into them. We should also recall that black noise involves the same objects on two separate levels. For if I interact with a rose or grasshopper, this occurs simultaneously on two distinct planes. First, these two objects must meet beforehand inside of another object, and second, they will play off against each other as black noise on the interior of their own relation. Put differently, they begin life as side-by-side caricatures on the inside of something else, and end up as side-by-side caricatures even on the interior of their relation with each other.

Let's also review briefly the features that belong to the two kinds of black noise and the third pseudo-kind. First, there is the relation of a sensual object to all its ambient objects—the streetcars and ice cream vendors that surround a mosque in Alexandria. We know that this occurs inside of an object, because contiguity requires that multiple things belong to the same whole. We have also noted the *binary* nature of contiguous or ambient objects: we take certain appearances to belong to the mosque or to a book, while others are simply excluded from these, though we might always change our minds later. An absolute decision of yes or no is made as to whether something is an independent ambient object or one that belongs on the surface of another object.

Second, there are accidents. These too can occur only on the interior of an object, since they are also in a contiguous or adjacent relationship with that of which they are the accidents. But by contrast with the previous case, accidents are not binary at all. They can exist in numerous different versions or degrees and still remain accidents belonging to the relevant thing—the monkey can seem to be faintly, moderately, or severely melancholic in its behavior without ceasing to be the monkey as we know it in each case. Not shut out from an object entirely, accidents cycle up and down along its surface.

The third case is the important oddball case: notes. Here too we are dealing with a binary phenomenon, since a note either belongs to an object or it does not. A dog can be more or less hungry or unnerved, but it cannot possibly be more or less doglike, more or less lacking in whatever is essential to dogs, as Aristotle already knew. But unlike the equally binary relationship between a sensual object and ambient objects, notes can be separated from the object to which they belong only by extending themselves into different levels of the world, or into the interior of different objects. This remains a puzzling difficulty for the moment, since notes are supposed to be utterly inseparable from that to which they belong. Our central doctrine is that a thing *is* its notes, and this seems to imply that there can only be one colossal note in the case of each thing, since the thing is always one. It needs to be discovered, then, how a plurality of notes seems to arise in a thing. We certainly know that this is possible, since a flame can affect some objects in one way and some in quite another, and this is not entirely due to differences in the affected objects. But what we have already learned is that the forms of black noise known as accident and ambient are inner features of the sensual bond, while the relation between a thing and its notes belongs to what we have called the causal/physical bond.

From this vantage point we can see that the phrase "vicarious causation" is to some extent a contradiction in terms. For once causation has occurred, the actors involved in it are no longer separate, but form a new object with its own new interior. And obviously, no object needs vicarious arbitration in order to be itself, once its existence has been established as a fait accompli in the universe. In fact, there is really only such a thing as vicarious *pre*-causation, in the sense that two objects can meet solely on the interior of another entity. Vicarious causation, then, is an issue of the interior of objects, of black noise, and of one kind of black noise in particular: accidents. For if two objects confront one another on the interior of another object and have not yet formed a relation, then there can be only one obstacle to this happening. It cannot be that they are not yet in immediate contact, since all sensual objects on the interior of the same larger object are adjacent to one another by definition. Given this, we can only ask what actually changes on the interior of any entity, what gives rise to shifting conditions that can make objects that were once merely adjacent suddenly catch fire in one another's presence. (The numerous erotic metaphors throughout this book are a deliberate echo of Empedocles, and his doctrine that love and hate are what join and separate the four elements throughout the cosmos.) As we already know, what really changes on the interior of an object are the changing surfaces of the sensual objects it contains. Something happens along the surface of objects to make them suddenly interact rather than merely remaining adjacent. There is a metonymic relation that transforms suddenly into metaphor, bringing objects deeply into play by severing them from themselves. If vicarious cause begins as a matter of contiguity and accidents, it ends its career as a matter of metaphor and objects, with the birth of nothing less than a new united object. Ortega's gem of an essay already brought us to the verge of a radically new vision of reality. He merely needed to expand his theory of objects and qualities from metaphor to the kingdoms of normal everyday perception and inanimate causal interaction. Nonetheless, his absolute distinction between executant and perceived reality must be preserved.

The same holds for Ortega's insight into "feeling-things," which are the same as what we have called sensual objects. The sensual world is filled with such "feeling-things," not with qualities bound together in some sort of bland substratum. We encounter horse, knife, and mountain. None of them are merely tangible profiles of color and sound to which deeper properties and powers are then subjectively affixed. Instead, the horse is immediately encountered in all its unity and all its power, including not just visible data in the narrow sense, but also all features whatsoever that I may rightly or wrongly ascribe to its essential core. These features are mostly unspoken and unarticulated, but they are there anyway—the mountain-object may contain a foreboding sense of mystery and a suggested whiff of cold thin air, just as the horse-object may entail a facility for being ridden or brushed or treated to sugar cubes. All of these complicated features are combined into the horse, instantaneously and in a single stroke, as soon as we sincerely recognize the horse as standing before us in some way. They are distinguished further into essential and accidental features, and we ourselves are the judges of this difference—essential features are simply those that cannot be removed without giving us the sense that we are in the presence of a different object than we had believed, whereas all shifting accidental features do not cause us to discard the belief that this horse is still before us. It is simply the sincerity of our judgment that decides whether we are really convinced that this is a horse or cow. We encounter total sensual objects in a single stroke, and this is exactly what Ortega meant by feeling-things. In this sense, a thing has only one note, which is identical with its total nonaccidental reality: horse-note, knife-note, mountain-note. A thing's notes can be considered plural only because they are separable, and they are separable only because they originate in the thing's parts. The separability is possible only because the thing has handles on its surface—accidental features that belong to its parts but which resist assimilation into the total thing. The fact that a mountain or watermelon can be cut up into numerous features stems from the fact that their components are not entirely appropriated by the total thing, but instead play a double game, with one foot in the door of the object and one outside it.

Of all the sensual objects currently before me, some fuse together into the knife, mountain, or horse, and others do not. Those that do not are what we call the ambient objects, such as the clouds above us and the breeze that wafts amidst us. The clouds and breeze are contiguous or adjacent to the knife or horse, since all of them are part of the same experience, and hence part of the same larger object. The black noise of ambiance simply stems from the other objects that belong on the same interior space of some larger relation. This leaves us with the theme of the black noise of accidents, and to discuss this we need to consider how the parts of an object fuse together in the first place. All the numerous components of a sensual house or melon are bound together by whatever features they might have that contribute to the reality of the total thing. The exact definite incarnation of doors, windows, or chunks of melon rind as distinct and overdetermined *elements* is irrelevant to the creation of the larger sensual object. What fuses together are only the portions of the parts that can play some role in the establishment of the larger object. These portions vanish into the thing as a whole, while the other portions remain as the accidental residue on the surface of the thing, as handles by which it can be grasped, broken apart, or altered. Somewhere, Levinas writes that violence means to take possession of what is strong in someone through what is weak in them—stabbing Caesar employs the frailty of human flesh as a means for destroying the greatness of the Emperor, not his weakness, since no Brutus conspires against the mediocre or attacks the strong suit of the strong. All objects are Caesars, however petty their empires may be. We commit violence against every last one of them so as to make use of them, or even merely to interact with them. We violate the melon by cutting in order to take possession of its sweetness, though its cuttability and its sweetness are two different things. We commit arson against an enemy's estate, exploiting the vulnerability of its expensive wood to low-budget kerosene flame, thereby destroying all that is powerful in the mansion through all that is flimsy in it. All forms of interaction in the universe occur insofar as objects leverage each other's peripheral features to inflict blows upon their deeper realities. This occurs between sensual objects as well as between real ones, though it may occur differently in the two cases. And at this point, we should note an important inversion between the two.

The entire problem of vicarious causation arose only because objects withdraw infinitely from any presence to one another. No miraculously perfect observation or measurement can make my perception of or causal interaction with tangerines and ravens equivalent to these objects themselves. But this kind of withdrawal belongs only to real objects. We now realize that the opposite happens when it comes to sensual objects, whose notes are fully present from the start, though somehow covered up with excess debris. If direct causation was impossible due to the secluded concealment of objects, it begins to look possible within the sensual realm, where no such seclusion exists. If the question addressed to real objects is how causation can occur at all, the question concerning sensual objects is precisely the opposite: namely, how can causation ever *fail* to occur? In other words, what prevents all contiguous sensual objects from immediately triggering all possible causal interactions in which they might possibly be involved? How do objects pass from merely contiguous to actually related? It is a basic philosophical principle that causation will occur as soon as it possibly can, that there is no delay of interaction once all the pieces are in place. This means that the interior of an object is now responsible for all buffering and delay. Black noise must not only link all the parts that stick their fingers into a new object, but also serve as the engine of hesitation and deferred gratification between things. Otherwise the universe would run its entire course in a flash, since all contiguous things that could interact would do so at once. But thanks to black noise, sensual objects are like allied ships too encrusted with barnacles to commence joint operations. They are like parted lovers in some matinee operetta, unable to recognize each other, for they are clothed in rags and their faces smeared with charcoal. They are radio transmitters set to each other's frequencies, but covered with sparkling dust or snow that reduces their transmissions to intermittent static and muffled code words. If we speak of vicarious causation between real objects, we ought to speak of something like *buffered* causation between sensual ones.

The key to further advance lies in the study of accidents. They are the route by which one object bleeds into another, but also the barricade preventing instant union between otherwise sympathetic objects. Contiguous objects are simply those that do not currently bleed into each other. Black noise refers to the paradoxical sense in which objects both belong to each other and fail to do so: if they belonged completely to one another then they would be the same thing, which is precisely what happens with the notes of a thing. In other words, black noise is always a matter of separation within a unity. And we must always remind ourselves that it consists of two forms, and only two forms: the accidental and the ambient. The manner of separation differs in these two cases. But in both cases it is a matter of objects, since the blackness of black noise entails that nothing but objects can be at stake. With accidents it is easy to see that the black noise comes from the unused residue of a thing's own parts; this residue is not shapeless color or some other quality, but has an object-like structure. The exact shimmering of the hairs on a centaur simply marks them as imperfectly deployed portions of the centaur as a whole. Our unified perception of this mythical beast contains a great deal of compressed information, but compressed so effectively as to be mashed up into a single point of unity, a single centaur-note. In this respect the centaur forms an inviolate singularity amidst our other simultaneous perceptions, effectively walled off from them. Yet this singular centaur does not utterly use up all of its components, which remain encrusted on its surface as passages and corridors from the centaur to its various parts. We easily move from one such object to the next—in fact, perception does nothing other than this.

The zone of perception is broken up in advance into separate objects, contiguous sectors of discrete sensual entities that have not fused into one another even though they belong to the same interior space. Where these objects come from, and how they might provide entryways to other such worlds, is another question entirely. But we have seen repeatedly that they are objects, not qualities. When Merleau-Ponty refers to the black color of a pen as a somber power comparable to the blackness of moral evil, he is already lifting objects to a higher status than before, one that cancels the reign of disembodied qualities. For ultimately, the blackness of my writing table is no more directly visible than its solidity or sturdiness; no one of these traits is more fully incarnate or less visible than the others. And insofar as such features can be detached and talked about at all, they are parts. They are objects in their own right, not spectral independent qualities. Now, some of these objects blend together while others do not. The ones that do not fuse together remain in relation to each other in the manner of the black noise of contiguity. Those that manage to blend into a new object also leave their leftover features as parts or handles on their surface, like exit doors allowing our attention to pass from one object to an adjoining one. In any case, some of them simply blend together while others simply do not: it is a purely binary issue, one that is judged solely by our own investment of sincerity in taking certain combinations seriously and others not. Either we sincerely invest our energy in seriously acknowledging some feature as belonging to another thing, or we do not. In any given moment there is no room for guile. (Ortega: "Every attempt to dislodge ingenuousness from the universe is in vain.") We simply recognize some things as being parts of an object and others as not being parts of it. Now, insofar as objects become parts of another, they do so by means of something essential that can be taken as belonging to the new object. Certain aspects of the parts necessarily blend into the new thing, while others are left in the cold as accidents, just as certain members of a school class are invited to a party and others not, or certain puppies and kittens are adopted and others not.

The unemployed residue of the parts is left in the form of accidents or handles on the surface of the newly created thing. They are what we call the inessential aspects of the new thing; they prevent the parts from being entirely used up by the whole and thereby vanishing from the cosmos. It might equally be wondered whether the essential notes of the new thing can also serve as handles on the surface of the thing, functioning as exit doors, or as entryways into the thing's inner chambers. The answer is no. Insofar as they are essential, they belong to the thing as a whole and are undetachable. The supportiveness of the table is a table-supportiveness; the succulence of a melon is always melon-juiciness. By definition these are undetachable from the thing, from the sensual object that Ortega calls a feeling-thing: it is a fully unified thing, and this means that ultimately it has only one note, not many. Insofar as qualities are essential, they are notes—or rather, part of the unified note—belonging to the thing as a whole. But insofar as they are graspable or detachable handles, they belong to the *parts* of a thing. In this sense, the duel between a thing and its notes is actually the opposition between a thing and its sensual parts.

Yet this type of combat is not really so violent, since we easily move from a thing to its parts and back again. The passage back and forth is smooth and easy to navigate. Even more importantly, it will be noticed that the parts are entirely independent. We easily move from the centaur to its head or even to its individual hairs, and each of these objects remains an independent part, porous or interlocking with respect to the others. In the sensual world of black noise or metonymy, no object is split off from its notes, but every object is easily split into its parts, which retain integrity without any protest from their neighbors. The situation is entirely different when it comes to allure, which belongs to a different order of being altogether. Allure is expressed in many ways, but each of its forms involves the separation of a thing from its innermost precious features: its notes. As a general rule of the universe, this is impossible; generally, a thing is identical with the system of its notes, or rather its single unified note. But this means that allure inaugurates something very special in the cosmos. Let's review the major cases of allure one last time, since it gives pleasure to keep these examples always in mind, and since the remainder of our discussions are condemned to such difficulty.

The most important case of allure we considered was metaphor. Here, one sensual object interferes with another by means of a forced attempt to make them coincide. From this process a new and distant object is created, while the notes of one of the original things are released into independent reality as objects. But unlike the mere parts of sensual things, these notes are not truly independent objects that separate from their neighbors without protest, easily walling themselves off in private reality. No; when man becomes wolf, the vague features released into the air are not simply wolf-qualities, but wolf-qualities of *man*. The heat and destructive power unleashed by saying "the cypress is a flame" are cypress-powers, not disembodied universal possibilities. They are notes, not qualities, and notes are always notes *of* something. In this way, they remain uncrossable viaducts to the other world, like enchanted bridges obstructed by locust swarms, excessive fog, or landmines.

Nor is metaphor the only tool at the poet's disposal for accomplishing this. The same already happens in cases of sheer poetic invocation in which no metaphor is present. When Georg Trakl ends a poem with the phrase "wolves broke through the gate," there is no metaphor here. Yet this sentence achieves poetic effect through the sheer bleakness of its isolation, separating it from its expected occurrence in a total context of information, such as when a historian writes: "As November of 1245 drew to a close, *wolves broke through the gate* at the northern edge of Paris and devoured the last remaining livestock of the citizenry." In this latter example, the magic words remain muffled by their relations with those surrounding them, and there is no fission of the words from the specific role that they are called upon to play. Or at least this is usually the case. For even this lengthy academic sentence about medieval Paris attains poetic effect if craftily employed through installation art—broadcast without context or explanation from the center of a massive beanbag or ominous ceramic cube, as I myself have witnessed in numerous obscure galleries.

We noted earlier that beauty entails the splitting of objects from their qualities, with the beautiful agent seeming to be a remote power in control of all its features. It was also mentioned that style is a surplus lying beyond any of its specific works, with only weak personal and literary styles unable to rise above their public track records so as to hint at a vaster reserve. (As a general rule, it is best to avoid both people and objects that fail to transcend their resumés.) Humor displays a similar structure, since it reduces the comic dupe to an underlying pawn of contemptible outer attachments. Tragedy works along the same lines, since Macbeth or Phaedra are severed from normal human adaptability and consigned to an irrevocable destiny that seems anything but accidental—after all, there is no real tragedy if a character mistakenly trips into a fire or is struck down at random by a stray bullet or nuclear strike. There may be countless other forms of allure. And though all of them deserve to be catalogued in a full work of aesthetics, allure reaches into realms far exceeding those of the arts, perhaps including the ethical and even the purely physical.

An additional form of allure reaching well beyond the arts is found in embarrassment. Here too, we find the separation of an agent from its qualities—usually the agent is we ourselves, though it may be any other creature for whom we feel some degree of basic sympathy. None of us are merely bare striving egos, since we are encrusted as well with numerous personal qualities and socially recognized achievements, and prefer that these features be certified as belonging inseparably to us. Embarrassment or humiliation occurs when we are stripped of these personal notes and publicly exposed as underlying nullities, or at least as much less than we claimed to be. Traits that seemed to be essential notes of our characters are suddenly unmasked as nothing more than easily detachable accidents, as pretenses or dress-up games. A talented violinist who slips and falls during a concert, or who panics and is unable to finish the concert, is exposed as someone not so intimately bound to her violinist-notes as she had silently claimed to be. The nation that fails in wartime, its capital falling to the enemy in a lightning offensive, undergoes humiliation from having its bluster and its military music removed from the list of efficacious powers in the world; the nation is reduced to a willful ego calling in vain for its lost place in the sun. A backstabbing gossip caught in the act by his victim not only fears retribution, but also feels acute embarrassment: his former charade of kindness and discretion has now been exposed as something less than an integral part of his character, so that he feels shame even before the naive weakling he thought he had exploited. Here too, the backstabber is systematically stripped of qualities he had publicly claimed, and is exposed as a bare manipulating ego. To make a fool of oneself on the golf course or dance floor is to be reduced to a bumbling *cogito* whose connection with publicly recognized merits is ruptured. When a sloppy operator mistakenly calls his friend by the name of an ex-lover, the inner workings of his unconscious designs leak from behind the facade of cool friendliness that he normally directs toward her—a facade now exposed as an extrinsic tool or detachable instrument in the service of his more candid designs.

All of this reminds us of an earlier observation: humans do not really want to be recognized as free and dignified rational agents. Instead, both humans and the higher animals would rather be recognized as stock characters, and secretly hope that others will recognize their talents and virtues as features welded directly to their inner being rather than connected to their souls only fleetingly or manipulatively. To be recognized solely as a bare consciousness is actually the root of all embarrassment. It is nakedness as such, of which the shame of physical nakedness is only one of countless forms. Humiliation strips a lowly central agent of its socially recognized powers, leaving only the hapless striving ego on stage, bathed in floodlights as all humane observers blush in horror. But the other side of the coin is the related virtue of humility, in which the bare poverty of our inner selves is offered to the public without shame. To cast away one's social capital to dine with lepers and sharecroppers, to renounce the throne of a kingdom to wander in the yellow robes of a beggar—in these cases, we give up all the diamonds and honors that glitter on our public facades and live closer to the bone. The allure of the ascetic is that of the human severed from all the striving and social climbing too often encrusted onto the human essence.

Another related case is disappointment. Here too, features that seem to be permanently welded to a person or thing suddenly fall aside like cobwebs, and the thing itself is revealed as a bare core of substandard reality. There is also the allure of loyalty, which faithfully upholds commitment to institutions now in decline, or to friends who have grown difficult. In such fidelity, the newly dubious qualities and relations of the thing are ignored, and we keep the faith with whatever is taken as the underlying dignified core of the thing. We could also speak of surprise in general, since any surprise splits off the previously recognized qualities of a person or thing from its living core, whether the surprise be pleasant or unpleasant. Normal perception simply moves around the exterior of an object or between objects, one step at a time, like a rock climber working his way around the face of a cliff. By contrast, allure initiates a rift in the thing that was lacking before, like a stonecutter making incisions in a granite surface.

All cases of allure are bound up with unusually strong emotions, which already points to their common root. In each case an object is severed from notes that seemed inseparably connected with it, while the notes retain some sort of lingering attachment to the exposed yet distant underlying thing. It would be tempting to say that perception does the same. But this is not the case, since perception merely allows us to move between objects and their independent parts, while allure grants us the power to move between entirely separate levels of the universe, navigating between objects and their notes. All of these events—beauty, humor, metaphor, tragedy, comedy, humiliation, disappointment, loyalty, surprise—make life worth living, and sometimes worth ending. Allure invites us into a world that seemed inaccessible, a world in which the object must be even deeper than what we had regarded as its most intimate properties. Whereas black noise unfolds entirely within a single world, allure resembles a whirlpool or black hole sucking us into another. A decisive question is whether causal relations between objects more closely resemble the black noise of perception or actual allure. But the answer is clear: causation can only resemble allure. For while causation has impact only on certain aspects of the object, its impact is on notes, not parts—and notes, unlike parts, are always inherently linked to the thing as a whole. Indeed, causation and allure are so closely related that they turn out to be one and the same. We should now consider the implications of this view of causation.

Consider what happens between the sensual elements that are buffered against one another in perception. A shaggy dog, a bicycle, a chessboard, and a water-pipe can belong to the same experience, yet all remain autonomous from one another, as only a paranoid visionary would deny. Perception moves from one sensual object to another, or from any given object to its parts: from the chessboard to individual rooks and bishops, or from the dog to its ears or panting tongue. Occasionally, we revise our beliefs as to which parts belong to which objects—for example, a piece of felt strapped to the bicycle might wrongly seem at first to be part of the nearby dog when viewed from across the room. These are all cases in which independent sensual objects either blend into one another, or remain steadfastly independent from each other as contiguous discrete districts. Yet allure can also occur in this situation, in any of the different ways we have reviewed, all of which involve the separation of an object from its own notes rather than its parts. This often occurs in an object that was already lying before us, such as when the chess-pieces sparkle with a feeble glow at dusk as we sit alone in the room, suddenly heartbroken. In other cases, the unity split by allure does not preexist the allure itself, as happens most obtrusively in the case of metaphor. But another such case is causation—here, two objects are brought together to affect each other despite their utter incommensurability, just as money translates food, air travel, books, musical instruments, and the labors of hitmen, mercenaries, courtesans, pie-bakers, and college professors into the same common language. The interior of an object is the site of every form of allure we have mentioned. It is also the place where causation in general arises, since two objects can interact only by first being translated into sensual objects on some larger interior. There are obviously two questions here. One question is how real objects take on the form of sensual objects in the first place. Another question is this: once numerous sensual objects are contiguous in the same space, what causes them to interact or fail to do so? We will begin with this second question, which applies both to allure and to causation in general.

The sensual objects on the interior of a sensual space may be adjacent to one another without coming into relation at all. Some of them already *are* in relation even while remaining merely adjacent for the senses, as in the earlier example of the various pieces of an airplane, which fuse together in reality while remaining perfectly distinct for the observer. But most interesting are the cases of buffer and delay, in which two sensual objects adjacent in the same space are somehow prevented from making contact. Without such obstacles there would be no such thing as time, since all possible relations would run their course in a single impatient flash. This principle of delay does not stem from the dark withdrawal of real objects from each other, because here we are speaking only of contact between sensual objects, and we have seen that these do not withdraw at all, so that real objects are in a sense outside time. But what happens with sensual objects is that they become encrusted with accidents. Such accidents must therefore provide the key to the buffered causation between sensual objects, which in turn is the key to the vicarious causation between real objects, and which in turn is the real key to temporality.

Black noise can only serve as a buffer for allure, and is never allure itself: it merely allows one sensual object to blend into another or remain separate from it. Sensual objects do not interact at all, but only blend into one another (leaving behind the residue of accidents) or fail to do so (leaving behind the residue of contiguous sensual objects). Interaction can only be that of real objects with one another, and hence allure must somehow bring real objects into play. This was the whole paradox of vicarious causation, in which objects must be able to touch without touching. The only way for such interaction to occur is if the object's sensual reality can somehow be reconverted into the notes of a deeper reality. Sensual paper and sensual flame lie entirely on the surface of the world, though encrusted with the brine of accidents, and seem to have no connection with any other reality that could be altered vicariously through their union. This happens only if the flame manages to alter not just the sensual paper that it confronts, but the very bond between this sensual paper and the real paper to which it is somehow linked. Yes, this would be a textbook case of vicarious causation—two real objects affecting one another by means of two sensual objects appointed as their agents or deputies. The question for now is what prevents these deputies from recognizing each other immediately in a crowd. What prevents two sensual objects from instantly functioning as notes of a real object in the first place? Somehow, black noise must provide the answer, because there is no alternative. The black noise of accidents must somehow hamper the energies of the notes of things, converting them into mere innocuous sensual objects, free of any immediate dangerous influence on each other.

For allure to be possible, the opposite must happen. Instead of one object simply blending into another as in metonymy, it must fuse together with it even while resisting it, as in metaphor. The black noise that separates objects must serve both as the dust preventing interaction between objects and also the multifarious entryway of these objects into one another. Somehow, objects are coated with black noise of a kind that leaves them unable to penetrate each other's mists. Yet somehow, these mists are parted, with the sensual objects making contact in such a way that a deeper interaction occurs. We must indicate how this happens. What characterizes all forms of human allure is that the objects it initially works with are all sensual objects, belonging in advance to the same world and not withdrawn from one another. They are present to each other, yet somehow too glazed over with accidents to make direct contact.

Now, we have seen that there are two forms of human allure. There is the kind that splits an already existent object—as when a dog becomes comical and is split from its notes, or a queen becomes tragic and is split from her notes, or a musician's new style disappoints us and she becomes split from her notes. We might call this type of allure "fission." But there is also metaphor, in which a previously nonexistent cypress-flame is summoned into existence for the first time at the very moment when it is split from its notes. We might call this type "fusion." The result of both fission and fusion is identical, and the amount of energy they release is equivalent. In both cases the result is an underlying object that eludes us but whose parts are converted into notes of the thing, notes which make no sense at all in isolation from that thing. In both cases, a bridge is extended toward another world that we cannot experience directly. What seemed to be merely independent sensual objects are now revealed as notes of a distant signaling pulsar—a real object that can never be perfectly translated into the terms of the world we currently inhabit. In both fission and fusion, something happens to unleash allure where there used to be nothing more than the harmless blending or serene detachment of distinct sensual objects.

To repeat, both fusion and fission in the sensual world have the same result, unleash the same energies. Both invoke a reclusive otherworldly object that we are unable to grasp, while also converting previously autonomous sensual objects into notes or marionettes of the otherworldly thing. The cypress-flame, the playful dolphin, or the no longer trustworthy friend orbit silently in the depths beneath us; their notes swarm directly in our faces even while proclaiming their dependence on the depths below. But while the results of fission and fusion are identical, their starting points are not. These two nuclear reactions in the heart of things begin by facing entirely different obstacles. When fusion fails to occur, this is because its objects initially have nothing to do with one another: the poet compares the cypress and flame precisely because they are so obviously *not* the same object, the comparison so obviously *not* banal. But when fission fails to occur, it is for precisely the opposite reason—namely, because a thing is so bound up with its notes that no separation seems to be possible. The notes appear to be one great giant note, with no deeper cryptic object at stake to which all of the notes might belong. The fission of a thing is not just a matter of breaking it up into parts, since perception already does this for us. On the contrary, what fission really does is split the object's single unified note into many.

If fusion is hindered by the black noise of contiguity, fission is obstructed by the black noise of accidents. What prevents all possible causation and metaphor from running its course in a single universal flash is the fact that the sensual world is carved up into different objects bearing at least some degree of autonomy. And what prevents the instantaneous global severing of sensual objects from their apparent notes is the fact that they seem attached to these notes quite closely. We need to consider how these two kinds of black noise occur, and how allure finally manages to surmount them. What we are speaking of is a form of buffered causation in which entities are somehow present in the same space and yet fail to affect each other anyway. We have already said two things about this situation. First, buffering occurs because of black noise, which prevents us from being in total contact with a sensual object, insofar as it is encrusted with jewels and barnacles lent by other entities. Second, buffering occurs because we are in contact with a sensual object only as sensual, and not *qua* note of a real object. These two points actually turn out to be one and the same. A fully exposed sensual object would be nothing other than the naked note of a real object. Yet we do not always come into direct contact with such a note, because its presence is blurred by its mixing and blending with other sensual objects. In other words, sensual objects inevitably become elements, and there is something inherently flat and caricatured about elements, however brilliantly they may sparkle. Elements do not reach toward the depths, toward other levels of the world, but simply act as facilitating links within the current level of experience. The personae swarming about on the interior of any object are primarily elements, not

sensual objects pure and simple. Sensual objects are present at any moment
in vast quantities, yet they mix together in ways that reduce them to what
they are for each other and for us, converting them into elements. When
elements are somehow partially pierced through, this is when sensual
objects come into direct contact with each other—and given that sensual
objects are also notes of real objects, vicarious causation is achieved.

Ultimately, fission and fusion are the same process. We already know
that they have the same result: a distant flickering object is created while
its notes become sensual objects in their own right. But their similarity
runs much deeper than results, just as fire and acid have more in common
than their ability to damage toys. Fission occurs when an object is revealed
to be something more than its sensual notes and thereby splits from those
notes. Fusion occurs because two sensual objects that were destined for
one another have finally managed to come into contact after piercing the
mists of black noise that had previously kept them apart. But notice that
each type of nuclear reaction also performs the function that was seemingly
reserved for the other. The fusion of cypress and flame first requires that
each of these objects be stripped of all the baggage that normally renders
them too dissimilar for union, thereby beginning with fission between the
man and whatever is so clearly not wolf-like about him that it must be left
out of the picture. But by the same token, the fission of the clown from his
colossal red nose requires that he be fused with something else—namely,
with me. For by definition there is no allure if we ourselves are not somehow directly involved in the action. To say that the clown as a cryptic agent
is severed from one of its own ludicrous features is really to say that I
myself have entered into relation with the shadowy subterranean clown
who lies beyond them. There is causal interaction between the clown and
me, as can be denied only by those who limit causality to a narrow range
of effects carried out by atoms. Clearly, all forms of allure resemble each
other in their strong emotional impact upon us. What this really means is
that we enter into relation with the objects exposed or created by allure,
and allow our world to be defined by their presence. To take seriously a
clown, a cute baby rabbit, a beautiful sunset, a treacherous or disappointing friend, or a humiliating situation, is to expend energy that could have
been expended elsewhere instead. To expend energy on one thing instead
of another is to enter into relationship with it. But this is no different from
what we called fusion. To respond to the metaphor of cypress and flame,
or to heed Trakl's words that wolves have entered the gate, is to enter into
causal relation with the object created in this way.

But unless we are wizards and witches, the act of saying "the cypress is
a flame" does not cause real trees to catch on fire. We are not speaking of
a causal relation between trees and flames themselves, but of trees and
flames as sensual objects for me. A metaphor is my problem, irrelevant to

the real cypress or flame and not affecting them in the least. The ultimate difference between allure and causation is simply that allure happens to me and causation happens to something or someone else. Certainly my body can be subject to sheer causal force without this force immediately registering in the domain of allure, such as when my body is quietly invaded by viruses with all symptoms still weeks in the future. But this is something that concerns my body rather than me directly; whatever I am, it is not just my body, or at least not just the part of my body that is attacked by the virus. Notice that allure is able to bring realities into contact that have little in common.

The clown and I make contact through a narrow film of visual and sonorous data, through my prior familiarity with the circus genre and its typical gags, and other intermediaries of this sort. The clown itself (does anyone think of a clown as having gender?) is some sort of withdrawn agent that I cannot touch. Meanwhile, I myself am an entire complex of moods and knowledge and bodily reactions that the clown does not directly touch. Yet somehow our interaction brings us into contact through whatever features do link us, and thereby has an impact on those that do not. The clown may be illiterate, for example, yet still be able to shake my intellectual life to the core with a sufficiently disturbing performance, as has happened to me in both Slovenia and Jordan. In this manner, the clown takes possession of what is strong in me (my cryptic inner life) through what is weak or vulnerable in me (my receptivity to visual data and to humor more generally). This causal relation is an act of violence, and like all violence it is asymmetrical.

Note that humor as such has no more special relationship with violence than do disappointment, humiliation, beauty, charm, metaphor, or gentle caresses. "Violence" here is nothing more than a nickname for causal impact as a whole, for any way in which one thing affects another. Causation in general is what allows one object to inflict blows on another, and causation is undeniably a form of violence, since it involves one thing touching the essence of another through the door of the inessential. Now admittedly, it is possible that I have a causal effect on the clown as well: my body will already have some sort of effect on the body of the clown, as when my breathing in the circus tent helps raise the temperature and make the clown sweat more profusely. But more likely I am just another anonymous spectator whose absence will not be noticed unless I am a famous guest or expected friend. But by contrast with my own irrelevance, the clown will lighten or disturb my own mood for hours to come. There is asymmetry of this kind in all causation, since even reciprocal violence has a different impact on each participant in the fray. The clown's effect on me would not be my effect on the clown even if the relation involved both of us.

All of this is allure. But what happens in allure is no different from what happens in any form of causation. Allure is not a special feature of human psychology that would be absent from plants and rocks, but a feature of me myself as opposed to plants, rocks, and even my own colleagues and brothers. Allure is simply causation in the first person, or executant causation. All other entities have their own experience of allure, and I cannot fill the shoes of any other object and experience life in its stead. When I myself am not on the scene and have no firsthand experience of the relation, then the term "causation" can be used instead of allure; otherwise, the words are equivalent. The inevitable resistance to this suggestion stems from the bias that allure must involve some sort of consciousness, and that only humans and a number of privileged animals have consciousness. To break the link between allure and human consciousness seems to invite the granola free-for-all of panpsychism or vitalism, and therefore we have no alternative but to proclaim human consciousness as the magic trumpet of all philosophy. Pay no attention to the stylistic contortions of those who claim to stand beyond "the idealist subject" or "humanism." Follow their deeds, not their words: they talk about propositions rather than fires and hailstorms; they analyze literary texts, not tornadoes striking villages; they view prisons as a set of documents *about* prisons, and say nothing concerning the thrust of iron bars into concrete and the beating hearts of doomed prisoners.

All of this is people-centered philosophy, whether declared or undeclared. Most readers are willing to overlook this bias as long as the only alternatives seem to be slave-driving positivism or the gullible dance of shamans around voodoo skulls and white buffalo calves. Nonetheless, both panpsychism and the ontologically privileged human subject are united in a single overpowering prejudice: the notion that psyche must be one of the key building blocks of the universe, with the sole disagreement being over how widely this priceless treasure should be distributed. Whereas objects as wildly different as flames, trees, rivers, and moons are all lumped together under the single useless category of "inanimate," the gap between me and my own collection of shirts is supposed to be so brutally vast that philosophy can only hope to deal with me, never the shirts. The more interesting alternative would be to say that minds or souls are simply one sort of object among others. They may be an especially interesting kind of object for those of us with minds or souls, but not objects that are necessarily suited to play a unique starring role in ontology. The key to allure is not consciousness, but *sincerity*. And rocks and dust must be every bit as sincere as humans, parrots, or killer whales. To clarify this requires a detour through the asymmetrical structure of causation.

Metaphor is asymmetrical, for it is I rather than the cypress or flame itself who experiences the cypress-flame. More than this, we saw that the metaphor is internally asymmetrical as well: "man is a wolf" is not reversible without changing the metaphor completely. It matters greatly which thing is robbed of its notes to let them serve another as their new master. Indeed, the asymmetry of every form of allure is usually obvious. Those who disappoint me are not necessarily disappointed by me. Recognition of beauty is often not reciprocal, and when dealing with inanimate objects is presumably never, so. We often fail to laugh at our own jokes, and only occasionally do our humiliations embarrass others as much as us. Actions quite often lack equal or opposite reactions, and when we gaze into the abyss it rarely gazes back. Now, asymmetry entails that one object is active and the other is passive or acted upon; in cases of mutual impact, we are really speaking of two different actions, with the active and passive roles simply reversible. Asymmetry also implies that only one of two objects in a relation is split from its qualities, its black noise cleared away from the scene. Somewhat ironically, it is the *active* participant that is split, while the passive one remains as it is. The clown undergoes nuclear fission before my eyes and is able to act on me precisely for this reason, while I remain a spectator—all surface and skin, no depth. Through various gags or sheer raw attitude, the clown loses its black noise within the relation even as I keep my own. Whatever fog of inessential traits may have hovered about me in this relation, this fog was sufficient to let the allure take place.

Initially there had been a relation between me and some human-shaped apparition, and we confronted each other face to face like two crossed swords. All sorts of shifting qualities swirled around this relation, none of them affecting the basic objects at stake. But suddenly the clown is split from its sensual note, changing everything. Like all sensual objects, the clown was previously both unified and entirely present to me in a flash, though to some degree obscured or encrusted by other sensual objects. It was always surrounded by free-floating parts such as nose, shoes, and hair, but these stood independently in sensual space and could either be focused upon or ignored at will. But afterward, the unified clown-nucleus is fragmented into a plurality of notes that also signal toward the depths, even in cases when the clown is a mere hallucination. This new relation between the clown and me had always been possible, since the necessary objects were all in place anywhere from seconds to decades beforehand. But somehow the relationship was buffered, obstructed by accidental accretions that were thrown into the mix. By contrast, allure draws me into a different universe by way of the actual notes of the clown. A new relation has occurred, and a new object is formed—one that links the clown with me, *but not the reverse.* We need to address two final points. First, how does the buffering of black noise occur? Second, how do the parts of a relation experience that relation? The asymmetry of causation provides the key to both questions.

This book has now spoken of vicarious causation, buffered causation, and asymmetrical causation. These are not three different kinds of causality, but simply three names for the only kind there is. Each of the names tells us something different about the impact that one entity has on another. The root of *vicarious cause* is that every object is a private reality that withdraws from any attempt to perceive, touch, or use it. An object cannot be fully translated or paraphrased; it simply is what it is, and no other object can replace or adequately mirror it. But if an object cannot be touched in its full reality, some portion of its reality must still be open to contact: otherwise, we would be stranded in a world of mutually isolated monads, bridged by a vaguely defined god drummed up into existence for the sole purpose of linking them. Vicarious causation means that objects touch each other's notes, or portions of each other's essences. Yet we have seen that an object is really only a single note rather than numerous ethereal qualities bound together in one physical substratum. The plurality of an object's notes does not belong to the object itself, but rises from the tension between an object and its multiple parts, which never fully commit to the object as whole. This tension plays out in sensual space, in the molten interior of an object or relation. Vicarious causation is possible because a thing's full reality withdraws from the world even as its multiple notes do not recede.

The root of *buffered* cause is that sensual objects are completely present in any relation from the start, but are encrusted with various capes, top hats, and rhinestones that prevent a sensual object from appearing in naked form. Whereas real objects withdraw infinitely from all access, sensual objects are available for contact in principle, but are muffled and shielded by irrelevant coats of glitter. In more technical terms, every sensual object is shrouded in black noise—carryon baggage attached to the object without being essential to it. Now, if the sensual object is shaken free from its black noise and becomes directly present, as happens in cases of allure, it becomes unstable and immediately breaks down into a relation between a distant real object and free-floating notes. This implies further that a sensual object is only truly present when split from its notes; on all other occasions, it wears the costume of an element, overdetermined by the specific accidental shimmerings along its face. On everyday occasions, the cypress as a naked sensual object never appears. We look straight through its irrelevant fluctuations and its various angular profiles toward the abiding sensual object lying underneath. The cypress is involved with other sensual objects, caressing them, negotiating with them, forever drawing and erasing new lines of armistice with them. The pressure of all this black noise seems to compress the notes of the cypress into some vaguely defined union that escapes our close scrutiny, just as atmospheric pressure allows a house to hold together until exploded by the depression of a passing cyclone.

Allure disrupts this union. Allure brings the sensual cypress itself to the fore, and when the ambient black noise is cleared from the vicinity, it also happens that the sensual notes of the cypress break away from its core—leaving behind only the radiation emanating from an apparent real cypress deeper than the one that had resided in our perception. A friend inhabits our daily lives as some sort of ill-defined constant presence amidst shifting events and conversations. But whether through betrayal or pleasant surprise, the friend brings us into a state of allure, separating from his or her notes, which the pressure of black noise had previously compressed into a sleekly unified whole. As a general rule, a sensual object directly appears only in the moment when it comes unglued. Buffered causation plays a crucial role in the world, since it prevents all possible relations and all possible allure from occurring in an immediate flash. It is the principle of temporality or delay. If sensual objects did not coat one another with black noise, the entire history of the world would already have run its course. In this sense, black noise is like the cosmic injustice of Anaximander, which prevents the featureless universe of *apeiron* from being always already achieved.

Asymmetrical cause is what unifies the vicarious and buffered aspects of causation. If vicarious cause means that a real object can never affect a real object, and buffered cause means that sensual objects are blocked from affecting other sensual objects, then asymmetrical cause points to the sole remaining option. Namely, a naked sensual object can still affect an element at times, and in this way a real one can vicariously affect it. Only for this reason can one object impact another without the reverse being true, since objects do not open up to one another directly, but only to concrete elements. To understand the role played by asymmetry, it is helpful to imagine what would happen if causation were regarded instead as symmetrical. If causality were symmetrical, it would be a matter of one sensual object touching another directly, and elements and hence black noise would lose all power to make things happen. All sensual objects in a relation would have to be entirely stripped of their encrustations for any relation to occur, and this would mean that black noise was purely useless noise or wasted energy, never an entryway into causation. More than this, causation simply would not be possible at all, since two objects cannot both become naked to each other—for in that case they would simply repel each other. A sensual object is entirely given from the start, yet in itself it still lacks anything that would allow it to share or interact with others, unless the black noise of its parts is allowed to play some sort of role. If man and wolf or cypress and flame were purely naked for each other, we would simply have two utterly incommensurable sensual objects, and metaphor would never occur: it works only when one splits apart another without itself being split. The asymmetry of causation means that one object uses its inessential radiation to get at the essence of another object. We saw this when wolf split man and flame split cypress, or when I split the clown.

This returns us to the two questions posed a short while ago. How does the buffering of black noise occur? And how do the parts of a relation experience that relation? Both questions should now be approached by way of the asymmetry of vicarious causation. Causation means that two objects interact with one another. Causation is always vicarious because the objects involved must withhold part of their reality from the interaction. And causation is asymmetrical because it is always one object that affects the other; mutual causation is never perfectly reflexive, but requires two separate processes that unfold along different paths. Another way of putting it is that causation always occurs between one sensual object and one real object. Yet somewhat paradoxically, it is the sensual object that is active and which breaks down in allure to point toward a deeper reality, while the real object is passive in the relation and remains stabilized in its sensual or elemental form. For example, the clown awakens allure by seeming to become a ghostly power lying at a distance from its fragmented notes; the clown is the active partner, working effects upon my mood without my being able to return the favor. It becomes alluring by splitting off from its notes, yet only as an object of the senses which splits from its notes—not as a real object, since the latter option would entail the actual death or destruction of the clown, and this seldom occurs even in the most avant-garde circus. In other words, the clown as a sensual object affects me as a real one. And yet this happens only through a strange reversal of roles: namely, the *reality* of the clown breaks through its purely sensual existence, while my own reality remains clothed by those *sensual* features that are receptive to the clown in the first place.

But we should return to the previous two questions, concerning the buffering of black noise and the relation of parts to their wholes. Whatever the details of its functioning, causal interaction does not occur at all times, and this is what buffering means. Objects are in constant proximity without affecting each other the way they would if circumstances allowed. Buffering or black noise are always symmetrical, since in this sphere one sensual apparition merely opposes another: my eyes and a volcano or tent have already come to terms in some specific way even while fending off each other's deeper unexpressed realities. By contrast, causation is asymmetrical, and reaches from one level of reality to the next. Asymmetry is possible because the sensual essence of a thing is already there before us, ready for the taking; it is hidden from us not by infinite withdrawal, but merely with jewelry and other cosmetic disguises, and at times these can be swept aside. To exist in the world is to be encrusted with accidents. Some of these accidents come from without: a volcano presents different aspects thanks to the nearby movement of helicopters or the sun, movements for which the volcano is not responsible. We have referred to these as contiguous or ambient qualities. Others we have referred to as accidents proper. These come from the thing's own parts and are ejected through the heart of that thing as through a wormhole, and come into sensual experience in this way. To relate to a clown, elephant, or snake is also to relate to its parts, yet these parts are processed through the thing as a whole and rendered sensual as notes of the thing, in such a way that the clown's hat or elephant's tail or snake's skin are already tinted with the style of the larger object, not encountered in their own right. These parts are reduced to the terms of the initial relation, so that my relation to the snake as a whole drowns out the parts. Asymmetry is what enables us to break through this buffering and let the parts speak for themselves, as when low-ranking citizens shout censored truths aloud at a passing monarch.

If two naked sensual objects were to appear, these would be pure notes of real objects, and hence could not come into contact. But asymmetry allows a naked note to come into contact with a full-blown encrusted element. In other words, causation uses accidents to get at the things themselves. Instead of seeing them as freestanding sensual objects, it sees them as clusters of notes distinct from a hidden underlying thing. When this happens, the notes cease to be the flat caricatures to which we reduce them, and instead seem to belong to a deeper underlying thing unknown to us previously. This also answers our earlier question as to whether inanimate causation is sincere, for it must be. Sincerity does not mean to stay at some surface level of enjoyment, because no such surface even exists. What it means is to enjoy objects, and the object is always encountered not in the flesh, but as a local ghost hiding in the beyond, dominating the notes that it now lends to our view. Yes, inanimate causation also involves asymmetry, and any asymmetrical relation is necessarily sincere, since it commits the passive component to opening up to the active component. Asymmetrical cause is the fact that multiple objects can share the exact same note. How this sharing happens remains a mystery, and any philosophy book worth its salt needs to end with at least one good unsolved mystery. The current mystery is particularly compelling, since the shared note of multiple objects is the glue of the world, and hence the explanation of all forms of causation. It is the vicarious medium between two separate objects. It is the possibility of black noise insofar as there is always more of it than any given object uses (thereby giving it the character of an accident as well), and finally it explains the asymmetry of causation because it breaks away from one object so as to relate to another.

To grasp how a naked note comes into sensual space at all, and how it additionally becomes shrouded with black noise, we have to understand the relation that the parts of objects have to their wholes. For black noise really comes from the parts of a thing. When two objects come into relation, their parts also enter a shared sensual space, though at first their contact is buffered since they are meeting each other only in terms of the larger relation. From time to time these parts encounter each other independently, no longer merely chaperoned by the larger relation, and set off independent reactions of their own. The plurality of notes in one thing also stems from the fact that its multiple parts are connected through the thing as a whole, and when released by allure are experienced in metaphoric relation to the thing rather than as freestanding independent parts. We have already described to some extent how the parts of a relation stand in relation to its interior. We stand in relation to an interior by experiencing black noise, and it is black noise emitted by the parts of all those objects that are involved in the relation. The essence of the relation is simply the relation itself, *not* the way it is experienced. For the essence consists in existing, not in being seen. And if the essence is hidden from outsiders by withdrawal, it is hidden from insiders by the encrustation of black noise. The responsibility for such encrusting lies with the currently irrelevant parts of the agents involved in the relation. The actual relation does not make use of all the parts, but the *experience* of the relation encounters them all as a kind of background noise, and one that eventually leads to new and surprising consequences. Experience, then, is a way of encrusting the essence of the world with the inessential, and it is from out of this sludge of the inessential or accidental that new relations and hence new objects come to be formed.

Amidst all these difficult concepts we should not lose sight of the theme of the fourfold, which lends the current chapter its title. In *Tool-Being* it was shown that Heidegger's fourfold originates at a shockingly early date (1919) from the intersection of two distinct axes of the world. First, there is the world-renowned Heideggerian difference between an object's presence and its active subterranean being, a schism better known as *Vorhandenheit* vs. *Zuhandenheit*. Second, there is the more obscure rupture between an object's particularity and the fact that it is something at all, something unified. Given that the second axis crosses both layers of reality—that which is present and that which is forever withdrawn—a fourfold structure of reality was the result. This quadruple reality refers to four dimensions found in every entity, not to four distinct types of entity such as gods, mortals, earth, and sky in the *literal* sense. Any specific deity, human, mineral, or moon will mirror all four dimensions, not just the one that seems most literally analogous to it.

A more understated version of the fourfold was also found in the system of Zubiri, one of the least recognized major philosophers of postwar Europe. For Zubiri, an object consists of both "transcendental" and "talitative" dimensions: that is to say, an object is both one thing (transcendental) and a specific thing (talitative). This is analogous to Heidegger's second axis, and also comparable to the difference between Husserl's second and first reductions. But for Zubiri there is an additional difference between a thing "of itself" or in its own right (*de suyo*) and the same thing as viewed merely logically or conceptively by a human mind. And here we encounter a parallel with Heidegger's first axis as well. Although Zubiri gives an interesting account of why he finds Heidegger insufficiently radical, we can ignore such criticisms for now. More important for us are the ways in which the two thinkers unluckily agree.

One point of agreement is that both see the difference between real and conceptive, between subterranean and present-at-hand, as a difference that occurs only once in the cosmos. There is one layer of reality or being, and then merely a second layer where human existence encounters those realities in their relational presence. By contrast, following the magnificent argument of Bruno Latour in *Pandora's Hope* (1999), I have insisted on an indefinite regress of substances, and most probably an infinite one. No object is only substantial or only relational. A chariot or wild dog is an inexhaustible unified mystery for all of the relations that make use of it, but each of these objects is also a relational system made up of countless parts in its own right. Any object can be considered simultaneously under both aspects.

A second and related point of agreement between Heidegger and Zubiri is that both regard human beings alone as having the capacity to double up the levels of the world. In other words, if all human beings were exterminated, there would be at most a single plane of interacting rocks, diamonds, flowers, clouds, and oceans. (Zubiri is enough of a realist not to think that mass human extinction would cause physical objects to disappear, while Heidegger merely gives us the noncommittal and pseudo-sophisticated claim that such objects would neither exist nor fail to exist in the absence of Dasein.) And on this point I follow Whitehead in countering that *all* objects must come to terms with each other, translating or caricaturing one another's reality whether humans are in the vicinity or not. As I see it, the annihilation of all human Dasein would merely kill off seven billion specific objects, and otherwise would not simplify the ontological rifts in the world at all. The difference between "conceptive" and "real," between "presence" and "readiness-to-hand," is not some special effect of human being, but is carved into the structure of relations as such.

Finally, both Heidegger and Zubiri are too restrictive in what they allow to count as real objects. Zubiri's prejudice is that of classical realism à la Aristotle and Leibniz: objects found in nature are granted an essence, whereas farms and butcher's knives are not. Heidegger's own bias stems from technophobic romanticism: a peasant's hovel or wooden shoe are granted philosophical dignity while sneering contempt is heaped upon plastic forks, nuclear reactors, satellite phones, and genetically modified corn. Against both positions, I have argued that an object can be natural or artificial, German, American, or Soviet in origin, and not be any less an object in any of these cases. An object is not that which comes from nature or from peasant handicraft—instead, an object is simply whatever unifies notes, creating a private inner reality that no other object ever exhausts.

But all these objections merely concern the range of application of the Heidegger/Zubiri fourfold. We also need to criticize something in the fourfold's very structure. There is no reason to complain about the first axis, since the present book also defends an absolute difference between the reality of a thing and the way it manifests to another object; I have merely insisted that inanimate objects are just as equipped as human Dasein to reduce other entities to presence-at-hand. But there is something wrong with the second axis and the way that it distinguishes between unity and particularity. The problem is that unity cannot actually be a distinct moment of an object: for unity is a mere concept, not a reality. The only reality is that of *specific objects*. The need to couple the specific features of an object with some sort of embracing unity makes sense only if one believes in separate disembodied qualities in the first place. Such a belief presupposes a difference between qualities and some unifying anchor ("transcendental," "something at all") that binds them—a model jettisoned by this book many pages ago. This book recognizes only objects, not qualities, and with this step there is no longer any room for the bare systematic unity of objects as endorsed by both Heidegger and Zubiri.

In other words, unity and particularity do not exist as separate moments in an object, but are one and the same moment: they are nothing more and nothing less than the object itself. The oneness of a sensual flame is no different from the particularity of that flame, because its notes (or rather, the single flame-note) exist only within that union. The flame-notes cannot survive being transported outside the flame. All unities are completely specific. All objects are both unified and completely specific in the same stroke, not by way of two separate dimensions, not even if these dimensions are termed "inseparable." No duel of two distinct moments is possible if both moments arise together and are utterly identical. Since the thing is always one specific thing, the duel is not between unified and specific, but only between the thing and its *parts*, which tends to pull apart the thing's single unified note into numerous notes. Stated differently, both Heidegger and Zubiri wrongly believe that particularity must always be a form of plurality; hence, both feel the need to introduce a moment of unity in the thing in order to hold together its plural abundance. By contrast, I hold that the individual thing is simply one, and that any plurality it might have actually comes from its parts, not from its notes. The thing actually has only one note, not many—it seems to have many only because it remains linked to its parts, which line it like handles or portholes.

Let's close this lengthy section by changing our terminology and speaking briefly of vertical and horizontal strife in an object. Vertical strife is the difference between real objects and the other real objects that play a role in creating them—namely, their parts, which are caricatured in such a way as to transform them into the notes of the new object. Horizontal strife, by contrast, is what occurs between sensual objects and the others that are grafted onto them—when the notes of a sensual object immediately lead us to other sensual objects as their parts. In one sense a strawberry is a withdrawn reality in the cosmos that both deploys and resists its components; in another sense, the strawberry is a relational caricature encountered by humans, birds, or sunlight, and this sensual strawberry is enmeshed in combat with the sensual parts that provide entry into its carnal essence. The present book tends to describe vertical strife as the combat of things and parts, whereas horizontal strife is generally termed the duel between things and their notes. But parts are involved in both cases, and so are notes. The relation between one level of the world and the next is a relation of parts that are converted into notes in a new unified thing, while the relation within the sensual cosmos is one of notes that lead directly into sensual parts. The interplay between these two axes is the worthy heir to Heidegger's fourfold. When the problem is elaborated in this way, his notoriously vague concept is transformed into something far more concrete, even if countless puzzles remain.

A different sort of puzzle arises when we reflect again on allure: namely, we still need to ask if allure is something merely human, or more than human. By opening a window onto other objects, other levels of the world, allure is a phenomenon within the sensual bond that nonetheless plays out as a form of the physical/causal bond. With the rise of allure, human experience seems to revert to the conditions of inanimate causation, as though humans had turned their backs on the long procession of higher animals from out of the amino acids and the mud, and thrown in their lot with rocks and flames—an act of treason against the other sentient creatures. With allure, the human seems to tend toward the mineral kingdom once more. Yet we are not speaking only of humans, since the allure of humor is already at work when dolphins toss plastic balls or ravens cackle while dropping clothes from a line. We will want to speak more generally about the principle guiding both animal sentience and the highest moments of human cognition. But first, there is old business to settle.

C. Four Questions in One

We can now give a preliminary answer to the four initial questions faced by object-oriented philosophy, transforming them into a simpler and perhaps more elegant problem. The first question was how any relation is possible at all between separate objects, given that objects are defined as withdrawn from each other. The second question was how a thing relates to its own parts. The third question was that of where the world of experience and relation actually occurs, given that a world of objects would seem to mean one made up of nothing but hiddenness, occlusion, withdrawal, utter darkness. The fourth question concerned the barriers that prevent all possible absurd relations from being regarded as real objects. These four problems were designated in shorthand as follows: vicarious causation, the whole and its parts, worlds in a vacuum, and firewalls.

The answer to the first question is that causation between real objects can *only* be vicarious. One such object never touches another, but interacts with its neighbors only by means of notes. These notes differ from the usual conception of qualities insofar as a note somehow already bears the inscription of the withdrawn object to which it belongs. Hence, vicarious causation is always a form of allure, whether this occurs in the experience of human beings or in causal interaction more generally. And if we ask where this vicarious causation occurs, the answer is that it lies on the *interior* of a further entity, in the molten core of an object. When two entities encounter each other as real objects, what this really means is that they encounter each other as *sensual* objects—in that carnal zone where objects brush against one another by way of their elements, rather than merely receding into private crystalline obscurity.

Second, we considered the relation of a thing to its own parts. No object ever exhausts or uses up its components, but merely unifies them to one specific end. But in order for these components to come into contact in the first place, they must already have extended their notes into some medium shared by both from the start, which converts this question into a question of the vicarious causation between the parts of any given thing. Beyond this, we have seen that the parts of an object actually descend into the very interior of that object, so that the nucleus of the thing is the unifier of part and whole in a second and converse sense. That is to say, in one way the parts of a thing are unified from above by coming into contact within the nucleus of another object, giving rise to their new relation which is also an object in its own right; in another way, those parts resist total expropriation by each other and bump up against one another in the interior of the new object in which both are deployed. In each of these cases, the solution to our problem lies once more on the inside of objects.

The third problem was that of worlds in a vacuum, and is easy enough to clarify here. Since objects have been defined as withdrawing from any relation, it has to be asked where interactions can occur at all. If objects were simply windowless monads, there would be an infinity of private worlds but no shared arena in which objects could strike one another with their magic spells or violent blows. The solution to this problem is that the relations of the world always unfold on the interiors of objects, and nowhere else. While every object exists in vacuum-sealed isolation from the others, the interior of each of these objects is anything but vacuous—it is a carnival of whirling sensual elements. Here as ever, the problem is sharpened by focusing on the molten or vaporous interior of an object, where relations are no more or less possible than the continued side-by-side coexistence of diverse elements that do not fuse with one another.

This brings us to the fourth and final problem: firewalls. The issue here was how to differentiate between a real object and mere random aggregates, such as why a specific laser or freight train should count as one thing, while the grand assembly made up of Kenya, the moon, Prince William, and a herd of zebras should not. The easy answer would seem to be that lasers and freight trains have real measurable effects on other things in the environment, whereas junkyard aggregates of the kind just cited do not. We could certainly try to dream up an odd scenario in which such a bizarre agglomeration of things would have a genuine effect—say, an obscure Kenyan holiday in which zebras are released from cages at the first new moon of the year, grievously injuring the visiting prince and increasing world tensions at a key historical moment. The problem is that we have tried to avoid letting external events serve as the criterion for the reality of objects, and if they were used to bail us out now, this would undercut object-oriented philosophy from the start and replace it with a philosophy oriented toward events or states of affairs. But at the same time, if we refuse to employ external efficacy to distinguish between real objects and pseudo-objects, then we might seem to be left with a glutted universe in which all possible objects exist, with only some of them being "actualized" in events, whatever that might mean. Obviously, this would not leave us with the strong sense of objects apart from all events that we require. The solution to the problem, yet again, lies on the inside of objects. For an object is to be defined not by its external efficacy, but rather by its internal reality. To be real is not to have an effect on something outside oneself, but simply this—*to unify notes.* It might be argued that an imaginary dog unifies notes just as much as a real dog. But this is not true, since what the real dog unifies are not the same sorts of notes as the pseudo-dog. In a sense, then, *being is a real predicate*, and one hundred real crowns do bring into play different notes from one hundred illusory crowns—not because being is something real that is added over and above the notes, but because

the metallic sheen of a real coin is not the same as the glimmering of phantom coins in the head of a mental patient. Notes are not interchangeable
from one object to the next, since we have seen that they belong entirely
to the object from which they emerge.

We return to the example of the zebra for a few final remarks. If we
regard the event of prince-being-trampled-by-zebra as an object, then it is
true that this object did not exist until the event actually occurred.
Admittedly, this grand trampling-event-object was only created when it
was created, and not beforehand. But this does not mean that the object
consists solely in its outer effects. After all, the trampling incident not only
has major world implications and numerous unforeseen side effects, it also
has an unfathomable reality not exhausted by its immediate impact. For it
could be interpreted in countless different ways by observers not yet born
or never to be born, could topple kingdoms never to be founded, and in
this way the event can be seen to hold something in reserve behind its current sum total of effects. An object is real when it has, not an outer effect,
but an inner one. Countless objects are real without having any current
impact, bending the notes of their components in terms of their own center of gravity even while these objects remain untapped or undiscovered up
till now, and in some cases perhaps forever. To call all of these untapped
and undiscovered objects merely "potentials" is to display the prejudice
that actuality means "to have an outer effect," which I have argued against
from the start. It should not be forgotten that the question of how we *ver-
ify* the existence of any of these currently suspended objects is quite different from the nature of their existence itself. Once again, we find the
solution to our problem in the interior of objects.

From all of this, we conclude that guerrilla metaphysics or object-oriented philosophy finds its sole topic in the molten dynamics of the interior
of things. All along we have sought to clarify two problems: the reality of
an object itself, and the possibility of relations between separate objects.
And both of these problems gain clarity only when we reflect on that cru-
cible, furnace, and alchemist's laboratory that the interior of a thing truly
is. The reality of a thing *is* its internal reality, which is nothing but a carnival or kaleidoscope of elements, and relations between separate things
become possible only within this smoldering, circus-like interior. These
relations occur vicariously by means of an allure that comes into contact
with a thing's elements and bring into play the entirety of that thing itself
even as it recedes into inaccessible distance. To offer another metaphor, we
need a kind of subatomic or nuclear metaphysics, but one that probes the
interiors of all sizes of objects, not just minute physical atoms. This metaphysics has also been described as a form of quadruple philosophy, since it
arises from the intersection of the aforementioned two axes of division,
which are not quite what Heidegger thought them to be. The

causal/physical bond pertains to each object insofar as it is walled off from its neighbors in vacuum-like isolation, even as each of them leaks a bit of radiation into the interior of the others. The sensual bond is what allows each of the sensual objects on the interior of another object to extend its tentacles in the form of elements, which then mutually interfere with one another. What we are confronted with is an infinite series of sealed chambers, but chambers showing countless trapdoors, slides, and portholes allowing movement from one entity to the next.

Stated more classically, there is no opposition between a single dank cave filled with shackled prisoners and a single well-ventilated outer wall where real objects are carried and from which they project their shadows. Instead, the universe resembles a massive complex made up of numerous caverns, outer walls, alleyways, ladders, and subway systems, each sealed off from the others and defining its own space, but with points of access or passage filled with candles and searchlights that cast shadows into the next. The cosmos is similar to a rave party in some abandoned warehouse along the Spree in East Berlin, where the individual rooms are each surprisingly isolated from all external sources of music, flashing lights, perfumed odors, and dominant moods—but in which it is quite possible to move from one space to the next, and in which the doorways are always flooded with faint premonitions and signals of what is to come.

The only way to get rid of the stale split between reality and appearance is to multiply their intertwining endlessly. This dualism cannot be escaped with sly, cutting-edge denunciations of reality, any more than with crusty insistence upon a perceptionless real world to which the mind adequates itself, and least of all with the vain trump card of pretending that we stand beyond both sides of the question. The first option continues to accept a flat plane of the world accessible to humans, and merely denies that there is a hidden second flat plane called reality; or at best, it concedes the possible existence of the hidden level but denies that there is anything to be said about it. Archconservative realism merely flips the domino, praising the second plane while dismissing the first as derivative. The third position is simply a less candid version of the first, faking an agnostic attitude on the question of reality while taking a hard line against it in practice, converting all meditation on the world into a philosophy of access to the world. But all three positions deny the *levels* of the world, the freshest metaphysical insight of the carnal phenomenologists. All three positions are Flatland philosophies rather than theories that illuminate the mysterious infrastructure of chutes, freight tunnels, and harbor beacons that link one object to the next. The philosophy of human access simply slices off one half of a dichotomy that was already stale to begin with, but eats the other half of the loaf although it is equally stale. To shift the metaphor, imagine an oppressed ocean crew staging mutiny against a sadistic captain, but then merely amputating one of the captain's legs before restoring him to power. The sailors would laugh drunkenly over their rebellion even while steered on the same dreary course that appalled them before, and with the delirious captain now more enraged and less surefooted than ever. Yo-ho-ho! This is all that happens when we congratulate ourselves for abandoning the naive doctrine of a world-in-itself. Like so many mutinies, it scores a quick sack of doubloons and sends a few elderly taskmasters to the gallows, but leaves the basic situation essentially unchanged.

From an initial theory of objects with molten cores, each providing passageways into other objects by means of some germinal form of allure, we have the beginnings of a philosophical method for examining the internal dynamics or carpentry of things. Ultimately, it ought to be extended into a complete system capable of shedding light on some of the traditional problems of metaphysics. Having already sketched the general outlines of vicarious causation, we can now end with a few rough cosmological remarks so as to pave the road just a bit further toward an object-oriented philosophy.

[12]

Some Implications

This book has now secured a new kind of subject matter through its discussion of the ceaseless alchemy underway in the interior of objects. We have abandoned every form of the philosophy of human access, along with all brands of traditional realism and their rigid distinction between real things and mere aggregates. Along the way, we have also assembled the rudiments of a distinct philosophical method, defining the bonds between objects and notes on the one hand and objects and parts on the other as the two fault lines of the universe, fissures that must be examined so as to seek out their laws of separation and compression. But this is still not enough. Our subject matter is still too global to be entirely satisfying. It is too similar to present-day ontology in providing general means for discussing any and all regions of the cosmos, while shying away from any discussion of key forms of *specific* entities in the world. In this sense it pulls up short of the highest task of any object-oriented philosophy: to illuminate those ultimate questions that the general public widely associates with philosophers, but which philosophers, partly through ascetic conceptual rigor but partly through lack of imagination, have been failing to address at all.

Examples of these specific topics are not hard to come by. Every intelligent child wonders about the nature of space and time, yet these topics are rarely considered by philosophers today—it is generally the human *experience* of space and time that is placed on the table rather than these realities themselves. The exact gradation of sentient intelligence among humans, animals, plants, robots, and cement is another question that mesmerizes the general public, which is then shocked when it turns to philosophy for guidance and finds little but metadiscourses about the conditions of possibility for posing the question in the first place. (For this reason I often prefer the books of hard-nosers such as Daniel Dennett and the Churchland family to anything emerging from the Valley of the Linguistic Turn.) When the problem of evil is raised following massacres or natural disasters, there are always interesting thinkers available to offer their views to magazines or talk shows, yet one always senses that there is a wide gulf between such pronouncements and the cutting-edge themes of both analytic and continental philosophy, as though it were somehow an act of slumming condescension to share such discussions with the public. A faint sneer always hangs in the air at such moments—the sneer of excessive professionalism.

Death is another key problem about which we learn little from contemporary philosophers, and I am not among those who hold that Heidegger contributes much to the discussion by reducing the theme of death to that of anxiety or nothingness. The nature of God has now fallen from the ranks of serious academic problems altogether, even though the knee-jerk atheism of contemporary intellectuals is as vulnerable to instant reversal as any high fashion at any time. Sexual difference is such a powerful rift in the cosmos that it affects us personally as much as any, yet the hundreds of philosophical studies of this theme too often paint it in the bland monochrome of oppression or power. The same holds for the pivotal experience of gliding into a foreign culture, which today's most fashionable philosophers now explain only by censuring all of our remarks about such cultures as tainted projections of ourselves coded by the stratagems of imperial mastery, an increasingly monotonous song. For against all expectations, we often learn more about foreign things from Marco Polo or T. E. Lawrence than from the most vehement technical orations on colonialism (though I am sickened by parts of Lawrence, and sickened by every one of Flaubert's letters from Egypt, with their snarling toasts to bigotry and physical aggression and their cruelty toward all living things from Coptic monks to stray dogs of the desert). *A fortiori*, we gain more energy from reading Freud than from the numerous complaints of his denigrators. This is not because such authors are right in what they say about barbarians or phalluses—they may often be brutally wrong—but because their style has a trace of that moral authority that comes from grappling honestly with the contours of things, rather than the pious official authority that comes from merely denouncing the hypocrisy of others. After decades of flailing ourselves for our intellectual crimes, it is time to put ourselves on the line by standing somewhere in particular rather than scoring repeated ironic victories by stripping masks from the faces of the mighty, and replacing the masks only to strip them away once more. The model of intelligence as *critique* and *opposition* has entered its phase of decadence.[19]

The problem to which I refer is philosophy's problem, not the world's, since the world does not need philosophy to ride to the rescue by providing intellectual foundations for it. The very idea that knowledge even needs a foundation gives too much credit to our own status as the source of knowing, and too little credit to the various planes of objects that compel knowledge to adapt to them on a level-by-level basis. The question is not how philosophy can ground new approaches to other disciplines, but rather how it can learn to distinguish between the brilliant, surprising work and the predictable, axe-to-grind, mediocre work that is already done in those disciplines. Human activity is object-oriented by its very nature: geologists respond to the evidence of strata exposed in a canyon, just as chefs adjust their actions to the level of pepper already tasted in a stew, and penitent friends respond to the exact degree of anger in our voices. Our specific knowledge of things is not "ontic," but object-oriented, and masonry and welding are no less in contact with the basic fissures of the world than is critical epistemology. What is proposed here is not a new onto-theology that would establish one entity as the highest of all and then judge the rest by how fully they incarnate the presence of this hidden god. What is proposed is simply an onto-*ontology*,[20] a theory that would map out key domains of specific objects and articulate where one ends and another begins. A full object-oriented philosophy could not be expected to deal with every possible object, just as phenomenology was never expected to describe all appearances in the world (though in quantitative terms it certainly could have done more). What could reasonably be expected is a renewed discussion of some of the traditional problems of metaphysics, as well as a wider range of objects perhaps including entities as specific as cats, millet seeds, Lebanon, salt, and the moon. For the near term these detailed topics lie too far from the conceptual equipment at our disposal. Philosophy is always compelled to start big, to deal with objects of far-ranging or even universal scope. We will begin with some rough suggestions about the nature of theoretical comportment and how it differs from the themes of allure, sheer sensation, animal life, and relationality in general. We should also offer a brief sketch of the cosmological problems of space and time, so central to philosophy. But progress in any of these areas is constantly threatened with relapse into *critique*, that most deeply rooted intellectual habit of our time. Let's begin, then, with a final warning against the model of intelligence as critique, freedom, transcendence, negation, clearing, or opposition.

A. Not Critique

What must be rejected from the start is the prevailing model of humans as transcending or negating the world, as critics who break loose from animal bondage and stand in a windy, starry space of freedom. We should be equally suspicious of those hermeneutic versions of critique that merely add the caveat that perfect transcendence is impossible. For even when this proviso is added, it is still a question of trying to rise above what is taken for granted and seeing it "as" what it is. Both models support the pedagogically influential idea that philosophy is a kind of critical thinking less attached to the world than other modes of dealing with objects, a style of cognition opposed to the gullibility of the unreflective. Some people put this model of philosophy to work by mocking the triviality of "ontic" acts, dismissing major political and scientific events as beneath their attention, perhaps even forbidding their children to read newspapers due to the merely superficial, ontic character of journalism. Others enact critical thinking by challenging their peers to endless oral disputes, assertively poking holes in each other's argumentation, competing to free themselves ever more decisively than their rivals from all naive presupposition—the sort of pushy, clambering atmosphere that would have crushed such melancholic loners as Plato and Spinoza. Indeed, there are many who think that philosophy amounts to nothing more than this: the ability to knock down all comers. In one sense, critical thinking deserves praise for acting as a corrosive fluid on dogmatic tradition, and our educational institutions must encourage this skill at the introductory level. But at a later stage it easily becomes counterproductive, for there is a sense in which the great thinkers are always far more childlike and gullible, far more involved with some mesmerizing central idea than all of the wary, uncommitted, replaceable critics. For contrary to popular belief, it is not philosophers, but only ironists, transgressors, blasé hipsters, lizards, and cows who remain relatively free of fascination with the world around them and reduce to dust whatever they might criticize or even eat, converting all objects into terms commensurate with themselves. To be a critic is to eat the world, leaving no seed left over to blossom in the spring.

This is not to say that only philosophers are able to avoid this temptation, since it is not a lower form of human who devotes herself to chemistry, opera, sports leagues, epic poems, fashion shows, or petroleum commodities. What distinguishes humans from animals is not some sort of critical distance from our surroundings, but rather an expansive fascination with all domestic and exotic things; no animal knows the gullible attachment to things that humans enact in the practice of religion or the labor of designing a submarine. We are not more critical than animals, but more object-oriented, filling our minds with all present and absent objects, all geographical and astronomical places, all species of animal, all flavors of juice, all players from the history of baseball, all living and dead languages. We do not remain in the holistic prisons of our own lives where things are fully unified by their significance for us, but face outward toward a cosmos speckled with independent campfires and black holes, packed full with objects that generate their own private laws and both welcome and resist our attempts to gain information. We even devote endless fascination to objects that turn out not to exist—empty fears, phantoms, rickety theories, cartoon characters, false friends, glacial highland monsters. No animal is ever duped or hypnotized as deeply as we ourselves can be. If we are critics and analysts, then we analyze only in order to gullibilize ourselves still further, inserting ourselves into worthier forms of naiveté than before. As we develop we become more innocent and more fascinated, not less so. This may be the ultimate lesson of the famous three metamorphoses of Nietzsche's *Zarathustra*.

The distinction between critique and fascination is no mere toying with words, but suggests a very different style of philosophy from the more popular model of critical/analytical thought—a kind of *constructive* thinking. While it is certainly better to train students to pick apart flaws in arguments than to leave them as easy prey for sophistry and propaganda, these are not the only two options, and both are too easy to improve us as thinkers. What we really need are not more critical readers, but more vulnerable ones, readers so hungry for the unexpected that they can "recognize a good [idea] when they see [it],"[21] to paraphrase William James's view of the essence of higher education. But this implies the rare ability to become dissatisfied with the dominant trench warfare of one's own age. For this reason, when asked by friends to define philosophy, I have taken to saying that philosophy means to find ideas that bore us and invent ways to make them obsolete. But this is difficult, and requires as much scrupulous respect for reality as the construction of bridges and power plants whose failure would result in the deaths of thousands. It cannot be allowed to degenerate into a kind of ultra-hip mannerism.

There is now available a useful English edition[22] of the early reviews of Kant's *Critique of Pure Reason*, which are shocking in their ability to miss the point. Reading these reviews we discover numerous reasonable criticisms of Kant that persist to this day, and even a number of discerning compliments. Yet none of the first reviewers is able to recognize the revolutionary kernel in Kant's now idolized book. There is plenty of "critical thinking" at work in these reviews; the authors are not fools. Their chief deficiency is subtler than this—they simply overlook the surprising treasure that lies before them, and enlist Kant's book into the existing leaden-paced trench warfare between well-known opponents that dominated their era as it does every era. Put differently: the reviewers had too little capacity for surprise, a capacity that Paul Berman has recently identified with wisdom itself.[23] Wisdom means the ability to be surprised because only this ability shows sufficient integrity to listen to the voice of the world instead of our own prejudice about the world, a goal that eludes even the wisest of humans a good deal of the time. While the critical intellect surveys the land from its lofty tower, punishing gaffes and discrepancies wherever it finds them, only inventive thinking is able to be surprised, because only such thinking stays in close contact with the contours of the world, listening closely and in silence to its mysterious intermittent signals.

Somewhere, Santayana writes that laughter and worship are the two things that take us beyond the boundaries of this world. I would say the opposite: that laughter and worship are what bind us to the world more tightly than anything else. The same holds for thinking as a whole, which cements us to the universe rather than freeing us from it, since freedom really occurs only in the self-absorption of laziness, indifference, selfishness, or animal need. In this sense, any engineer who invents a new electronic device is already far more of a thinker than the critical Heideggerian intellectual who complains vaguely that we should "stop and think" before using the tool. If the machine in question is truly an abominable invention, then it is best opposed not by some anemic critical proofreading of its possible misdeeds, but rather by a compelling invocation of all the counter-machinery threatened by the new device (marshland, folk dances, the autonomy of local farmers).

For similar reasons, it is a weak criticism of a historical work to complain loosely that it has not "proven" all of its claims; a stronger critique would be to summon up all of the major historical actors that were downplayed or omitted in the historian's account. Likewise, it is relatively fruitless to scan through a philosopher's book and expose its numerous redundancies and non sequiturs as analytic philosophy trains us to do; far more devastating is to place before the reader a series of questions that the philosopher never posed, the neighboring ideas never ventured, the ignored new alternatives never considered, or the simple predictability, nitpicking tedium, and lack of gambler's spirit in the work lying before us. While relatively few books are hopelessly riddled with errors, numerous books are too boring to be worth our time.

What is most important is never critique, but invention and counter-invention. As Michel Serres puts it: "philosophy is an anticipation of future thoughts and practices . . . Not only must philosophy invent, but it also invents the common ground for future inventions. *Its function is to invent the conditions of invention.*"[24] To invent always means to put oneself in motion along with what is invented, to hitch oneself to the wagon wherever it goes, to travel elsewhere than one was. By contrast, to critique without innovating implies that we remain where we already stand and merely chop down the trees planted by others, the reactionary gesture par excellence. If enlightenment was once a matter of debunking traditional pieties, it should now be a matter of creating new ones—not arbitrarily, but rigorously and in accordance with the demands of the tectonic plates of the world. Unfortunately, there are moments when it seems that the most treasured whipping boy of the critical intellectual is still the Wizard of Oz, the hypocritical zero who manipulates the world with illusions until his curtain is finally torn to shreds and his deceptions exposed. While such debunking may be necessary work at times, we should not forget that it is mainly the work of dogs (*cynics*, to say it in Greek). And instead of releasing seven hundred dogs from the city pound to tear away even more curtains and expose ever more frauds by the mighty, the work of the thinker should be to find the counter-wizard, or to pave the way for him oneself.

But the time has come to ask about the nature of sensation. If the difference between humans, animals, and rocks is not an absolute ontological distinction, we want to know what sort of distinction it actually is. If laughter and worship bind us deeply to the world, we also want to explain theoretical comportment in terms of bondage rather than freedom. We need final escape from the tyranny of the as-structure, even from the hermeneutic kind that claims to be haunted by a hidden depth. We need an account of theory that no longer views it as separated by a colossal gap from all other relations in the world. We seek a form of invention no different in kind from the blossoming of cherry trees or the compression of carbon into diamond.

B. Gradations

The theme of representation is one of the recurrent problems of philosophy. Certain special entities known as sentient organisms are granted a unique ability to perceive images of the world, rather than merely responding to it with blind causal force as subsentient entities are supposed to do. The hermeneutic school of Heidegger and his successors claims to have left the problem of representation in the past. For hermeneutics there is supposedly no magical gap between humans and the world, since humans are always already involved with objects, and hence there is no pure representation of the world free of the prior interpretation and use of objects. In one sense this is a clear step forward, but in another it yields no progress at all. For with the notion that human beings are rooted in a specific factical life rather than standing at a distance from the world and observing bloodless images of it, we do come one step closer to dethroning the privilege of human beings in philosophy. Yet hermeneutics still ascribes to humans (and perhaps even to animals) an apparently miraculous power: the ability to convert the sheer impact of the world into pictures or simulacra of such impact. Humans still transcend the world and contemplate it, even if only partially, and this makes humans different in kind from mere paper, sand, or gold. It is still humans alone who can perceive the world, and the philosophical gap between sentient and inanimate or object and appearance is still taken as a given. This in itself would not be so bad, since most of us would willingly concede important differences in the structure of conscious and unconscious objects. But the question is whether the gap between conscious and unconscious entities is so unspeakably vast that it needs to be built into the very foundation of ontology in a way that the chasms between mammal and reptile or plant and fungus never are. For hermeneutics, there is still an absolute gulf between two types of entities, with humans and possibly animals on one side and all remaining objects on the other. A crucial ontological structure—the as-structure—is ascribed to certain entities and denied to others. But this means that Heidegger grounds his ontology in an ontic rift between specific *types* of objects. And in fact, he has no hope of explaining how the as-structure magically arises only for certain objects and not others. Nor does he ever attempt such an explanation.

I have suggested that the real stakes in ontology lie at a far more primitive level than any of the well-known special properties of human being. The as-structure is found even in inanimate matter; the dual axes of the world are everywhere and not just in some anxious, mournful human space that would exclude such supposed inferiors as almonds and glass. One possible antidote to this bias would be to embrace panpsychism and claim that even rocks and milkweed must already show crude traces of cognitive power. Such doctrines are now wildly out of fashion, and are generally exiled to the wastelands and gullies of the philosophical world, the eternal homeland of renegades, outliers, pariahs, hermits, vagabonds, and unemployable cranks. It would take a short memory to think that such theories will remain unfashionable forever: most abandoned concepts return someday in modified form, as the crop rotation of history brings every fallow field back to life sooner or later. Yet reviving panpsychism would not solve our current problem, since this refreshingly freewheeling theory actually preserves the central problem of human-centered philosophy: namely, it still assumes that cognition is something so poignantly special that ontology cannot live without it. After all, no one ever claims that inanimate matter must possess other human features in germinal form, such as five-fingered hands, a spinal cord, taste buds, laughter, or musical skill. I have yet to hear anyone speculate that rocks and maple sap display a primitive form of language. In this respect, even philosophical cranks have proven themselves to have limited imaginations. For some reason it is sentient perception alone that is deemed so important that certain fringe schools allow it to balloon into an ontological feature of objects as a whole.

And this merely displays the well-worn assumption that there is something magically unique and inexplicable about the ability to create images of things rather than merely submitting to their blows. When hunters and gatherers came to develop agriculture, few historians deny that this change is of staggering importance for human history. This shift is much more than a difference of degree: it is a revolution that triggers the unforeseen rise of cities, armies, monarchies, and bureaucratic specialists. Even so, no one tries to convert agricultural life into some sort of magic ontological principle; no philosopher carves up reality into entities that farm and entities that do not. When birds first developed wings at some point in their evolutionary history, this was a crucial shift that opened a new reality and new lifestyle to these creatures, inviting them for the first time to long-distance migration and the building of nests in trees. Despite this landmark step in the history of animals, no philosopher sees the gap between winged and nonwinged creatures as immeasurably vast. No school of "panpterists" steps forth to claim that even dirt and sunlight must have wings in some imperceptible, germinal form.

Heidegger makes an important mistake by locating one of his pivotal ontological features (the as-structure) in certain kinds of objects at the expense of others. For him, only one kind of entity transcends, nihilates, or rises above the world to see it "as" what it is, and that entity is human Dasein. To use a term that Heidegger himself avoids, only one kind of entity is conscious, and for this reason the very existence of human beings is supposed to introduce a vital cleft into being itself. This is not only a typical case of human arrogance in philosophy, but also has an air of voodoo or fetish about it—like some tribal myth in which the world was a lifeless soil until sprinkled with talking magic beans. We will never overcome this voodoo ontology by joining forces with the panpsychists and demanding that the special powers of human consciousness also be divvied up among dust, cactus, water, and melons. Instead, we overcome it only by denying that the special features of human consciousness are built into the heart of ontology at all. The history of the universe is packed with numerous fateful revolutions: the emergence of the heavier elements from hydrogen; the birth of solar systems; the breakup of Pangaea into multiple continents; the emergence of muticellular life, the beaks of birds, and the gills of fish; the first dreams in early animals; the domestication of cows and dogs; the shift from papyrus to paper; navigation across open sea rather than playing it safe along the coasts; electricity and telephones; phenomenology, quantum theory, and psychoanalysis; the atomic bomb, smart weapons, credit cards, steam engines, atonal music, internal combustion, and blood transfusions. My claim is that sentient consciousness, human theory, and language all belong on the same list with these other examples, and not on some sanctified ontological throne from which they might proclaim that conscious images of the world are infinitely different from the inanimate causal impacts of that world. There is no absolute gap between objects and images, but only ubiquitous gaps between one object and the next. Images are merely sensual objects, and sensual objects lie always and only on the interior of real ones.

Object-oriented philosophy is not panpsychist, but only "panallurist," to coin a ridiculous and linguistically inept term. I have argued that allure exists in germinal form in all reality, including the inanimate sphere. This by no means implies that rocks can think and feel, just as it never entails that mulberry bushes have wings in germ or that sand grains tacitly know how to manage farms or fabricate stone tools. Allure is something far more primitive than any of these revolutions: indeed, allure is the principle of revolution as such, since only allure makes quantum leaps from one state of reality into the next by generating a new relation between objects. Without allure, we are trapped amidst the swirling black noise of any given sensual space. Even if the world were filled with nothing but dust, allure would already be present, and the whole of ontology would already be operative. Human consciousness, perception, language, or "death-drive" (Žižek) are certainly revolutionary in their own way, but they do not cause the sort of fateful rupture in the world that all idealists imagine. The ontological structure of the world does not evolve or undergo revolutions, which is precisely what makes it an ontological structure. Only objects undergo revolutions— and human beings make up just a few billion objects among others, and are not special guests at the table of Being whose absence would simplify the universe immeasurably. Our dignity lies elsewhere than in some wizard-like power to see the world "as" it is. The cosmos is vast, and we are just one chemical in the lab, one species of leopard in the zoo, one atom in the haystack. We are one kind of object among others, and like the others we have our characteristic glories and defects. But this is our own problem and the problem of the objects that live near us. It makes no difference to Being itself whether humans die off or not; the axes of the world will continue their strife long after we have all succeeded in murdering each other.

Every corner of the world is torn asunder by two axes of division; the world is a kind of fourfold, tetrad, or quadrate. The inhabitants of this fourfold are objects, and between objects there are always gradations. We distinguish between animal, vegetable, and mineral, between pre-Mohamedan and Islamic poetry, England before and after the Norman conquest, pre- and post-Kantian philosophy, and Manhattan before and after 9/11. Each of these differences involves a change in tenor of some specific region of the world, yet none of them are basic ontological distinctions: they are ontic distinctions, and I aim to convert the word "ontic" into a term of approval. The world is made up of countless gradations, and allure is the only principle we know of that can explain such gradations. It must be differences in allure that somehow account for the different lives of animals, plants, rocks, mushrooms, jesters, artists, sophists, merchants, tyrants, guardians, and philosophers. In order to take a first crude speculative crack at this theme, let's briefly review everything we know about allure—which is already far less than we would wish.

Allure splits an object from its sensual notes. It cannot split an object from its real notes, since this would require that the object be destroyed. By splitting apart sensual objects, allure generates two byproducts of almost radioactive intensity: the distant real object signaling from beyond, and the sensual notes that had previously been implicit and compressed into a single point of unity, but which are now fragmented and drawn toward the deep real object to which they seem to belong. We also saw that allure must occur even in the inanimate realm, since otherwise causation would be impossible, and the world would be made up of frozen and isolated monads. But even this could not happen, since without allure the levels of the world would never communicate, and without communication no object could ever be built up out of parts, meaning that nothing would have any specific qualities in the first place. Allure turned out to be the key to all causation, which is always vicarious, buffered, and asymmetrical. There is no need to revisit the technical aspects of the theme here. The important thing for now is that allure openly places at stake objects that were formerly muffled, acknowledges them as forces to reckon with, rendering the object itself distant while giving us intimate contact with a plurality of notes. We have seen repeatedly that one entity does not gain direct access to another, and neither can it approach the other entity gradually, as though each view of the object were somehow measurably closer to it than the previous version. Instead, one object translates another in more or less adequate way, and does so precisely by allowing the object to manifest itself as something more than all of its current effects in our world. Perception, intelligence, and language all serve as ways of translating objects into a sphere where objects come to be at issue for us. Somehow, different ranges or quantities of allure provide the basis for different quantities of sentient or cognitive power. Our bodily organs are nothing but translation machines, transforming various energies from the outer world into terms that we can grasp or fail to grasp, allowing objects to show their faces in new and more compelling ways than before. Even when our digestive system translates bread into fuel and our nerves reduce pin-pricks to pain, this is not sheer appropriation or destruction, but rather a way of leveraging all that is strong in these objects by way of their most vulnerable points. Somewhat paradoxically, to appropriate something is also to pay tribute to it—precisely by acknowledging that its frailty is a door through which we hope to enter and participate in its mysteries, even in those cases where mastery is our aim.

All consciousness is allure, but not all allure is consciousness. What we find in allure are absent objects signaling from beyond—from a level of reality that we do not currently occupy and can never occupy, since it belongs to the object itself and not to any relation we could ever have with it. Allure is the presence of objects to each other in absent form. It is the alpha factor of the universe, found in all objects from the ground up, but gradually built up into increasingly larger and more intricate shapes. While allure has no hope of ever getting us closer to the objects themselves, it can unleash objects that had been largely muffled in their relations with us, and can translate already recognized objects into more potent form. Allure is the fission of sensual objects, replacing them with real ones. It is also the principle of all concreteness, insofar as it points to objects apart from all relational impact that they have on us. In this way we invert the notion of concreteness found in Whitehead, who holds that an object is concrete only when we consider all of its prehensions or relations with other objects. Without this maneuver, Whitehead fears we will be left with an abstraction or vacuous actuality rather than a concrete object. But quite the contrary— the only truly concrete thing in the world is an object, and its relations with other objects can only reduce it to abstraction, even if new objects manage to be created in the process.

The primary way in which allure expands its scope is simply through building up a physical body with organs capable of alerting us to that which was previously buried. To develop eyeballs, wings, upright posture, an opposable thumb, or a central nervous system is to take stock of a whole range of new objects that were never sensed before. Inevitably, it also means to lose contact with some previously attained sensual objects, such as the scents or chemical traces that play a large role in the lives of dogs or ants. Physical changes of this kind continually shift the range of objects that have an impact on us. But for animals as for humans, to sense objects is not to transcend or rise above them: it is to descend into their depths, lured away from all the sheer manifestations by which they make themselves known to us. When dogs approach and smell a dubious stranger, they do not remain at the level of odors, but identify a potent withdrawn individual behind those odors; real poets compose lines not to add to their total corpus of pro- ductivity, but to wipe away a bit more of the dust obscuring a style that has already announced itself vaguely but is still concealed by extraneous clutter or the lingering echoes of mentors; real philosophers make arguments not to knock down the positions of rivals, but to establish the compelling char- acter of the model of the universe that generates their arguments in the first place. As humans come to terms with objects such as fossils, ozone, or oil, they may well go on to manipulate those objects, and may do so wisely or demonically or in some combination thereof. But humans do not thereby become sheer nihilistic manipulators turning objects into a stockpile or standing reserve enslaved to our predetermined purposes. To become an oil baron, a eugenicist, or a blitzkrieg commander is also a kind of sincerity, one that transforms the life of the person in such a way as to involve new daily habits, reading materials, research trips, hometowns, even new colleagues and heroes. The object may be altered or demolished by the force of our will, but we are altered by the contours of the object as well, even if we shatter it with a single blow.

By coming to terms with an increasing range of objects, humans do not become nihilistic princes of darkness, but actually the most sincere creatures the earth has ever seen. Anthropologists sometimes describe humans as apes frozen in arrested development, in perpetual childhood. We are the most childlike of creatures, and our violence is the wrath of children even when we are equipped with especially dangerous toys. Wolves are haunted by cries in the night in a way that sand grains are not, and humans are haunted by metaphysical concepts and fantasy tales in a way that wolves are not. What distinguishes humans from animals is not some sort of arbitrary shift in the power of the as-structure, but simply a new range of access to objects, one that plays out in the first instance through our sheer physical differences from the animals. And unlike most animals, we continue to increase our bodily organs with the external proxy of mechanical and electrical devices, and the day may come when these proxies are no longer external. The question concerning technology is not the theme of how objects are transformed into mere fuel, reduced to reservoirs of presence and incinerated in various furnaces. Technology is really a question of translation, of changing long-dead ferns into the motion of school buses, and the vibrations on embassy windowpanes into transcripts studied by spies (as shown most clearly in the case studies of Bruno Latour, that true metaphysician of case studies). The printing press does not convert truth into stockpiled information, but brings the world of dead queens and knights into my living room in twenty-first-century Cairo. It does not reduce objects to standing reserve any more than my fingers and eyes already do. And the atomic bomb, that poster child of the Heideggerian stockpile, arguably changes our patterns of life no more than did agriculture or the longbow.

Efforts are frequently made to locate human uniqueness in language or tool-making, in the ability to plan for the future, or in our having a history rather than a fixed essence. But some of these features are arguably found among the higher animals, and in a few cases the evidence seems fairly obvious. Beyond this, none of these features alone is sufficient to explain human peculiarity. We can state far more generally that humans are the most object-oriented animals. We are the most nihilistic creatures only because we are the most gullible, only because our powers of destruction survey a wider field to which to apply their childlike energies, whereas sharks or scorpions never dream of eating empires and moons.

Throughout the ages it has been said that the uniquely human attribute is abstraction, that we humans can pick out universals from the fog of perception where dogs and birds see only specific cases. But allure is always the allure of concrete objects, not of universals. It is a process of concretion and not abstraction, as Hegel already knew when he wrote that the uneducated person thinks abstractly, not the educated one. Perception and relation are already abstractions; they are a reduction of the full reality of objects to a limited range of effects that they have on us or on other components of their surroundings. The concreteness of objects (as already seen in Aristotle's primary substance) refers to something so real that no description or definition ever does it justice. Whatever it might be that humans do, it is not abstraction, but rather an exposure of their surfaces to an increasing variety of concrete objects—and concrete objects, like classical substances, are what always *elude* the senses. If paper and fire tend toward a kind of allure that exposes them to objects of direct physical effect on their parts, sensation is already a principle of distance. It creates a zone of safety, sensitive to objects but not immediately giving way to their force. It does this by annexing numerous organs or tools and using them to hoard the signals of countless objects in a single treasure chamber. An animal organism is the first great translation-machine, rendering the motleyest crew of objects into a single mother-tongue: the language of the *soul*, which Aristotle regarded as the ultimate organ of the senses. The tendency of any soul is to assemble a single holistic mass in which the sensual parts of objects mix together and unify. But this sensual tendency is countered from the start by the inverse movement of intelligence, which tends toward antiholism, chopping apart incarnate elements and leaving us with a forest of ghosts—phantom objects that never show themselves. If sensation is the principle of unity, intelligence aims to split the world into districts, into isolated objects flickering independently from beyond. And like every exercise of intelligence, philosophy is less a creation of concepts than a creation of objects. Ultimately, the phrase "object-oriented philosophy" is redundant.

C. Time and Space

The classic philosophical controversy over time and space concerns whether these structures of the world are independent realities or merely networks of relations between entities. More simply put, the question is whether time and space would still exist even if all objects were suddenly annihilated. This debate occurs in magisterial form in the correspondence between Leibniz and Samuel Clarke (acting on behalf of Newton). For Clarke and Newton, space and time are absolute containers that would continue to exist even if completely drained of all entities; time would still move forward at a uniform rate even if all its contents were incinerated into vanishing smoke. Leibniz regards this view as incoherent, holding instead that time and space have meaning only as a kind of relative ordering among the individual things that exist. Echoing earlier Islamic debates, Leibniz decries the absurdity of claiming that the universe could have been created twenty days earlier than it was, or seventy meters further to the west. For under these scenarios everything would move in unison, and there would be no relative change among objects at all.

The question can be rephrased slightly to ask whether time and space are autonomous substances or only interlocked systems of events. When stated in this way it forms an exact parallel to the question of whether objects should be regarded as indivisible and substantial ultimates, or whether they are merely a nickname for a certain series of tangible effects or bundle of qualities. In the case of objects we were forced to reject both alternatives, since both turned out to be exaggerated and untenable. For precisely the same reason, we must reject both the Leibnizian and Newtonian views of space-time. On the one hand, we must agree that space and time cannot be empty objective containers, and that all of the paradoxes Leibniz ascribes to absolute space and time remain insoluble. On the other hand, it cannot strictly be true that space and time are merely relational: this is at best a *half*-truth, for if the whole of space and time were relational, all objects would be sucked into these relations entirely and could not be carved up into districts in any way at all. Sheer relation without barricades and boundaries would mean the pure totality of *apeiron*, and this is not what experience shows us. If space and time are relational in one sense, there is another sense in which they must be *anti*-relational, since we can easily speak of parts of space or eras of time in the plural.

Objects shift about us as we advance and retreat in their midst. Yet there is also a sparkling and glittering along the facades of objects that does not alter them in their core. The appearance of the Taj Mahal changes minute by minute after sunrise, and this happens even more rapidly with a glass bottle set before a fire or a piece of pottery spinning on a wheel. Numerous gradations are possible in the shadings of light projected on barns, warehouses, statues, and armies. Everything from whirling dervishes to pencils can be viewed from numerous angles and at numerous distances and in every imaginable mood. None of these fluctuations change the object we are looking at, and all show us merely differences in degree, not binary shifts from one sensual object to another. Time itself flows gently from one state of such objects to the next, and these states can circle back repeatedly to give us more of the same profiles that we encountered before. Notice that these observations are clearly analogous to the internal life of an object—the interior world in which the black noise of accidents, relations, and notes shimmers on the surface of sensual objects. When we speak of time, we are not speaking of an absolute constant force that wheels onward regardless of the deployment of specific objects. But by the same token we are also not speaking of a mere relation between things: for if relational systems told the whole story, they would give rise only to sleek and instant cosmic unity, the ultimate exaggeration to which every form of holism leads. Finally, when we speak of time we are also not speaking of the *consciousness* of time. Nor are we referring to a special ecstatic feature of human beings whose own projections of futuricity first set static objects trembling in a dynamic threefold.

Instead, to speak of time is to speak of the black noise on the interior of any object, in which the sensual notes of that interior endure through all accidental fluctuations along their faces. Time cannot be a mere system of relations, but must also be something in itself. But instead of one universal time pushing everything forward with monotonous grinding clockwork, we find that there are countless times, one for every object. More specifically, there is a separate time on the interior of every object that exists, in which the internal notes of those objects are showered with a varying succession of different floodlights, strobes, confetti, and glitter, while nonetheless remaining the same. Time is the strife between an object and its accidents or contiguous relations. Time is black noise: not the condition of possibility of this noise, nor the ecstatic structure through which humans encounter it, but simply this noise itself.

But not only time pertains to the inside of an object—as we have seen, there is nowhere else to be but on such an inside. Space is always the space of a specific interior. But unlike time, this is always a binary question: we are either inside of a certain object or not; each note either belongs to a certain object or not. We can pass from some objects into others, but we are never both inside and outside a space simultaneously. To move from one space to another is to move from the inside of certain objects or relations to the inside of certain others. Once again, there is no fluctuation here: we are either inside an object or relation by virtue of belonging to it, or we are closed off from its inner sanctum, in which case we either remain unaware of it or capture its signals only from afar. Space is not an empty universal container unchanged by whatever happens to drop into it. But it is also not equivalent to the relations between things, because what is truly spatial is that which *resists* being devoured by a system of relationships, so that space actually has more in common with hollow or vacuous autonomous zones of reality than with any set of relationships. Still less can space be an alias for the referential assignments in which things are encountered by human Dasein, since objects are spatial quite apart from human existence. When we speak of space, we are speaking only of the interior of an object, whatever the scope of such an entity may be. We are speaking of the way in which objects are set off from their parts, or from other objects in general. Space is the absolute mutual exteriority of all objects from each other, not their relationality. Whereas time flows gently or violently but always by gradations, space is utterly quantized, its parts broken up into cleanly-hewn chunks, so that space is not even really a continuum in the way that time is. Space is the strife between objects and their parts.

From all of this, it should be clear that time and space are simply the two axes of the world under different names: time and space, taken together, are equivalent to the fourfold structure of reality. They do not belong solely to human *experience* of the world, since they belong to objects themselves, including both those in which humans are involved and those from which they are excluded. On this basis we must resist all recent theories—whether of Husserl, Heidegger, or Bergson—that propose a strict distinction between dynamic lived time and the scientific time of clocks. Here as always, it is a bad idea to save philosophy from the sciences by turning philosophy into a fortified ghetto or incestuous canton walled off from its surroundings. The more radical way of avoiding scientific naturalism is to realize that nature is not natural and can never be naturalized, even when human beings are far from the scene. *Nature is unnatural,* if the world "natural" is meant to describe the status of extant slabs of inert matter. The life of gravel and sandpaper is every bit as troubled by inner ambiguities as human existence ever was. For this reason, metaphysics still has a long future.

Another way of stating the opposition is to say that time unfolds on the inside of objects, but that space *forms* the inside of objects. Or still differently, if space were defined as the hard wall or external carapace of an object, time would be its molten interior plasm. This also brings us to the verge of an unexpected theme. The usual assumption is that spatial movement is reversible but temporal change is not; after all, I can travel to Dubai and back again as many times as I wish, but can never do this with my childhood years. Everyone puzzles over "time's arrow" and why and whether it only flows in one direction, but no one has ever asked about "space's arrow," since reversibility seems to belong to the very essence of spatial movement. But we can now see a way in which the opposite is true. Namely, time is *always* reversible, because on the interior of a relation it makes no difference when the Taj Mahal cycles from pink to blue to yellow to orange to black and finally to pink again. The sequence can go in any order and reverse itself any number of times without shifting the regime of objects. But this is not so with space. When I move from Chicago to Davenport and back to Chicago, it is space that has changed, since objects are to some extent no longer what they were: houses have been torn down or rehabilitated, brain cells have developed or died, friendships have formed or decayed, old wounds have healed slightly. Schopenhauer senses this when he advises us not to revisit familiar past sites for nostalgia's sake, since we are actually nostalgic for times rather than places. Time can always be reversed on the interior of an object, because the shifting gales of black noise within have no direct consequence for the regime of objects. But space can never be reversed, and we can never return to the same airport twice—the regime of objects will have shifted.

If someone now rephrases the traditional question and asks whether "space's arrow" can flow in both directions, the answer must be in the negative. The reason for this is interesting. When objects enter into a relation, the relation cannot necessarily decompose again into the same objects: two chemicals might necessarily mix to form a third, but this does not imply that the new fluid is able to break down into its original parts. There is an asymmetry of cause and effect, and this is why space is irreversible. There are lasting consequences to space, but none to time, that transient fulguration along the surface of things—or rather, in the molten cores of things. Time itself creates nothing, while spatial changes create lasting monuments. The irreversibility of space stems from the dominance of an object over its own history, just as the child does not decompose into its parents. Every new object lies on the far side of the Rubicon, whereas time only swirls midstream without lasting damage.

All of this suggests a specific theory of how to read the passage of time: among other things, it obviously suggests some variant of a "monumental" form of history, if not quite in Nietzsche's sense. The mere flow of time changes nothing, and what we are measuring when we measure progression are changes in the actual regime of objects, also known as changes in *space*. As a result, the gradualism of sheer temporal forward motion gives way to a quantized world measured in epoch-making incidents or substantial changes. In yet another notable passage, Schopenhauer observes that the tumult of current events and best-selling books changes nothing in the real advance of literature, which progresses slowly at the rate of only a dozen or so significant books per century. A quick glance at the history of philosophy or music shows that decisive events often occur in rapid sequence (with puzzling regularity, great figures in all fields tend to come in groups of three) followed by long periods stranded on a plateau established by earlier seismic events. There may even be revolutions trapped within revolutions: the decisive shifts introduced by Husserl and Heidegger may be only smaller local events within the general Copernican Revolution of Kant, just as the still narrower field of Heidegger studies may contain numerous small but decisive moments well worth recounting. One can split the history of Cairo or Prague into numerous distinct periods, yet none of these transitions are as revolutionary as the final sacking of these cities by wild barbarian hordes. It is now common to mock the practice of referring to every new book or idea that appears as a "revolutionary" or "epoch-making" breakthrough, but there is a sense in which there are far more revolutions than we suspect. Every object is a revolution, since it necessarily makes a new cut into the other objects of the world and reorganizes them accordingly. Space is made up of quanta, because space is the absolute mutual exteriority of objects. By contrast, time is an oscillating backward and forward flux on an entity's interior. More attention needs to be paid to the mysteries of space, since it is too often taken for granted as obvious, even as armies of philosophers try their hand at the all too evident paradoxes of time. And there is a sense in which mere spatial displacement is an adventurous act that shifts us abruptly from one world into another: to be lured toward the distant end of a tree-lined street is in some sense already philosophy. Let this serve as a first orientation as to the model of time and space proposed by object-oriented philosophy. Time and space are the double axes of the world: the interlocking duels between an object and its notes, and an object and its parts.

D. The Carnival of Things

In a noteworthy fragment, Pythagoras declares that life is like a festival, with some people seeking honors and others creating wealth, while the superior ones stand removed from the fray and contemplate. A contrary note is struck by the young Leibniz, who proposes a carnivalesque theme park where theory would not stand apart and alone, but would be fully immersed in the rest of the fair. Here the advancement of science, engineering, and philosophy would mix freely with more trivial amusements: magic lanterns, artificial meteors, strangely shaped boats, counterfeit gems, chess games, archery contests, ballets of horses, perilous leaps, and a machine able to throw objects to a prespecified point. The entire institution would be funded by gambling tents, though curses and blasphemy would be forbidden to prevent political interference. If all went well, branches of the circus would eventually be opened in Rome, Venice, Vienna, Amsterdam, even Hamburg. In the same droll but earnest spirit, the present book also began with the scenario of a carnival or circus, and the metaphor has echoed several times in the meanwhile. It may be asked what is gained by this image of the universe as a circus, carnival pageant, or ontological world's fair.

The carnival of things is meant to replace the Pythagorean concept of philosophy as a uniquely transcendent liberation that rises above the world. In fact, philosophy is also an absorption in the world, no less than is true of charming snakes, eating fire, selling popcorn, juggling, lifting immense weights, or displaying freak animals. Instead of showing off mutant rabbits or albino crows, philosophy exhibits strange overarching structures that are suppressed by the given dogmas of the day. At any given time, its showcase oddities may have the names of occasional cause, eternal recurrence, perfect forms, transcendental conditions of possibility, monads, atoms, an infinite God with infinite attributes, or threefold temporality. In this sense, philosophers always resemble freaks or carnival hands—not less involved with the world than the others, but involved instead with more strange, more unsettling, or more far-reaching topics. The image of the carnival is meant as a reminder that the world is far more bizarre than we usually remember: philosophy is above all else an exile amidst strangeness and surprise. It is not just "wonder," as the Heideggerians put it with pompous mock-Greek solemnity, since this word places too much emphasis on us ourselves and our own intermittent states of special attunement, when it is really a question of the objects lying about in the world. The universe is not made up of dull, block-form, solid slabs of matter which only human moods and projects can bring to life. Nor is it built out of power or language, since it is far more disturbing than either of these.

This book has offered several overhead glimpses of the carnival of things—or alternatively, the carpentry of things in which objects join into one another even while retaining their independence and integrity. It will be helpful to return to these cross-sections of the world one last time. We first learned that the world of perception is filled neither with objects nor with qualities, since objects elude all access, and formless qualities divorced from an object do not exist. Hence the world of perception is filled only with sensual objects and their notes, or with notes structured into sensual objects. This cannot be solely a human experience, since any relation will have this structure, including inanimate relations. The world is already split up into independent zones: humans do not shatter a monotonous rumble of being into districts for the first time, since this has happened long before we arrive on the scene. Stated differently, the world is made up of levels, and the passage from one level to the next is made possible by way of elements or notes. We then discussed allure, which splits objects from their notes while preserving or even inaugurating the connection between them. In so doing, it connects the upper and lower floors of an object in the manner of a trapdoor or spiral staircase. Allure, in other words, is what allows passage from one level of the world to the next, and human allure seems to be only a special case of such transition. Finally, the interweaving of these two basic themes (object-oriented sensuality and allure) provided a fresh glimpse of the carpentry of things and its fourfold structure. At all times we are on the inside of an object, since there is no other place that one can be. *The interior of an object, its molten core, becomes the sole subject matter for philosophy.* More than this, it turns out to be *the only theme of life as a whole*, and not just life in the narrow sense of sentient consciousness. The interior of an object is demarcated as a specific space, and swirls with all the reversible oscillations of time. It is a chunk of space-time, and space-time is always local, always broken up into isolated chambers.

Existence on the interior of an object is defined by sincerity and involvement, not transcendence and critique. This is true for all objects at all times, but in particular it suggests a different model of the philosopher than is usual. The thinker does not have fewer naive beliefs than the fool or the hack, but actually believes in even more things, and more surprising things. Note that I say more surprising things, not more crazy or distempered things: the real thinker is no contrarian. Like Meno's stingray, contrarians live to shock others; like Socrates's stingray, thinkers and adventurers live primarily to shock themselves. They hope to discover that the world is not what they thought it was, that the dreary alternatives of the trench warfare of the day have covered up far more stunning possibilities, overlooked until now. Instead of asserting one's own unique critical liberation in the world and trying to burn down traditional or reactionary temples, the key is to listen closely to the faint radio signals emitted by objects—so as one night, alone, to hear what was never heard before.

This book has not offered a systematic metaphysics, but only a kind of electron microscope or bacterial culture from which such a system can be developed. The method employed has been to isolate the fluctuations and contradictions on the interior of objects. By studying this strange new chemical—the molten interior of things—we can develop approaches to a number of key traditional problems. For instance, we have said little about the problem of universals, and almost nothing about whether the numerous levels of the world require an infinite regress into ever tinier parts and infinite progress into ever more gigantic universes enclosing one another endlessly. The taste for cosmological vastness reaches us from Buddhist scripture and the roar of the sea and the probes launched toward Saturn, but the philosophy of human access persuades us to forget these astonishing spaces, or to leave them to other university departments. We also want to know what it means that objects endure through time, and what this endurance signifies. Everyone wants to discover whether human freedom really exists, and we can no longer be satisfied with philosophical strategies that place this question forever beyond our reach. Furthermore, although we have tried to undercut all claims for the preeminence of language in philosophy, it would still be important to know a thing or two about language even if it is no longer destined to play the starring role it has enjoyed for the past one hundred years. The existence of God and the fate of the soul, the struggle between good and evil, remain the most important philosophical questions for the majority of humankind, yet these very questions now strike most intellectuals as deeply naive, or at best as exiled to the no man's land of faith. While such metaphysical problems are not ignored entirely, they continue to strike most observers as lying beyond the pale of rigorous technical philosophy—a view now even more widespread in continental circles than among the analytics, some of whom are taking a renewed crack at these problems. The first impulse is always to fend off such questions with a reflexive, critical, even defensive attitude, since our professional trademark is the instinctive step backward to rephrase any question in terms of our very possibility of posing the question. But in this way we lose contact both with reality and with the general public, as we retreat ever further into the idiom of the guild.

We have been trained, in other words, not to wonder in public about the most overpowering cosmological mysteries, even as some of us continue to wonder about them in private. We are now penned up safely in a narrow range of verifiable and technically precise meditations on human access, ranging from stylish to dry. The present book has urged another attitude toward the world. The term "guerrilla metaphysics" is meant to signal both this attitude and my full awareness that the traditional cathedrals of metaphysics lie in ruins. Let the rubble sleep—or kick it a bit longer, if you must. But new towers or monuments are still possible, more solid and perhaps more startling than those that came before. We have now surveyed the interiors of objects with their quadruple structure, a structure also known as space-time. It is from this strange initial material that object-oriented philosophy must be built.

quadruple structure of objects = space-time

Notes

PART ONE
THE CARNAL PHENOMENOLOGISTS

Chapter One
CONCRETENESS IN THE DEPTHS

1. See the compact anthology by Dominic Janicaud et al., *Phenomenology and the "Theological Turn": The French Debate.*
2. Ibid., 103.
3. Ibid., 26.
4. Ibid., 36.
5. Ibid., 49.
6. Ibid., 38–39. (Modified by Prusak from p. 12 of the Lingis translation of *Totality and Infinity*.)
7. Ibid., 38.
8. Ibid.
9. Ibid.
10. Ibid. Italics added.
11. Ibid. (The portion cited from Levinas is modified by Prusak from p. 26 of the Lingis translation of *Totality and Infinity*.)
12. *Phenomenology and the "Theological Turn*," 27.
13. Ibid.
14. Cited by Janicaud from *Totality and Infinity*, p. 90 in the English version.
15. *Phenomenology and the "Theological Turn*," 46.
16. Ibid., 37.

Chapter Two
TWO BORDERLANDS OF INTENTIONALITY

17. Martin Heidegger, *Prolegomena zur Geschichte des Zeitbegriffs*, 30.
18. See the student transcript of the 1924 Marburg Lecture Course, Martin Heidegger, *Grundbegriffe der aristotelischen Philosophie*, 5: "[Ein Philosoph] war dann und dann geboren, er arbeitete und starb."
19. Edmund Husserl, *Logical Investigations*, Investigation V, vol. 2 of the English edition, 558.
20. Heidegger, *Prolegomena zur Geschichte des Zeitbegriffs*, 216–26.
21. Franz Brentano, as cited in *Logical Investigations*, vol. 2, 556.

22. See the whole of Heidegger, *Grundbegriffe der Metaphysik: Welt-Endlichkeit-Einsamkeit.*
23. Husserl, *Logical Investigations,* vol. 2, §64.
24. Ibid., 648. Italics modified.
25. Ibid., 649.
26. Ibid., 572.
27. Ibid., 565.
28. Jean-Paul Sartre, *Being and Nothingness,* 5.
29. Husserl, *Logical Investigations,* vol. 2, 592.
30. Ibid., 680. Punctuation modified.
31. Ibid., 559.
32. Ibid., 670.
33. Ibid., 542.
34. Ibid., 729.
35. "It is accordingly clear, and evident from the mere essence of perception, that adequate perception can only be 'inner' perception, that it can only be trained upon experiences simultaneously given, and belonging to a single experience with itself." But naturally, not *all* inner intuitions are to be regarded as adequate. (Ibid., 542.)
36. Ibid., 709.
37. Ibid., 561.
38. Ibid., 685.
39. Saul Kripke, *Naming and Necessity,* throughout.
40. Husserl, *Logical Investigations,* vol. 2, 684.
41. Husserl actually uses "quality" in the opposite sense, as a term pertaining to our own intentional acts rather than to sensual material. But I will retain the traditional usage of "qualities" to refer to the specific attributes of a thing.
42. Aristotle, *Metaphysics.* 1052b15–17, 186 in the English. Italics added.
43. See the collection G. W. Leibniz, *Philosophical Essays,* 213–14.
44. Husserl, *Logical Investigations,* vol. 2, 558.
45. Brentano, as cited in Husserl, *Logical Investigations,* vol. 2, 554.
46. cf. Graham Harman, *Tool-Being,* 296.
47. Husserl, *Logical Investigations,* vol. 2, 795.
48. See Edmund Husserl's *Ideen* I §49, §85. See also the lucid remarks on this theme by the young Emmanuel Levinas in *The Theory of Intuition in Husserl's Phenomenology,* especially 47–49.

Chapter Three
BATHING IN THE ETHER

49. Cf. Harman, *Tool-Being,* ch. 1.
50. Levinas, *Totality and Infinity,* 122.
51. Ibid.
52. Ibid., 123–24.
53. Ibid., 34.
54. See Emmanuel Levinas, *Existence and Existents* and *Time and the Other.*

55. Levinas, *Totality and Infinity*, 125.
56. Ibid.
57. Ibid., 127.
58. Ibid., 128. Punctuation and italics modified.
59. Ibid., 129.
60. Ibid.
61. Ibid., 130.
62. Ibid., 133.
63. Ibid.
64. Ibid.
65. Ibid., 134.
66. Ibid., 131.
67. Ibid., 132. Italics added.
68. Ibid.
69. Ibid., 135.
70. Ibid., 134.
71. Ibid., 132.
72. Ibid., 131.
73. Ibid., 132.
74. Ibid.
75. Ibid.
76. Ibid., 135.
77. Ibid.
78. Ibid., 136.
79. Ibid., 135.
80. Ibid., 132.
81. Ibid., 140.
82. Ibid., 137.
83. Ibid., 135.
84. Ibid., 132.
85. Ibid., 142.
86. Ibid.
87. Ibid. Italics added.
88. Ibid.
89. Ibid. Translation modified for consistency.
90. Ibid. Translation again modified for consistency.
91. The technical term "alterity," while not the only horrible piece of jargon to have emerged from postmodern philosophy, surely ranks among the worst. (My own list of candidates also includes the antiseptic term "performativity" and Derrida's barely forgivable "hauntology.")
92. Ibid., 135–36.
93. Ibid., 136.
94. Ibid.
95. See Alan Sokal and Jean Bricmont, *Fashionable Nonsense*, 212–58.
96. Thanks are due to Sadeem el Nahhas for noting the pre-Socratic simplicity of much of the philosophy of Levinas.
97. Levinas, *Totality and Infinity*, 139.

98. Ibid., 140.
99. Ibid.

Chapter Four
THE STYLE OF THINGS

100. From the bogus article "The Structural Paradigm of Discourse and Realism," randomly generated from my home computer on the evening of April 5, 2003. The postmodernism generator was modified by Josh Larios from the "Dada Engine" of Andrew C. Bulhak, and can be used by all interested parties at http://www.elsewhere.org/cgi-bin/postmodern/
101. Friedrich Nietzsche, *Human, All Too Human*, §131 of "The Wanderer and His Shadow."
102. Maurice Merleau-Ponty, *Phenomenology of Perception*, 27.
103. Ibid., 264.
104. Ibid., 265.
105. Ibid., 271.
106. Ibid., 376.
107. Ibid., 360. Punctuation and italics modified.
108. Maurice Merleau-Ponty, *The Visible and the Invisible*, 150.
109. Maurice Merleau-Ponty, *Phenomenology of Perception*, 356.
110. Ibid., 454.
111. Merleau-Ponty, *The Visible and the Invisible*, 144. Punctuation modified.
112. Merleau-Ponty, *Phenomenology of Perception*, 3.
113. Ibid., 14.
114. Merleau-Ponty, *The Visible and the Invisible*, 131.
115. Merleau-Ponty, *Phenomenology of Perception*, 15.
116. Ibid., 42–43.
117. Levinas, *Totality and Infinity*, 123.
118. Merleau-Ponty, *Phenomenology of Perception*, 471.
119. Ibid., 355.
120. Ibid., 439.
121. Ibid., p.378.
122. Ibid., p.436.
123. Merleau-Ponty, *The Visible and the Invisible*, 132. The word "porous" is marked as uncertain in Merleau-Ponty's handwritten manuscript, but certainly fits the passage well enough.
124. Ibid., 45.
125. Ibid., 370.
126. Ibid., 10.
127. Ibid., 370.
128. Ibid., 168.
129. Ibid., 165.
130. Ibid., 176.
131. Ibid., 296.
132. Ibid., 363.

133. Ibid., 275.
134. Ibid., 96.
135. Ibid., 97.
136. Ibid., xi.
137. Ibid., 375.
138. Ibid., 72. Bergson's position strikes me as more sophisticated than this. See Henri Bergson, *Laughter*, ch. 3, first section.
139. Merleau-Ponty, *The Visible and the Invisible*, 54.
140. Ibid., 373.
141. Ibid., 430.
142. Ibid., 431.
143. Ibid., 432.
144. Merleau-Ponty, *The Visible and the Invisible*, 47.
145. Ibid.
146. Ibid.
147. This may explain Merleau-Ponty's little-recognized appreciation for Whitehead in later years, noted most recently by Isabelle Stengers in her outstanding *Penser avec Whitehead* (cf. p. 14). One would hope that Stengers's book would provoke a resurgence of genuine speculative metaphysics in the Francophone countries after their long servitude in Heidegger's shadow.
148. Merleau-Ponty, *Phenomenology of Perception*, 77.
149. Ibid., 79. Italics added.
150. Ibid.
151. Ibid.
152. Ibid. Italics added.
153. Ibid., 81
154. Ibid., 350.
155. Ibid., 377. Italics added.
156. Ibid., xxii.
157. Ibid., 423.
158. Ibid., 82–83.
159. Ibid., 375.
160. Ibid., 477.
161. Ibid.
162. Ibid., 478.
163. Ibid., 502.
164. Ibid., 308.
165. Ibid., 310.
166. Merleau-Ponty, *The Visible and the Invisible*, 139.
167. Ibid., 83–84.
168. Ibid., 135.
169. Ibid., 127.
170. Ibid., 136.
171. Ibid., 114.
172. Ibid., 132–33.
173. Ibid., 134.

174. Ibid., 140.
175. Merleau-Ponty, *Phenomenology of Perception*, 407.
176. Ibid., 237.
177. Ibid., 174.
178. Ibid.
179. Paul Verlaine, *Selected Poems*, 113.
180. Merleau-Ponty, *Phenomenology of Perception*, 175.
181. Ibid., 153.
182. Ibid., 208.
183. Ibid.
184. Ibid., 321.
185. Ibid., 267.
186. Ibid., 266.
187. Ibid., 372.
188. Ibid.
189. Ibid., 376.
190. Ibid., 372.
191. *The Visible and the Invisible*, 152.
192. Ibid.
193. Ibid., 160–61.
194. Ibid., 100.
195. Ibid., 110–11.
196. Ibid., 139.
197. Ibid.

Chapter Five
THE LEVELS

198. Alphonso Lingis, *The Imperative*, 3.
199. Ibid., 2.
200. Ibid., 44.
201. Ibid., 90.
202. Wes Swedlow, from a remark to the author in May 2000.
203. Lingis, *The Imperative*, 1.
204. Ibid.
205. Ibid., 3.
206. Ibid., 4.
207. Ibid., 2.
208. Ibid., 21.
209. Ibid., 126.
210. Ibid., 48.
211. Ibid., 52.
212. Ibid., 51.
213. Aristotle, *On Memory and Reminiscence*, 609. In *The Basic Works of Aristotle*, ed. R. McKeon.
214. Lingis, *The Imperative*, 3.
215. Ibid., 126.

216. Ibid., 21.
217. Ibid., 63.
218. Ibid., 62.
219. Ibid., 99.
220. Ibid.
221. Ibid.
222. Ibid., 5.
223. Ibid., 25.
224. Ibid.
225. Ibid., 27.
226. Ibid., 37.
227. Ibid., 113.
228. Ibid., 66.
229. Ibid., 122.
230. Ibid., 106.
231. Ibid., 37.
232. Ibid., 49.
233. Ibid., 55.
234. Ibid., 69. Italics added.
235. Ibid., 105.
236. Ibid., 114–15.
237. Ibid., 78.
238. Ibid., 107.
239. Ibid., 105.
240. Ibid., 64. Italics added.
241. Ibid., 64–65. Italics added.
242. Ibid., 122.

PART TWO
SETTING THE TABLE

Chapter Six
OBJECTS

1. I am referring, respectively, to Heidegger's *Geviert*, Plato's divided line, Aristotle's four causes, and Marshall and Eric McLuhan's fascinating but underutilized concept of the tetrad. Any philosophy that recognizes two basic principles of division will always result in some sort of fourfold structure, as will any superstition or any brainwashing swindle that meets this criterion. This does not mean that they are all connected, any more than Aztec or Egyptian sun-worship are truly connected with Louis XIV the Sun King or the NBA's Phoenix Suns.
2. G. W. Leibniz, *Monadology*, §9, §14.
3. In correspondence with the author of January 2003. Cf. David Skrbina, *Panpsychism in the West* (Cambridge, MA: MIT Press, 2005).

4. John Locke, *An Essay Concerning Human Understanding*, book II, ch. XXIV, 424.

Chapter Seven
THE PROBLEM OF OBJECTS

5. See all of the works of Bruno Latour, and especially *Pandora's Hope*, for a fascinating empirical account of this process.
6. This, of course, is Aristotle's view in the *Metaphysics*, book VII, ch. 10.
7. José Ortega y Gasset, "An Essay in Esthetics by Way of a Preface," in *Phenomenology and Art.*

Chapter Eight
METAPHOR

8. Thanks are due to William Melaney for first pointing out the surprising degree of overlap between Ortega and Black.
9. In Jacques Derrida, *Margins of Philosophy.*
10. In Ortega, *Phenomenology and Art*, 127–60.
11. Ibid., 140.
12. Ibid., 133.
13. Ibid., 134.
14. Ibid., 136.
15. Kripke, *Naming and Necessity*, throughout.
16. Ortega, *Phenomenology and Art*, 138. Italics added.
17. Ibid.
18. Ibid., 138–39.
19. Ibid., 140.
20. Ibid., 141.
21. Aristotle, *Poetics*, 1457b33–1457b35.
22. As cited by Ortega, *Phenomenology and Art*, 142.
23. Ibid., 143.
24. Ibid., 144.
25. Ibid., 145.
26. Jacques Derrida, "White Mythology," 213.
27. Ibid., 243.
28. Ibid., 271.
29. Ibid., 246.
30. Ibid., 247, cited from Aristotle, *Poetics*, 1457b3–4.
31. Ibid.
32. Ibid. I have eliminated the word "essential" from this citation and "essence" from the one that follows so as not to complicate the present discussion further. Let it simply be said that I agree with Derrida's accurate observation that the terms *proper* and *essential* are closely related but not identical. But whereas Derrida views this a bit too piously as some sort of crippling contradiction that haunts the oppressive West, I simply regard it as one of the most inevitable and most fruitful puzzles of phi-

losophy. It is the very riddle of the second axis, of the strife between a thing and its qualities—a chasm that Derrida cannot recognize, given his unspoken agreement with Russell that the name of a thing is an abbreviated definite description of its qualities and never points to anything beyond them.

33. Ibid. See also the preceding note.
34. Aristotle, *Poetics*, 1448b5–9.
35. Ibid., 1459a5–8.
36. Derrida, "White Mythology," 246.
37. Ibid., 247.
38. Ibid., 247–48.
39. Ibid., 248. Italics added.
40. *Metaphysics*, 1006a34–1006b1, 1006b6–1006b10.
41. Ibid., 1006b17–1006b18.
42. Ibid., 1006b2–1006b24. Italics added.
43. Ibid., 1007b19–1007b21, 1007b24–1007b26.
44. Derrida, "White Mythology," 269–70.
45. Ibid., 244. Italics added.
46. Ibid., 213.
47. Included in Max Black, *Models and Metaphors*, ch. 3.
48. Black, "Metaphor," 30–31.
49. Ibid., 34.
50. Ibid.
51. In I. A. Richards, *The Philosophy of Rhetoric*, 117.
52. Black, "Metaphor," 39. Italics added.
53. Ibid., 37. Emphasis added.
54. Ibid., 41.
55. Ibid., 40.
56. Ibid.
57. Ibid., 41. Italics added.
58. Ibid.
59. Ibid.
60. Ibid., 42.
61. Ibid.
62. Ibid., 43.
63. Donald Davidson, "What Metaphors Mean." See p. 264, and also the bottom of p. 254.
64. Ibid., 260.
65. Ibid, 262.
66. Ibid. Italics added.
67. Ibid., 261. Italics added.
68. Ibid.
69. Ibid., 262. Italics added.
70. Ibid.
71. Ibid. Italics added.
72. Ibid., 263. Italics added.
73. Ibid., 263–64.
74. Ibid., 245.

Chapter Nine
HUMOR

75. Davidson, "What Metaphors Mean," 245.
76. Available on-line at www.theonion.com.
77. George Meredith and Henri Bergson, *Essay on Comedy/Laughter*.
78. Sigmund Freud, *Jokes and their Relation to the Unconscious*.
79. Sigmund Freud, *The Interpretation of Dreams*.
80. Aristotle, *Poetics*, 1448a18–1448a20. Translation modified. Emphasis added.
81. Bergson, *Laughter*, 65.
82. Ibid.
83. Ibid., 124.
84. Black, "Metaphor," 36.
85. Bergson, *Laughter*, 141.
86. Ibid., 157–58. Translation modified.
87. Ibid., 158.
88. Ibid., 160.
89. Ibid., 158.
90. Ibid., 159.
91. Ibid.
92. Ibid., 163.
93. Ibid.
94. Ibid., 162.
95. Ibid., 161. Translation modified.
96. Ibid., 62. Translation modified.
97. Ibid., 66.
98. Ibid.
99. Ibid., 63.
100. Philip Fisher draws a strikingly similar conclusion in his newly published book *The Vehement Passions*, pp. 38–39. He even uses the very example of people slipping and falling on the ice. I agree completely with this portion of Fisher's analysis, which displays his dark but humane imagination at its finest.
101. This an actual scene from the film *Duck Soup*.
102. Bergson, *Laughter*, 72.
103. Ibid., 118.
104. Ibid.
105. Ibid., 80.
106. Ibid., 69.
107. Ibid., 81.
108. Credit is due to Raven Zachary for this inspired comic vision, which has entered my mind often since I first heard it. I have never been able to improve upon this particular pair of characters, despite many attempts to do so.
109. Bergson, *Laughter*, 187.
110. Ortega, "Preface for Germans," 65.
111. Jean Baudrillard, *Seduction*.

PART THREE
QUADRUPLE PHILOSOPHY

Chapter Ten
THE ROOT OF VICARIOUS CAUSATION

1. Porphyry, *Isagoge*, 1.
2. Husserl, *Logical Investigations*, vol. II, 812. This progression by stages is also a key preoccupation of Heidegger in 1919, as I have already shown in chapter 1, §8 of *Tool-Being*. The young Heidegger already contended that while the *qualities* of objects can be analyzed by interlocking stages, the *being* of objects can be invoked without progressing only one step at a time. Instead of saying "forest green is a kind of green, green is a kind of color, color is a kind of thing," I can say simply that "the forest green *is*." This is important insofar as it shows that the being of a thing is always a private objective unity, whereas qualities, proceeding by way of stages, are engaged in a kind of interlocking dialogue or collision between adjoining levels of the sensual world.
3. Husserl, *Logical Investigations*, vol. II, 819.
4. Ibid., 782.
5. Ibid.
6. Ibid., 437.
7. Ibid., 474–75.
8. Ibid., 475. Italics modified.
9. Ibid., 443.
10. Ibid., 480. Italics modified. If we were to strike out the word "categorial," these words could easily pass for Leibniz's own.
11. Ibid.
12. Ibid., 444.
13. I am referring to his point in *Metaphysics* Book Theta that dirt is not a potential human being or a potential box, since too many intervening layers need to be spoken of first: "the next thing following is always simply potentially the one that precedes it. For instance, the box is not made of earth, nor is it earth, but is wooden, since this is potentially a box" (176, 1049a22–1049a25).
14. cf. Husserl, *Logical Investigations*, 470–74.
15. Although the Husserl of the *Logical Investigations* uses his theory of intentional objects to oppose the passive sensory matter of the Kantian tradition, there is a sense in which Kant fully endorses an infinite regress in the perceptual field (and not just *indefinite* regress, which for him pertains only to chains of causality leading outside the present moment). What I have in mind are the passages on intensive magnitude in the section of the *Critique of Pure Reason* on the Anticipations of Perception. (See especially pp. 204–6, A 169/B 211–A 173/B 214.) Even so, Kant does insist on an absolute distinction between sensibility and understanding, so that there is still a kind of raw givenness at the basis of perception, even if humans are never able to encounter it in a form untainted by the

categories. In this sense, Husserl's jab against the neo-Kantians remains both illuminating and useful.

16. We get a small taste of such a theory in *Camera Lucida*, Roland Barthes's interesting book on photography. Barthes distinguishes between the overall tonal *studium* of a photograph and its *punctum*—an inessential detail that manages to capture our attention and set the entire photograph into motion. Stated in terms of the present book, every case of allure functions by way of some sort of *punctum*.

17. Cf. Aristotle, *Metaphysics*, Book Zeta, ch. 6, beginning at 1031a14. Found on p.125 in the Sachs translation.

Chapter Eleven
VICARIOUS CAUSATION

18. Harold Bloom, *The Western Canon*, 172.

Chapter Twelve
SOME IMPLICATIONS

19. See Bruno Latour, "Why Has Critique Run Out of Steam? From Matters of Fact to Matters of Concern."

20. The term "onto-ontology," of course, is far too ugly and absurd to deserve prolonged use, and is employed here only as a passing joke.

21. The full original quote runs as follows: "The best claim that a college education can possibly make on your respect, the best thing it can aspire to accomplish for you, is this: that it should *help you to know a good man when you see him*." William James, "The Social Value of the College Bred," 1242.

22. Brigitte Sassen, ed., *Kant's Early Critics*.

23. Paul Berman, *Terror and Liberalism*, see p. 112 and p. 149, among other passages.

24. Michel Serres and Bruno Latour, *Conversations on Science, Culture, and Time*, 86.

Bibliography

This list includes books that are explicitly cited as well as those that are loosely invoked. In most instances I have preferred to list English translations where available; exceptions to this rule occur in cases where fresh translations have been made from the original text.

Aristotle. *On Memory and Reminiscence*. In *The Basic Works of Aristotle*. Edited by R. McKeon. New York: Random House, 1941.
———. *Metaphysics*. Translated by J. Sachs. Santa Fe, NM: Green Lion Press, 1999.
Barthes, Roland. *Camera Lucida*. Translated by R. Howard. New York: Hill and Wang, 1981.
Baudrillard, Jean. *Seduction*. Translated by A. and M. Kroker. New York: St. Martin's Press, 1991.
Bergson, Henri. *Creative Evolution*. Translated by A. Mitchell. New York: Modern Library, 1944.
———. *Laughter*. In Meredith and Bergson, *An Essay on Comedy/Laughter*. New York: Doubleday, 1956.
Berkeley, George. *A Treatise Concerning the Principles of Human Knowledge*. Indianapolis: Hackett, 1982.
Berman, Paul. *Terror and Liberalism*. New York: Norton, 2003.
Black, Max. "Metaphor." In Black, *Models and Metaphors*.
———. *Models and Metaphors*. Ithaca, NY: Cornell University Press, 1962.
Bloom, Harold. *The Western Canon*. New York: Riverhead Books, 1995
Bruno, Giordano. *Cause, Principle, and Unity*. Translated by R. de Lucca. Cambridge, UK: Cambridge University Press, 1998.
Bulhak, Andrew C. *See* La Fournier, Andreas J.
Clarke, Samuel. *See* Leibniz, G.W. and Clarke, Samuel.
Davidson, Donald. *Inquiries Into Truth and Interpretation*. Oxford, UK: Oxford University Press, 1984.
———. "What Metaphors Mean." In Davidson, *Inquiries Into Truth and Interpretation*, 1984.
Derrida, Jacques. *Margins of Philosophy*. Translated by A. Bass. Chicago: University of Chicago Press, 1982.

————. "White Mythology." In *Margins of Philosophy*, 1982.

Fisher, Philip. *The Vehement Passions*. Princeton, NJ: Princeton University Press, 2002.

Freud, Sigmund. *The Interpretation of Dreams*. Translated by J. Crick. Oxford: Oxford University Press, 1999.

————. *Jokes and their Relation to the Unconscious*. Translated by J. Strachey. London: Routledge and Kegan Paul, 1960.

Harman, Graham. *Tool-Being: Heidegger and the Metaphysics of Objects*. Chicago: Open Court, 2002.

Heidegger, Martin. *Grundbegriffe der aristotelischen Philosophie*. [Gesamtausgabe Band 18.] Frankfurt: Vittorio Klostermann, 2002.

————. *Grundbegriffe der Metaphysik: Welt-Endlichkeit-Einsamkeit*. [Gesamtausgabe Band 29/30.] Frankfurt: Vittorio Klostermann, 1983.

————. *Prolegomena zur Geschichte des Zeitbegriffs*. [Gesamtausgabe Band 20.] Frankfurt: Vittorio Klostermann, 1988.

———— *Zur Bestimmung der Philosophie*. [Gesamtausgabe Band 56/7.] Frankfurt: Vittorio Klostermann, 1987.

Husserl, Edmund. *Ideen zu einer reinen Phänomenologie and phänomenologischen Philosophie*. Tübingen: Max Niemeyer Verlag, 1993.

————. *Logical Investigations*. 2 volumes. Translated by J. N. Findlay. London: Routledge and Kegan Paul, 1970.

James, William. "The Social Value of the College Bred." *Writings: 1902–1910*. New York: The Library of America, 1987.

Janicaud, Dominique. "The Theological Turn in French Phenomenology." In Janicaud et al., *Phenomenology and the "Theological Turn": The French Debate*, 2000.

Janicaud, Dominique et al. *Phenomenology and the "Theological Turn": The French Debate*. Translated by B. Prusak [Part 1] and J. Kosky and T. Carlson [Part 2]. New York: Fordham University Press, 2000.

Kant, Immanuel. *Critique of Pure Reason*. Translated by P. Guyer and A. Wood. New York: Cambridge University Press, 1998.

Kripke, Saul. *Naming and Necessity*. Cambridge, MA: Harvard University Press, 1996.

Kuhn, Thomas. *The Structure of Scientific Revolutions*. Chicago: University of Chicago Press, 1970.

La Fournier, Andreas J., real name Larios, Josh. "The Structural Paradigm of Discourse and Realism," mock article generated on April 5, 2003 by Larios's postmodernist modification of Andrew C. Bulhak's "Dada engine," available at www.elsewhere.org.

Larios, Josh. *See* La Fournier, Andreas J.

Latour, Bruno. *Pandora's Hope*. Cambridge, MA: Harvard University Press, 1999.

————. "Why Has Critique Run Out of Steam? From Matters of Fact to Matters of Concern." *Critical Inquiry* 30, no. 2 (Winter 2004).

Lawrence, T. E. *Seven Pillars of Wisdom*. London: Penguin, 2000.

Leibniz, G. W. *Monadology*. In *Philosophical Essays* and *Selections*.

————. *Philosophical Essays*. Translated by R. Ariew and D. Garber. Indianapolis: Hackett, 1989.

————. *Selections.* Edited by P. Wiener. New York: Scribner, 1979.

Leibniz, G.W. and Clarke, Samuel. *Correspondence.* Edited by R. Ariew. Indianapolis: Hackett, 2000.

Levinas, Emmanuel. *Existence and Existents.* Translated by A. Lingis. The Hague: Matinus Nijhoff, 1988.

————. *The Theory of Intuition in Husserl's Phenomenology.* Translated by A. Orianne. Evanston, IL: Northwestern University Press, 1985.

————. *Time and the Other.* Translated by R. Cohen. Pittsburgh: Duquesne University Press, 1987.

————. *Totality and Infinity.* Translated by A. Lingis. Pittsburgh: Duquesne University Press, 1969.

Lingis, Alphonso. *The Imperative.* Bloomington, IN: Indiana University Press, 1998.

Locke, John. *An Essay Concerning Human Understanding.* 2 vols. New York: Dover, 1959.

Marion, Jean-Luc. *Reduction and Givenness.* Evanston, IL: Northwestern University Press, 1998.

The Marx Brothers. *Duck Soup.* Aired frequently on cable television and also easily available in DVD format.

Meredith, George, and Henri Bergson. *Comedy: An Essay on Comedy/Laughter.* Edited by Wylie Sypher. New York: Doubleday, 1956.

Merleau-Ponty, Maurice. *The Visible and the Invisible.* Translated by A. Lingis. Evanston, IL: Northwestern University Press, 1968.

————. *Phenomenology of Perception.* Translated by C. Smith. London: Routledge, 2002.

Newton, Isaac. *Principia.* Translated by A. Motte and revised by F. Cajori. Berkeley, CA: University of California Press, 1966.

Nietzsche, Friedrich. *Human, All Too Human.* Translated by R. J. Hollingdale. Cambridge, UK: Cambridge University Press, 1996.

The Onion. Weekly satirical newspaper. Available on-line at www.theonion.com, new issues posted Wednesdays.

Ortega y Gasset, José. "Preface for Germans. In *Phenomenology and Art,* 1975.

————. *Phenomenology and Art.* Translated by P. Silver. New York: Norton, 1975.

Plato. *Euthyphro, Meno.* In *Five Dialogues.* Translated by G. M. Grube. Indianapolis: Hackett, 1981.

Polo, Marco. *The Travels of Marco Polo.* London: Wordsworth Editions, 1997.

Porphyry. *Isagoge.* In *Five Texts on the Mediaeval Problem of Universals.* Translated and edited by P. V. Spade. Indianapolis: Hackett, 1944.

Quine, Willard van Orman. *From a Logical Point of View.* Cambridge, MA: Harvard University Press, 1980.

Richards, I. A. *The Philosophy of Rhetoric.* Oxford, UK: Oxford University Press, 1936.

Sartre, Jean-Paul. *Being and Nothingness.* Translated by H. Barnes. New York: Washington Square Press, 1984.

Sassen, Brigitte, ed. *Kant's Early Critics: The Empiricist Critique of the Theoretical Philosophy.* Cambridge, UK: Cambridge University Press, 2000.

Serres, Michel, and Bruno Latour. *Conversations on Science, Culture, and Time.* Translated by R. Lapidus. Ann Arbor, MI: University of Michigan Press, 1995.

Skrbina, David. *Panpsychism in the West.* Cambridge, MA: MIT Press, 2005.

Smolin, Lee. *The Life of the Cosmos.* Oxford, UK: Oxford University Press, 1997.

Sokal, Alan, and Jean Bricmont. *Fashionable Nonsense: Postmodern Intellectuals' Abuse of Science.* New York: Picador USA, 1998.

Spade, P. V., ed. *Five Texts on the Mediaeval Problem of Universals.* Indianapolis: Hacketrt, 1994.

Stengers, Isabelle. *Penser avec Whitehead.* Paris: Seuil, 2002.

Verlaine, Paul. *Selected Poems.* Translated by C. F. MacIntyre. Berkeley, CA: University of California Press, 1989.

Whitehead, Alfred North. *Process and Reality.* New York: Free Press, 1978.

The Wizard of Oz. Aired frequently on cable television and also easily available in DVD format.

Zubiri, Xavier. *On Essence.* Translated by A. R. Caponigri. Washington: Catholic University Press, 1980.

Index

273